The Language of Canadian Politics

COMPLIMENTARY	TERRITORY	MO	DATE DAY	YR	NUMBER
	1005	7	24	80	U1153

QUANTITY	PRODUCT CODE	DESCRIPTION	SUBJ. AREA OR PRICE
1	C99839	MCMENEMY LANG CAN POL PA	

JOHN WILEY & SONS
CANADA, LIMITED
22 WORCESTER ROAD, REXDALE, ONTARIO M9W 1L1
TEL. 675-3580   TELEX 06-989189

The Language of Canadian Politics:

A Guide to Important Terms and Concepts

John McMenemy
WILFRID LAURIER UNIVERSITY

John Wiley & Sons Canada Limited
Toronto   New York   Chichester   Brisbane

Cover design by Blair Kerrigan/Glyphics

Canadian Cataloguing in Publication Data
    McMenemy, John, 1940–
        The language of Canadian politics
    ISBN 0-471-99839-7
            0-471-79948-3 (bound)
    1. Canada – Politics and government – Dictionaries.
    I. Title.
    JA61.M33   320.971   C80-094027-X

Printed and bound in Canada
10 9 8 7 6 5 4 3 2 1

Preface and Acknowledgements

This book is designed to meet an academic and a general need. In the 1970's, the discipline of political science in Canada experienced considerable growth in many fields. This was reflected in the establishment in universities and colleges of many new courses – for example, provincial politics, federalism, parties, public policy, political communication, political sociology, and political attitudes and behaviour. There has also been the development of interdisciplinary programs such as Canadian studies, which include government and politics.

In many of these cases, especially when the courses are of one-term duration, the lecturer faces the difficulty of "assuming" satisfactorily a level of knowledge or body of information held by the entire class whose students have widely differing levels of formal education in Canadian politics. Even in a comprehensive two-term Canadian government course, the development of the subfields with a large body of literature has created an *embarras de richesse* for the instructor who has the increasingly difficult task of deciding what to include or emphasize in lectures. This book, therefore, was designed in part to provide students with a comprehensive summary of terms and concepts in Canadian government and politics, with reference to some of the current or standard academic works on these subjects. Thus, in a Canadian Studies lecture or in a provincial government course, for example, an instructor might remark that the "convention" of "parliament-cabinet" government is observed in the provincial and federal political systems, without necessarily having to explain the terms to a class which includes students already familiar with the terms as well as those who are not. The book may also be of assistance to the instructor in the comprehensive Canadian government course who may wish to concentrate on certain aspects of the political system in lectures and leave other matters generally for the student to become familiar with on his or her own initiative.

The academic utility of this book has a counterpart in the general community. What does a journalist mean when he reports that "the department's estimates are in committee," that the federal government will "abate several equalized tax points" to the provinces, or that "the formula for calculating equalization payments has been revised"? The language of Canadian politics is sufficiently unfamiliar that reference to this book can be useful to non-academics.

The entries are intended to introduce the reader to the subject. The references to works by academics, journalists, and government bodies will direct the reader who wishes to pursue a particular matter. In some cases, especially those entries about government agencies, readers should consult the *Canada Year Book, 1978-1979*, which is published under the authority of the minister of industry, trade, and commerce (available from Publications Distribution, Statistics Canada, Ottawa K1A 0T6), and *Organization of the Government of Canada*, prepared by the interdepartmental committee on the organization of the government of Canada (available from Canadian Government Publishing Centre, Supply and Services Canada, Hull, Quebec K1A 0S9). In some cases, the information will be dated and certain matters discussed will lack an important political context. In this volume, I have tried to provide that context; in any case, the two government references contain much valuable information that could not be included here. Finally, in 1979 the federal Task Force on Canadian Unity published *Coming to Terms: The Words of the Debate*, which contains definitions of key words and concepts related to what the commissioners call "the Canadian debate." The volume also contains extracts from important historical and contemporary constitutional documents (available from Canadian Government Publications Centre, Supply and Services Canada, Hull, Quebec K1A 0S9).

To attempt to compress the accumulated knowledge and wisdom of many careers into a few paragraphs at least borders on the absurd. I wish to acknowledge, therefore, the debt owed implicitly to those whose work comprises the body of literature from which I have learned, however imperfectly. I would like to thank Marsha Chandler and Frank Peers for their important comments on the entire manuscript. I also appreciate the assistance of colleagues in my department who commented on parts of the manuscript and made suggestions – in particular Steven Brown, P.K. Kuruvilla, and Harvey Pasis.

I would be surprised if the selection of terms and concepts, their definitions, and the citation of particular references met with only a few objections. The very nature of the subject matter makes the compilation of successful definitions difficult in some cases. There are bound to be items missing which some might have expected to find. In some cases, I decided to exclude a term if its meaning was so subjective that it could be understood only if a user placed it in context. I also tried to avoid seemingly "localized" items unless, like "Maritime union," they had implications for the larger political system. I also included historic items, such as "Lord Durham's Report" and "Conscription," if they continued to have contemporary political significance. I certainly take responsibility for the final product and thank those whom I have mentioned above for making it better than it might otherwise have been.

Finally, I would like to thank Helen Macnaughton and Dianne Gilchrist, students who provided important assistance in this project. Thanks are due Joan Dawson, Arvis Oxland, Susan Planta, and Angelika Sirois for assistance in preparing the manuscript. I benefitted as well from the encouragement, counsel, and skills of James Rogerson, editorial director, Francine Geraci, production co-ordinator, and Dee Pennock and Kathryn Dean, copy editors, of Wiley Publishers. Also, Wilfrid Laurier University deserves thanks for a grant which assisted the development of this project, and for computer facilities and personnel who made the editing and presentation of the manuscript an efficient procedure.

John McMenemy
Waterloo, Ontario

The Language of Canadian Politics:
A Guide to Important Terms and Concepts

Accountability. The requirement that an individual or group explain and accept responsibility before another individual or group for actions taken by them and by those under their supervision. In the Canadian parliamentary system, the principle of responsible government requires the political executive (that is, the prime minister or provincial premier and the cabinet) to respond to criticism in the legislature and to retain the "confidence" of the House of Commons or provincial Assembly in order to remain in office. Executive accountability is both collective and individual. Not only is the cabinet collectively responsible to the House, but each minister is personally accountable for administrative behaviour in his or her area of designated responsibility. Within the administration, deputy ministers (the senior civil service) are accountable to the ministers, who must assume publicly the political consequences of accountability. It is possible, however, that practice at the federal level may change to require deputy ministers to appear before legislative committees to answer questions and criticism. See *Collective responsibility; Ministerial responsibility.*

While accountability is a central component of the Canadian constitution, legislatures have seldom defeated governments or precipitated the resignation of ministers. The disciplined party system and the secrecy which has traditionally enveloped the cabinet and public administration have enabled governments and ministers to survive Opposition criticism. Nonetheless, the principle of accountability is sufficiently strong to allow the Opposition to make a public case which the electorate will subsequently decide. Also, a freedom-of-information act as well as changes in the Official Secrets Act at the federal level will strengthen the principle of executive accountability. See *Freedom of information; Official Secrets Act; Responsible government.*

Act (statute). A Bill which has passed three readings in the legislature and received royal assent. Legislation, or bills, are printed after first reading. When royal assent is given, bills become acts; they are given chapter numbers, with the name of the sovereign and the year, and are published. They are then statutory law. Acts are not effective until proclaimed, and in some cases not until invoked by the governor-in-council through an order-in-council which is also published in the *Canada Gazette*. Some acts delegate authority to particular government bodies to make regulations which have the force of law. These regulations, or statutory instruments, are also published.

Activists, party. People who, in terms of political participation, are involved with party activity beyond simply voting for a party but who do not make important decisions in party councils pertaining to election campaigns or parliamentary conduct between elections. Specifically, an activist is a person who holds membership in a party, contributes money to a party, serves as an officer of a party, attends local party meetings or party conventions, and works for a candidate during an election campaign or is personally a successful or unsuccessful candidate. It is debatable in the case of some parties whether "backbench" legislators are activists or elites; one might describe them leading activists.

Activists of all parties tend to be of higher standing than the passive supporters of their respective parties in terms of education, occupation, and income. Nationally, Conservative and Liberal activists are preponderantly high-ranking professionals. Lawyers are numerous among the ranks of all party activists, particularly Conservative and Liberal activists; business managers are more numerous among Conservatives and Liberals than among New Democrats; trade union officials are much more numerous among New Democrats than among Conservatives and Liberals. Women and young people tend to be underrepresented among activists in all parties.

For an analysis of political activists, see Allan Kornberg, Joel Smith, and Harold D. Clarke, Citizen *Politicians – Canada: Party Officials in a Democratic Society* (Durham: Carolina Academic Press, 1979).

Administrative (executive) federalism. A term which describes Canada's federal system, in which federal-provincial relations are characterized by a high level of interdependence which puts great emphasis on multilateral and bilateral consultation, negotiation, and functional operations. See *Federalism*.

Aeronautics Case (1932).   A decision by the Judicial Committee of the Privy Council which declared the federal Aeronautics Act *intra vires*. The court confirmed federal jurisdiction over air transportation under Section 132 of the British North America Act – power related to imperial treaties. In 1952, the Supreme Court upheld federal jurisdiction, although the British Empire treaty on which the Aeronautics Act had been based had been replaced by the non-imperial Chicago Convention. In this case (*Johannesson v. Rural Municipality of West St. Paul*, [1952]), the Supreme Court noted Lord Sankey's implication in the Aeronautics Case that federal jurisdiction over air transportation was a matter of national importance under the "Peace, Order and good Government" clause in the preamble of Section 91 of the British North America Act. See *Treaty power*.

Agency corporation.   A type of federal crown corporation which is responsible for quasi-commercial management of trading or service operations and the management of procurement, construction, or disposal activities. The "limited" agency corporations are established under the Company's Act, and their shareholder (the governor-in-council) appoints their boards. The budgets of the agency corporations appear before Parliament as an item in departmental estimates. The minister designated responsible tables the corporations' annual reports in the House of Commons. The agency corporations hire their own employees, who are subject to internal personnel management procedures. Agency corporations vary in financial condition. Some operate at a profit, while others operate entirely from parliamentary appropriations; some have large capital assets, while others have none. See *Crown corporation*.

On agency corporations and crown corporations generally, see R.A. Ashley and R.G.H. Smails, *Canadian Crown Corporations* (Toronto: Macmillan Co. of Canada, Ltd., 1965.)

Agrarian Socialism.   The title of a book by Seymour Martin Lipset which examines the socialist Co-operative Commonwealth Federation (CCF) and its government in Saskatchewan (Berkeley: University of California, 1950). According to Lipset, the success of the CCF came from the involvement of better-off farmers of British origin who had considerable experience in farm organizations such as market co-operatives and farmer-education programmes. Their socialism was not so much radical as conservative in respect to their desire for government intervention in the wheat-based economy. They wanted to preserve land tenure and stabilize farm income in the face of hostile forces in eastern Canada and in the international marketplace. See *Quasi-party system*.

Lipset's analysis of this prairie-based "third party" can be compared with C.B. Macpherson's more deterministic interpretation of Social Credit in Alberta (*Democracy in Alberta: Social Credit and the Party System* [Toronto: University of Toronto Press, 1953]). See the exchange between Lipset and Macpherson in *Canadian Forum*, November and December, 1954, and January, 1955.

Agricultural Rehabilitation and Development Act (Administration) (ARDA) (1961). A federal act to encourage more productive use of marginal and submarginal farmland and to improve employment opportunities and income in such areas. The act empowered the federal minister of agriculture, through provincial agreements, to assist financially projects designed to achieve rural developmental objectives. Initially focussed on soil conservation, water supply, and other land-management propositions, the programme later emphasized employee retraining in non-primary industry in depressed marginal and submarginal agricultural areas.

The Act represented the perspective of the Conservative Government of westerner John Diefenbaker which replaced a 22-year-old Liberal administration in 1957. The Liberal Government had been criticized for its "Ottawa-bound" view of Canada and an excessive concern with the interests of central Canadian manufacturing, industry, and finance.

Later federal legislative outputs with similar objectives included the Fund for Rural Economic Development (FRED) established by the Pearson Government in 1966 and the Regional Incentives Development Act (1969) under the Trudeau Government. All these measures represented attempts by the federal government to redistribute wealth through stimulating regional (that is, periphery, or non-core) development. See *Regional disparity*.

Air Canada. A federal crown corporation affiliated with Canadian National Railways, designated a proprietary corporation under the Financial Administration Act; it provides passenger, mail, and freight air service in and outside of Canada. Incorporated in 1937 as Trans-Canada Airlines, Air Canada came under criticism in the 1970's for financial mismanagement and for attempts to enlarge its activities in regional air services. See *Proprietary corporation*.

Alberta Press Bill Reference (1938). A reference by the Supreme Court concerning Alberta's Accurate News and Information Act (1937). The Court denied provincial governments the power to restrict traditional forms of the right of free speech and discussion. Feeling itself unjustly dealt with by a hostile press, the Social Credit Government of Alberta passed the Act requiring newspapers to correct, at the insistence of a government body, "misleading" and "inaccurate" articles. With the consent of the federal government, the lieutenant-governor reserved the measure.

The chief justice of the Supreme Court declared that the preamble to the British North America Act (1867), which committed Canada to a constitution "similar in Principle to that of the United Kingdom," assumed parliamentary government with freedom of expression. Thus the legislature, at least at the provincial level, could not violate such fundamental constitutional principles as free speech and an unregulated press. See *Duff Doctrine.*

Anti-Inflation Programme (Act, Administrator, Board) (1975-1978). A federal programme, initiated without prior provincial consultation in 1975, designed to reduce the rate of inflation through fiscal and monetary policies. It limited the growth of government expenditures and the rate of increase in government employment, and it introduced a policy to restrict increases in prices and incomes. In response to some provincial opposition, the Supreme Court ruled that the federal legislation "for the restraint of profit margins, prices, dividends and compensation in Canada" was valid under the "Peace, Order and good Government" clause of the British North America Act (Section 91). While the programme had these several objectives, most public debate centred on the "wage and price controls" which were directed against the more powerful groups in the economy. The Act provided for an Anti-Inflation Board to administer "guidelines" for prices and compensation, to monitor changes, and to identify increases which would have a significant impact on the economy, as well as to consult and negotiate modifications in those changes. When such negotiations failed, the matter was referred to the administrator for mandatory action and possibly to the Anti-Inflation Appeal Tribunal. A phasing-out of the controls policy began in 1978.

A report published in 1979 indicated that the anti-inflation programme had only a modest impact on prices and profit margins, but had a more substantial effect on wages (R.S. Letourneau and Claude Simard, *Inflation and Income Policy in Canada* [Ottawa: Conference

Board in Canada]). On the constitutional aspects of the federal action, see Peter H. Russell, "The Anti-Inflation Case: The Anatomy of a Constitutional Decision," *Canadian Public Administration* 20 (1977), 632-65.

Aspect Doctrine.   An assertion by the Judicial Committee of the Privy Council that "subjects which in one aspect and for one purpose fall within section 92 of the British North America Act (1867) may in another aspect and for another purpose fall within section 91." In *Hodge* v. *The Queen* (1883), the appellant argued that a conviction under an Ontario statute which regulated liquor trade in the province was invalid, despite clear enumeration of tavern licences in Section 92. The appeal was based on *Russell* v. *The Queen* (1882) in which the Judicial Committee of the Privy Council upheld a federal statute which provided for local prohibition under the "Peace, Order and good Government" clause of Section 91, as the question of prohibition was not specifically enumerated under provincial jurisdiction in Section 92. The two statutes dealt with different aspects of the same thing (the liquor trade); and the use of the "Peace, Order and good Government" clause in the Russell case was not allowed to deny a province's jurisdictional competence clearly stated in Section 92. See *Russell* v. *The Queen* (1882).

Assistant deputy minister.   The rank of permanent senior officials in the civil service. Their job classification and recruitment are the responsibility of the Public Service Commission. See *Deputy minister.*

Atlantic Provinces Adjustments (Additional) Grants.   Unconditional federal grants to the Atlantic provinces from 1958 to 1967 in addition to the equalization payments as an extension of the equalization principle. When the grants were discontinued in 1967, a special grant was made to the sum of what would have been the Additional Grant if continued. See *Equalization grants.*

Atomic Energy Control Board.   A federal crown corporation established in 1946 to regulate the development, application, and use of atomic energy. Through licensing and regulations, the Board controls all dealings in prescribed atomic energy substances and equipment, with regard for health and safety and for national and international security. The Nuclear Plant Licensing Directorate is responsible for licensing and regulating reactor, heavy water, and other projects. The Administration Division is responsible for the administrative aspects of radioisotope licensing and the Board's administration. The Material and Equipment Control Directorate is responsible for licensing and regulating the production of fissionable substances, radioisotopes, equipment, transportation activities, the procurement of raw materials, and the disposition of waste.

The AECB is a key government agency in the debate over nuclear policy. In 1978, the AECB and Atomic Energy of Canada Limited (which the Board regulates) were criticized in a draft report of the Organization for Economic Co-operation and Development (OECD) for the secrecy with which they have operated "outside the forum of major public debates and within the narrow world of the nuclear industry and electric utilities." In his draft report, K.G. Nichols of the science and technology division of OECD said the Board had "not always maintained effective regulatory compliance procedures" in its otherwise close relationships with AECL. See *Atomic Energy of Canada Limited.*

Atomic Energy of Canada Limited (AECL). A federal crown corporation established as an agency corporation in 1952. It is responsible for research, development, and marketing of technology for peaceful uses of nuclear energy, including the establishment of nuclear power stations. The development of the CANDU (Canadian Deuterium Uranium System) nuclear reactor took place under AECL.

In 1976 and 1977, AECL was under examination by the House of Commons committee on public accounts because of commercial practices disclosed by the auditor general. In its zeal to market CANDU reactors successfully in a highly competitive international market, AECL had dispersed more than $22 million to foreign bank accounts. The money was paid for the undisclosed and unaccounted-for services of foreign agents in the sale of reactors to Argentina and the Republic of (South) Korea. High-level staff changes occurred in AECL at this time; and in December 1976, the Government announced policy and guidelines to clarify the standards of business conduct by government corporations, agencies, and departments.

In 1978, the agency was reorganized as a holding company, with four quasi-autonomous subsidiaries, to achieve commercial and marketing as well as research and engineering objectives. The Atomic Energy of Canada Engineering Company is responsible for the design and marketing of CANDU reactors; the Atomic Energy of Canada Chemical Company is responsible for operating AECL's three heavy water projects; the Atomic Energy of Canada Research Company is responsible

for the research laboratories; and the Atomic Energy of Canada Radio-
chemical Company is responsible for the processing of radioactive isotopes and equipment for the application of radiation and radioactive
isotopes.

Also in 1978, AECL and the federal regulatory agency, the Atomic
Energy Control Board, were criticized in a draft report of the Organization for Economic Co-operation and Development for the secrecy with
which they had traditionally conducted their business. See *Atomic Energy Control Board*.

AECL reports to the House through the minister of energy, mines,
and resources; and its estimates are considered by the House's standing committee on national resources and public works. See *Agency
corporation*.

Auditor General. The federal officer who post-audits public accounts, investigates the financial affairs of most agencies of the federal
government, and reports annually to Parliament. The auditor general is
appointed by the governor-in-council, with the rank of deputy minister
for a ten-year renewable term until the age of 65, and is removable
within-term only with the approval of both houses of Parliament. The
revised Auditor General Act (1977) included recommendations in the
Report of an independent review committee established by Auditor
General J.J. Macdonell. The auditor general is to report to the House of
Commons regarding: any cases of accounts and "essential records" not
"faithfully and properly maintained"; money spent for purposes other
than those for which it was appropriated by Parliament; money spent
"without due regard to economy or efficiency"; and any failure to
establish "satisfactory procedures . . . to measure and report the effectiveness of programmes. . . . " Moreover, the auditor general can make
special reports, in addition to the annual report, on "any matter of
pressing importance or urgency. . . . " To achieve these objectives, the
auditor general and the auditor general's staff have "free access" to all
records relating to the accounts of the government and are to receive
any information and explanations from civil servants which the auditor general deems necessary. The staff is appointed under the Public
Service Employment Act, but the auditor general is responsible for personnel management within the office and may also contract for professional services from outside the civil service.

The auditor general's report is transmitted to the House and sent to
the committee on public accounts, which an Opposition member of
Parliament chairs. In turn, the secretary of the Treasury Board provides

a formal response to the report of the auditor general for the committee. The committee may receive the assistance of the auditor general's staff during its examination of the auditor general's report. The auditor general's office is itself audited by the Treasury Board.

Earlier in the 1970's, Auditor General Maxwell Henderson was particularly vocal about the laxity of financial controls in the government. The phrase "report the effectiveness of programmes" which is in the revised Act, may be seen in part as a response to Henderson's criticism and to the independent review committee's concern that the Government had failed to achieve "value for money" spent in particular programmes.

The review and the subsequent revision came during the tenure of Henderson's successor, J.J. Macdonell, who described the 1977 Act as "landmark legislation" (Conspectus of the Report of the Auditor General to the House of Commons ... [November, 1977], 3).

In his report in 1976, Auditor General Macdonell charged that the Government had lost control over its spending, and he recommended the creation of an office of comptroller-general to pre-audit spending. At the same time, he reported on the commercial practices of Atomic Energy of Canada Limited and Polysar, by which millions of dollars were unaccountably spent and double billing took place. In response, the Government announced guidelines for the business conduct of government bodies and established the Royal Commission of Inquiry of Financial Management and Accountability in the Government of Canada. The Government also announced in 1977 its intention to create the office of comptroller-general, giving the official rank of deputy minister. This office would be responsible to the president of the Treasury Board for the "quality and integrity of the financial control systems and administrative policies and practices" in the federal public service (Report of the Auditor General to the House of Commons . . . [November, 1977], 8).

Harry Rogers was appointed comptroller-general in 1978. In his report in 1979, the chairman of the Royal Commission, Allan Lambert, confirmed the auditor general's view of the Government's financial affairs. Lambert was critical of the tradition of budget secrecy, the technique of parliamentary scrutiny of the budget proposals, and the use of supplementary estimates. See Budgetary process; Comptroller-General; Treasury Board; Treasury Board Secretariat.

On the office of auditor general, see Sonja Sinclair, Cordial but Not Cosy: A History of the Office of the Auditor General (Toronto: McClelland and Stewart Ltd., 1979).

B

Backbencher. A member of a legislature who is neither a member of the cabinet nor, on the Opposition's side, a designated party critic. The public role of backbenchers in the House is basically to support their party leadership. The main outlets for parliamentary activity by backbenchers are the committee system and private member's legislation. However, the strictures of party discipline may still apply in committee. Backbenchers themselves sometimes cite the in-camera sessions of the party caucus as an arena of independent activity. See *Caucus.*

Bank of Canada (central bank). A crown corporation established by Parliament in 1935; it is responsible for monetary policy, for regulating the quantity of money in circulation, and for protecting the external value of the currency. The central bank achieves these objectives by determining the fixed amount of cash reserves and secondary cash reserves which chartered banks must maintain in the form of deposits with the Bank or through the holding of Bank of Canada notes. Primarily by buying and selling government securities, the central bank alters the level of chartered banks' assets and deposit liabilities. The central bank does not engage in commercial banking.

When the Bank buys government securities in the market, this adds to the cash reserves of chartered banks and allows them to expand their assets and deposit liabilities. Conversely, when the Bank sells securities, there is a reduction in the chartered banks' cash reserves, and they must reduce their assets and deposit liabilities. The Bank also achieves a particular monetary policy by altering the rate at which it will make loans or advances to chartered banks and institutions regulated by the Quebec Savings Bank Act (bank rate). Because the credit policies (interest rates and terms of borrowing) of private banks exert great influence on saving and spending decisions in the economy, the central bank's ability to affect chartered bank policies constitutes a powerful force in monetary policy. M-1 represents currency in circulation and demand deposits in chartered banks. If M-1, which indicates trends in gross national expenditure, is growing faster than desired, the Bank will dampen inflationary growth rates by raising interest rates.

On the international level, the central bank protects the value of the currency by entering into transactions to buy and sell foreign exchange and gold and silver bullion. It opens accounts in, and accepts deposits from, other central banks and international monetary agencies. Interest is received and paid on such accounts. Thus, when there is a "run on the dollar," the Bank may "prop up" the dollar's value on foreign exchange markets through purchases of Canadian dollars with foreign, notably United States, exchange and by raising the bank rate.

Until 1967, there was some uncertainty over the relationship between the minister and the chief executive officer of the Bank (the governor), and hence the independence of the Bank from the Government. The central bank began as a privately owned corporation in 1935; but since 1948, the federal minister of finance has held all share capital issued by the Bank. A difference of opinion between Governor James Coyne and Minister of Finance Donald Fleming in 1961 over appropriate monetary policy resulted in a confrontation which eventually led to Coyne's forced resignation. The decennial review of the Bank of Canada Act in 1967 clarified this relationship. After a period of consultation, the minister is required to give the governor a specific, written directive on monetary policy to be made public, "and the Bank shall comply with such directive" (Section 14). In 1979, for example, federal Conservative Minister of Finance John Crosbie resisted Opposition pressure to so counter Governor Gerald Bouey's policy on increases in interest rates.

The Bank's board of directors includes the governor, the deputy governor, and twelve directors. The minister of finance appoints the directors with the approval of the governor-in-council. The directors appoint the governor and deputy governor for seven-year terms with the approval of the governor-in-council. The deputy minister of finance sits on the board without a vote. See *Proprietary corporation*.

Bar (of the House).   A barrier at the entrance to a legislative chamber, beyond which no "stranger" or non-member may go. In the Senate, members of the Commons are summoned to the bar to hear the Speech from the Throne. Miscreant persons may be "summoned to appear before the bar of the House" to answer charges that they have slighted the dignity of the legislature or violated the privileges of members.

Bicameral.   An adjective denoting two chambers in the legislative system, as opposed to only one chamber (unicameral). The federal Parliament is bicameral by virtue of possessing the House of Commons and the Senate, while all provincial legislatures in Canada are unicameral.

Bicultural cleavage. A social division based on ethnic, religious, and linguistic factors. In federal politics in Canada, the cleavage is usually expressed in terms of the French-speaking and Roman Catholic community on one side and the English-speaking and Protestant community on the other side.

The bicultural cleavage is generally considered the most powerful of cleavages in federal politics because of the cohesive political force of French Canadians. Certainly it is the most historic cleavage, originating in the conquest of New France by the British in 1759-60 and being expressed in the subsequent, at times uneasy, cohabitation of the two communities.

Following disturbances in Lower Canada in 1837, Lord Durham recommended to the British goverment a policy of assimilation. However, the political cohesion of French Canadians and the achievement of responsible government in the 1840's resulted in a pattern of bicultural accommodation, which became the model for post-Confederation Canada. Since 1867, each cultural community has been sensitive to changes which might put it at a disadvantage in relation to the other group, and many issues have arisen to create anxiety and to heighten tension on the bicultural cleavage. The earliest such issues in post-Confederation Canada were the hanging of Louis Riel in 1885 and the passage of the Jesuit Estates Act in Quebec in 1888. Recent issues include the provisions following from the Official Languages Act of Canada (1969) and the language and constitutional policies of the *Parti Québécois* Government of Quebec which was elected in 1976.

At the federal level, the historic formula of political accommodation still holds. A party will generally possess the support of French Canada if its leadership in Quebec is integrated in that society and its leadership in English-speaking Canada is sympathetic to the cultural aspirations of French Canadians. Judging by the success of the Conservatives in the late nineteenth century and of the Liberals in the twentieth century, electoral success on this cleavage tends to be reinforced in subsequent elections. The party of French-Canadian favour is usually in office and able therefore to reward that favour in concrete terms. The party which does not hold the support of French Canadians often appears by contrast to harbour unfavourable attitudes toward French Canada. The leadership of the successful party naturally magnifies and exaggerates these attitudes in order to maintain the electoral allegiance of French Canadians and thus to style itself the party of national unity.

The literature on the bicultural cleavage is extensive. For bibliographies on French Canada and the bicultural cleavage, see *Canadian Journal of Political Science* 1 (1968), 107-18, and Richard J. Van Loon and Michael S. Whittington, *The Canadian Political System: Environment, Structure, and Process* (2nd ed.; Toronto: McGraw-Hill Ryerson Ltd., 1976), 506-09. See also the *Report* and studies published by the Royal Commission on Bilingualism and Biculturalism. For a list of published and unpublished work submitted to the Commission, see *Canadian Journal of Political Science* 7 (1974), 709-20.

Bilingualism and biculturalism. Terms which describe the French-English language programme of the Liberal Government of Canada during the 1970's, following from the provisions of the Official Languages Act of 1969. The Act basically declared French and English to be the official languages of Canada, with equal "status ... rights and privileges as to their use in all the institutions of Parliament and the Government of Canada." To achieve equal status for both languages, the Act required that federal departments and agencies provide service in both languages in designated bilingual districts. The Act also provided for a commissioner of official languages, commonly known as the language ombudsman, to oversee the enforcement of the Act.

The most evident impact of the Act has probably been the extension of French-language radio and television service across Canada in the 1970's. The most contentious aspect of the implementation of the Act involved recruitment to, and promotion within, the federal civil service to create a functionally bilingual service. The modification of the merit system – by the introduction of language requirements and the creation of single-language units within the civil service – was also designed to increase French-Canadian representation in middle- and upper-level positions where historically French Canadians had been underrepresented.

By the mid-1970's, the Liberal Government had begun to reduce its goals for bilingualism within the civil service, and in 1977, it decided to phase out its language training programme. Keith Spicer, the departing commissioner of official languages, declared the language training programme to have been costly and of limited success. However, his successor, Max Yalden, disagreed; he put the blame on poor provincial second-language training in the schools, the failure of senior civil servants to give language training a high priority, and the failure of the Government to explain its policy adequately. See *Commissioner of Official Languages; Official Languages Act.*

Bill 101 (Charter of the French Language). Legislation enacted in 1977 which, embodying the language policy of the *Parti Québécois* Government, made French the sole official language of the government, courts, schools, and economy of Quebec. The Charter was the culmination of debate in Quebec on language policy involving three party governments and their proposed laws: earlier, Bill 63 of the *Union nationale* Government in 1969 and Bill 22 of the Liberal Government in 1975. In 1979, the Supreme Court declared the sections relating to the Legislature (that is, government) and to the courts to be unconstitutional.

Under Bill 101, legislators could debate in English in the National Assembly, and litigation could be heard in the courts in English. However, only French versions of debates, documents, and court proceedings were to be official.

In the economy, businesses employing more than 50 persons were required by the end of 1983 to possess certificates indicating that they had converted their operations to French. In 1978, the Quebec Government proposed regulations to allow companies whose head offices for Canada were in Quebec to retain English as their working language, through a special agreement with the province, if they conducted 50 per cent of their business outside of the province. To obtain a special agreement, a firm had to indicate acceptable arrangements to make use of French inside the head office and to recruit francophone staff. Companies with most of their business in Quebec could still qualify for a special agreement if they conducted business outside the province frequently, used complex technology, required specially trained personnel, or feared that a "francization" programme would detract from their competitive position. Determination of the proportion of business done outside Quebec would be based on gross income for three years prior to the application for special agreement. Also in 1978, signs, posters, advertising, and catalogues were required to be in French.

In education, the law restricts school instruction in English to children who had siblings in English-language schools in the province when the Bill was enacted, or who have one parent who has studied in an English-language school in Quebec. Exceptions are made for temporary residents of the province, and Indians and Inuit. Temporary residents can claim exemption up to six years. The law does not affect post-secondary college and university education.

In 1978, the chief justice of the Quebec Superior Court ruled the section making French the official language of Quebec's courts and Legislature to be a violation of Section 133 of the British North America Act.

The provincial government argued that Section 92:1 of the BNA Act, which allows the provinces to amend their constitutions, was the relevant section in the case of the language law. The judgment, which was upheld on appeal in Quebec and by the Supreme Court in 1979, does not pertain to the law's application in education and business. On the contrary, the chief justice of Quebec ruled in a separate case that the provincial government could withhold funds from the Protestant School Board of Greater Montreal if the government determined that the Board violated regulations of the Department of Education, in this case with respect to Bill 101.

The *Office de la Langue française* is the government agency responsible for overseeing the implementation of and adherence to the Charter, which contains numerous exemptions and an appeals procedure.

Bill of Rights (Canada, 1960). A federal statute which enumerates the "human rights and fundamental freedoms" of Canadians. Canadians, the Bill declares, possess: equality before the law; freedom of speech, assembly, the press, and religion; freedom from arbitrary arrest and cruel punishment; and the right to *habeas corpus*, counsel, a free trial, and presumed innocence in court actions against them.

The Bill applies to federal jurisdiction only, and effective enforcement of some rights is ensured only by provincial legislation and regulations (for example, under Section 92:13 of the British North America Act ["Property and Civil Rights . . . "]). The Bill is not entrenched in the constitution; as an "ordinary" parliamentary statute, it can be amended or repealed by a parliamentary majority. It can also be made ineffectual by the invocation of legislation (such as the federal War Measures Act) which operates "notwithstanding the Bill of Rights."

The Bill has been the subject of confusing and seemingly contradictory judgments by the Supreme Court. For example, in *Drybones* v. *Regina* (1970), the Court declared the Indian Act to be in contravention of the Bill in the matter of racial discrimination. However, in the Lavell and Bedard cases in 1975, the Court upheld sex discrimination in the Indian Act. On the positive side, the requirement under the Bill that the minister of justice must ensure that new legislation does not violate the Bill suggests some value to the Bill. See *Civil liberties; Drybones case; Lavell and Bedard cases; Supreme Court.*

Block Payments. Unconditional federal transfer payments to the provinces introduced in 1977, in contrast to conditional transfers by the federal government on a dollar-for-dollar-expenditure basis. From the federal government's perspective, the new formula, based on a moving average of growth rates per capita, was preferable to the blank cheque of "fifty-cent dollars" by which it had earlier supported provincial expenditures in approved social service programmes. From the viewpoint of some provinces, block payments "disentangled" the federal government from provincial policy-determination in allocating funds for certain programmes. Critics of block financing were primarily among the public in those provinces whose governments decided in the late 1970's to underfinance post-secondary education and medical insurance programmes in particular. See *Federal-provincial tax-sharing agreements.*

British connection.   A reference to the political and sentimental ties between Canada and the United Kingdom, emphasized by the continued role of the British monarch as Canada's monarch and head of state and by Canada's membership in the Commonwealth of Nations, which includes most of Britain's former colonies.

The British connection has meant less in politics and sentiment throughout the twentieth century. In the late nineteenth and early twentieth centuries, Britain was the dominant foreign model of domestic behaviour. The national economy was then dependent on British capital. But as the glory of the Empire receded and the United States replaced Britain as the main external source of capital and became the model of domestic behaviour, the British connection was relegated to largely symbolic importance.

The last occasion on which the British connection created division among Canada's federal parties was during the Suez crisis of 1956. The Liberal Government then refused to support the British military intervention in Egypt. The Conservative Opposition objected particularly to Prime Minister Louis St. Laurent's reference to the "supermen of Europe" no longer being able to dominate the world. However, when the Conservatives were in power a few years later, their attempts to reaffirm the connection actually worsened relations between the two countries. For example, the Canadian Government at that time actively opposed the British Conservative Government's intention to enter the European Economic Community (Common Market).

British North America Act (U.K., 1867, and subsequently amended).   An act of the British Parliament which created Canada with originally four and ultimately ten provinces in a federation. It describes the components of the federal, or central, government and distributes power between the two levels (federal and provincial) of government. As the major written element of the Canadian constitution, it is not a document as complete as the written constitutions of some other countries. Indeed, a literal reading of the Act would give one a wholly inaccurate view of the country as a federal, but centrally directed and autocratic, régime. The succinct-phrase in the preamble declaring Canada to have "a Constitution similar in Principle to that of the United Kingdom" is a better indication of constitutional behaviour than much of what follows in the Act.

Other components of the Canadian constitution include: principles of common law; certain British and Canadian statutes which have had an important impact on the political process (for example, the Dominion Act of 1875 which created the Supreme Court, the Canada Elections Act, and the War Measures Act); orders-in-council; judicial interpretations of the BNA Act by the Judicial Committee of the Privy Council in London (until 1949) and by the Supreme Court of Canada; and informal practices established in Canada by custom, usage, and convention.

In *The Government of Canada* (5th ed., rev. by Norman Ward [Toronto: University of Toronto Press, 1970], 58-60), R. MacGregor Dawson contrasts a literal reading of the BNA Act with the actual operation of the constitution. Under the BNA Act, the governor general exercises supreme executive authority in Canada on behalf of the sovereign. The governor general is advised by a privy council which the governor general selects, summons, and removes. The sovereign is the commander-in-chief of the military. The governor general appoints the Speaker of the Senate, all senators (who hold office until 75 years of age), and almost all judges. The governor general summons and dissolves the House of Commons and issues writs for general elections. Bills involving the expenditure of money can be introduced in Parliament only on the governor general's recommendation. The governor general may refuse assent to bills passed by Parliament and may disallow a provincial act. Generally, the same powers possessed by the governor general are also possessed at the provincial level by lieutenant-governors, whom the governor general appoints.

The unwritten component of the constitution, however, contradicts this literal reading of the BNA Act. In fact, the governor general rarely acts according to personal judgment but acts instead on the advice of a small component of the Privy Council – the cabinet – which is not mentioned in the Act and which, in turn, is selected by the prime minister, who is also not mentioned in the Act. The prime minister and other cabinet members, the Government-of-the-day, must retain the support, or confidence, of the House of Commons to remain in office and must themselves have seats in the House of Commons (although some ministers may be in the Senate in addition to the Government's leader there). Should an election result in another party's winning a significant plurality of constituencies, the prime minister would in all likelihood resign; and the governor general would ask the party-determined leader of the new leading party to form the Government.

Under the BNA Act, each level of government retains specified jurisdictional competence. Acting within their jurisdictional spheres, the legislatures in Canada are supreme. The judiciary (before 1949, the Judicial Committee of the Privy Council in London, and since then the Supreme Court of Canada) is the final arbiter in disputes about the constitutional validity of legislation. The judicial rulings from London historically reduced the federal power asserted in the "Peace, Order and good Government" clause of Section 91 in favour of the provincial power asserted in the "Property and Civil Rights" clause in Section 92 (see *Judicial Committee of the Privy Council; Supreme Court*). The development of administrative, or executive, federalism since 1960 has reflected a preference of the governments to accommodate differences in a consultative, bargaining process rather than resorting to the winner-take-all route of judicial conflict resolution. References from the Supreme Court on the validity of proposed government action are sometimes used in the bargaining process.

The unwritten component of the Canadian constitution can be amended by establishing new forms of practice or by statutes; some of the written components, such as certain Canadian statutes or orders-in-council, can be simply superseded by new statutes or orders. Section 92 of the BNA Act conditionally permits the provinces to amend their own constitutions. Until 1949, the BNA Act itself could be amended only by an act of the British Parliament. Customary practice is for the British Parliament to amend the Act only when requested to do so by a joint address of the two houses of the Canadian Parliament. The British Parliament has never amended the Act on the request of a single or any number of provinces unless their wishes were expressed in a joint address by the Canadian Parliament. Also, the British Parliament has never denied a request by the Canadian Parliament for amendment, even when there has been provincial opposition. In 1949, the British Parliament amended the Act to allow the Canadian Parliament to determine its own structure and operation apart from provisions for official languages, annual sessions, and a five-year term. The federal government acquired the 1949 amendment without provincial consultation and consent (Section 91:1). Although it did not touch on provincial jurisdiction, the amendment established a distinction between matters to be amended by the Canadian Parliament and those to be amended by the British Parliament with, by convention, the consent of the provinces. In 1979, the Supreme Court ruled that the Canadian Parliament could not unilaterally amend the BNA Act with respect to representation in, and the role of, the Senate, matters which would fundamentally alter the constitution.

Since 1960, there have been several attempts by the eleven federal and provincial governments in Canada to "patriate," or domicile, the constitution by establishing a domestic amending formula. Such formulas as the Fulton-Favreau Formula (1964) and that included in the Victoria Charter (1971) have failed to achieve the support of all eleven governments. See *Fulton-Favreau Formula; Victoria Charter.*

In 1978, in a pre-federal election climate and before the anticipated referendum in Quebec on sovereignty-association, the federal Liberal Government abandoned its multilateral approach to constitutional reform and announced a timetable for a new constitution by 1981. Phase One included changes by 1979 in the composition and method of appointment, status, and powers of the Senate (later declared unconstitutional, as mentioned above), the Supreme Court, and federal tribunals; it further proposed an entrenched bill or charter of rights and freedoms, including minority language rights. Phase Two would have involved redefining the powers of the two levels of government. The proposals embodied in the constitutional amendment bill (1978) died, however, with the dissolution of Parliament in 1979. The minority Conservative Government which replaced the Liberals briefly in 1979-1980 was prepared to be more conciliatory to the provinces.

On the Canadian constitution, see J. Noel Lyon and Ronald G. Atkey (eds.), *Canadian Constitutional Law in a Modern Perspective* (Toronto: University of Toronto Press, 1970). On judicial interpretation of the BNA Act, see Peter H. Russell (ed.), *Leading Constitutional Decisions: Cases on the British North America Act* (rev.; Toronto: McClelland and Stewart Ltd., Carleton Library No. 23, 1973). See also J.R. Mallory, *The Structure of Canadian Government* (Toronto: Macmillan Co. of Canada Ltd., 1971), especially 1-31.

Brokerage politics.   Political behaviour based on practicality, which in politics means on actions best suited to achieving and maintaining power. Thus, according to J.A. Corry and J.E. Hodgetts, brokerage politicians and parties act as "middlemen who select . . . ideas . . . that can be shaped to have the widest appeal and . . . try to sell a carefully sifted and edited selection of [them] to enough members of the electorate to produce a majority in the legislature" (Democratic Government and Politics [Toronto: University of Toronto Press, 1959], 221). Both conservative and liberal thinkers justify brokerage politics as management of social tensions in a heterogeneous society through pragmatic decision-making to maintain social peace. Thus, R. MacGregor Dawson states: "The merit and general usefulness of political parties need not be elaborated here. In all democracies they [in part] are the outstanding agents for bringing about co-operation and compromise between conflicting groups and interests of all kinds . . . " (The Government of Canada [5th ed., rev. by Norman Ward; Toronto: University of Toronto Press, 1970], 415). Left-wing social scientists challenge the concept, questioning who benefits most from brokerage politics. These critics suggest that brokerage politicians deliberately magnify the importance of traditional social cleavages involving ethnicity and religion, thus discouraging the public from developing a class perspective on society and demanding appropriate public policies. Such a development presumably would not favour the wealthy and powerful interests in society which have historically financed the two most "practical" political parties, the Liberals and Conservatives.

Budgetary process.   The establishment of the Government's priorities for spending among existing and proposed programmes by the public administration and the cabinet and its committees, with parliamentary scrutiny and approval. The process is complicated and varies in detail among jurisdictions. The description here is of the federal Government recently. Constitutionally, the prerogative of introducing money or supply bills (appropriation acts) belongs to the cabinet alone. Parliament's role is to examine and approve departmental estimates and the Government's budget. The crucial decisions in the budgetary process take place in a highly competitive environment within the private confines of the administration and cabinet.

The focus of financial administration and control is the cabinet committee on the expenditure budget, or Treasury Board, and the Board's secretariat, a central executive agency. However, the process begins in the complex pattern of demands made on the Government from groups in society. These demand pressures are accommodated in the cabinet (under Prime Minister Joe Clark in 1979-1980 in the inner cabinet; under Prime Minister Pierre Trudeau earlier in the 1970's in the committee on priorities and planning, which he chaired) and in lower-level functional cabinet committees which receive and evaluate policy priorities from the departments and government agencies. It is from the decisions of these cabinet committees that the Treasury Board under the Liberals in the 1970's developed an annual expenditure plan and co-ordinated the estimates process. Although the Board functions as a cabinet committee, it has special status as a committee of the Canadian Privy Council established by statute. It has a minister, the president of the Treasury Board, as head; its members include the minister of finance and four other cabinet ministers. In 1979-1980, the Conservative cabinet included a minister of state to assist the president of the Treasury Board. The Board, which was separated from the Department of Finance in 1969, also has a secretariat which acts as its operational arm. A former secretary of the Treasury Board has written that what distinguishes the decisions of the Board from those of other cabinet committees is that the former "represent those hard choices which finally must be made in arriving at an expenditure plan" (A.W. Johnson, "The Treasury Board of Canada and the Machinery of Government of Canada," *Canadian Journal of Political Science* 4 [1971], 346).

In the 1970's, the Department of Finance submitted to the cabinet its proposals for fiscal policy for the budgetary year based on the department's evaluation of likely revenues and expenditures. This evaluation occurred approximately 18 months before the relevant fiscal year. The acceptance of this policy by the Government represented the fiscal framework within which the Treasury Board then allocated projected revenue.

Given the high level of competition within the administration, the Liberal Government in the 1970's had established two budgets: "A" budgets represented departmental forecasts one year in advance of needs to maintain current levels of service on established expenditure programmes for three years; "B" budgets were forecasts of requirements for new or expanded activities. Having considered departmental and agency requests, the Treasury Board Secretariat then prepared recommendations for consideration by the Board and the cabinet. Several months prior to the fiscal year, departments were advised of allocations approved by cabinet. Departments and agencies then drew up and submitted detailed estimates to the Treasury Board. In 1979, the Conservative inner cabinet established a ceiling for federal expenditures and blocked out specific sums, or "envelopes," for policy areas (economic development, social and native affairs, justice and legal affairs, Parliament, general services to government, defence, and external affairs). Cabinet committees and individual ministers were then expected to work within the fixed expenditure ceiling. Following review by the Treasury Board and approval by the cabinet, the Government tables the estimates in Parliament. In 1979, the ill-fated Conservative budget included five-year expenditure projections and an accounting of tax expenditures (that is, revenue foregone as a result of various tax concessions) as government spending.

The final and public stage of the budgetary process is parliamentary scrutiny and approval (or, on rare occasions, rejection, as in 1979). Main estimates and supplementary estimates are referred to committees of the House of Commons. Standing orders of the House deal with the timing of consideration of both main and supplementary estimates with respect to the current and the forthcoming fiscal years. There are three supply periods in which the Government's supply motions, or appropriation acts, are debated. On allotted days, motions made by the Opposition take precedence and motions of non-confidence are debated. On the last allotted day in each supply period, the Speaker interrupts debate and asks for a vote on all supply business then before the House. Party discipline among members makes the outcome of the division of the House predictable.

The governor general's warrant is an important exception to parliamentary examination of government expenditures prior to actual disbursement of money. On the report of the Treasury Board that there is no appropriation for an expenditure which, according to a report by the relevant minister, is urgently required, the governor-in-council may order a warrant authorizing the expenditure. Warrants must be reported in the *Canada Gazette* within 30 days of issue and reported to Parliament within 15 days of the next session when debate can take place.

The minister of finance presents the Government's annual budget in an address to the House of Commons at no specified time; but it is usually after the main estimates have been introduced, debated, and passed. The budget address reviews the state of the economy from the Government's point of view, the operation of the government in the previous financial year, and the forecast for the next year – the economic "outlook." The minister will also announce revenue measures, changes in the existing tax rates and tariffs. The budget speech is given within the context of a motion approving the Government's "handling" of the economy, which then leads to a wide-ranging debate lasting six days. When the motion is passed, budget resolutions and tax bills are introduced. Commodity taxes, such as sales tax, are usually in effect from the time of their announcement on "budget night," although they still require parliamentary approval. Bills which incorporate budget proposals are considered by the House as a whole in the committee of ways and means. In 1979, the minority Conservative Government accepted the passage of an opposition sub-amendment to the finance minister's motion as a vote of no confidence. Prime Minister Clark advised the governor general to dissolve Parliament and issue writs for a general election (which the Government lost).

Traditionally, Parliament considers the budget (revenue proposals) and departmental estimates (expenditure proposals) separately. Consequently, approval for expenditures is sought before the revenue implications are clear. Suggestions for improving parliamentary scrutiny of government expenditures include the simultaneous consideration of estimates and the budget. See *Estimates; Treasury Board; Treasury Board Secretariat.*

For a critical analysis of the federal budgetary process prior to the Conservative Government of 1979, see H.V. Kroeker, *Accountability and Control: The Government Expenditure Process* (Montreal: C.D. Howe Institute, 1978). See also G. Bruce Doern and Allan M. Maslove (eds.), *The Public Evaluation of Government Spending* (Scarborough: Institute for Research on Public Policy, 1979).

Bureaucracy.   For social scientists, an administrative system associated with large social organizations and involving the tenured careers of individuals characterized by hierarchy and status, specialized training, clear lines of supervision and accountability, objective judgmental criteria for career advancement, and the maintenance of records. In popular usage, bureaucracy is a pejorative word, often used with reference to the public service and signifying excessive size, formality and inflexibility, jurisdictional concerns, specialized vocabulary or jargon, and a tendency to self-perpetuation – traits described collectively as involving "red tape." See *Public service (administration).*

See Max Weber's classic statement on bureaucracy in *The Theory of Social and Economic Organization,* trans. by A.M. Henderson and Talcott Parsons (New York: Free Press, 1957). For an introduction to Canadian public administration, see T.J. Stevens, *The Business of Government* (Toronto: McGraw-Hill Ryerson Ltd., 1978).

By-elections.   Elections held to fill vacancies which occur in legislatures from time to time between general elections. The timing of federal by-elections is left to the prime minister, who, within six months of formal notification to the Speaker that a vacancy has occurred, may name any date. Thus, a by-election may occur within a short time of the notification of the vacancy or may be postponed so long that it is not held, due to an eventual issuance of writs for a general election. A by-election may be called quickly if, for example, the prime minister or provincial premier has engineered the vacancy for his own purposes or otherwise sees advantage in a by-election.

By-elections may be important if the Government does not have a solid majority in the House. Otherwise, they are exercises which test in a limited way the Government's popularity during its term of office without threatening its existence.

For analyses of federal by-elections, see Harold A. Scarrow, "By-elections and Public Opinion in Canada," *Public Opinion Quarterly* 29 (1961), 79-91, and Barry J. Kay, "By-elections as Indicators of Canadian Voting," a paper presented to the annual meeting of the Canadian Political Science Association, 1980.

C

Cabinet.   The political executive which formulates government priorities and policies. It is responsible for the introduction and passage of public legislation embodying government policies, the execution and administration of the policies, and the finances of the government. There is no statutory basis specifically for the cabinet. The federal cabinet is the active part of the Canadian Privy Council; provincial cabinets are known formally as Executive Councils. The following describes the federal cabinet, a model which is followed in the provinces except in the specific examples of power of appointment.

The cabinet consists of the prime minister (premier) and ministers who have a relationship in one direction with the governor general (lieutenant-governor) and, in another direction, with the House of Commons (Assembly). The prime minister is the dominant member or leader of the cabinet, the Government-of-the-day. A person becomes prime minister after the governor general invites him or her to form a Government. The prime minister then selects people for the cabinet and "advises" the governor general on appointments to the judiciary, the Senate, and many senior posts in the administration. The prime minister also effectively determines the date of the dissolution of Parliament and the issuance of writs for the next general election. It is effectively the prime minister's Government, which, though defeated in an election, may still remain in office to face the new House. Only when the prime minister – and not any individual or group of ministers – submits his or her resignation to the governor general, does the Government cease to exist. There are at least four types of ministers: ministers with portfolios, that is, political heads of government departments; ministers of state, responsible for policy areas but without departments to administer; ministers without portfolio, who have no statutory responsibilities; and the Government's leader in the Senate.

Custom, usage, and convention restrict the prime minister's choice of ministers. Currently numbering about 30, the federal cabinet ministers must have seats in the House of Commons or, constitutionally possible but less politically acceptable, in the Senate. Moreover, according to the principle of responsible government, they must retain the support of the House in order to stay in power. The House, however, is organized on the basis of a disciplined party system. Thus, the MP whom the governor general invites to form a Government is the party-selected leader of the party which holds a majority of seats in the House or, lacking a majority, is able to win the support of a majority of MPs on important policy votes. The ministers then selected by the prime minister are usually from his (or her) party. In addition, the selection of cabinet colleagues will often be the result of the prime minister's attempts to have people in the Government from as many regional, ethnic, and religious groups as possible.

Not having any legal status other than as part of the Privy Council, the cabinet acts formally as the Privy Council. Thus, the governor-in-council is the governor general acting on the advice of the cabinet through an order, or minute, of council which has the force of law. The cabinet is a collective body whose members are bound for life by the Privy Council oath of secrecy. Opinions which a minister expresses publicly are those of the cabinet. A minister may disagree publicly with the cabinet's view only after resigning from it, and even then must not disclose details of cabinet discussions or documents.

The disciplined party system in the House, along with the custom of cabinet behaviour based on an historic relationship to the Crown, gives the Government-of-the-day an outward appearance of strength, efficiency, and single-mindedness with which to fend off the Opposition. Political patronage associated with government (see examples of appointments listed above) also facilitates the operation of the cabinet. Perhaps the most notorious use of the historic, but largely formal, relationship between cabinet and Crown to protect the Government in its

more critical relationship with the House of Commons is the use of the
Official Secrets Act. This Act enjoins all Canadians – but in particular
public employees, Opposition critics, and investigating journalists –
from possessing, distributing, and publicizing information deemed to
be injurious to the state. This pressure may be applied against those who
are only embarrassing a cabinet which, in such circumstances, prefers
to pose as privy councillors to the Crown rather than as a Government
which is responsible to the House.

The cabinet is also protected by parliamentary custom. For example,
ministers need not answer questions about activities in portfolios no
longer held by them. (In 1979, the federal Conservative Government
proposed that cabinet ministers [but not former ministers who were
still in the House as backbenchers] be answerable for activities in pre-
viously held portfolios.) Basically, the Government and individual
ministers remain in office as long as they have the support of the majority of MPs, or as long as public opinion fails to rally behind the Opposition's criticism. The governor general is not likely to ask for a
prime minister's (that is, a Government's) resignation except in a clear
case of malfeasance and unless there is another MP available who
would have the support of the House. Canadian cabinets are not
known for disposing of their prime ministers; but prime ministers occasionally purge their offending ministers or bring them into line with
allusion to the satisfying post-cabinet careers to which the prime minister can appoint them. See *Budgetary process; Cabinet organization;
Inner cabinet; Regulatory agencies (regulations).*

On some of these matters, see W.A. Matheson, *The Prime Minister
and the Cabinet* (Toronto: Methuen Publications, 1976); Albert S. Abel,
"Administrative Secrecy," *Canadian Public Administration* 11 (1968),
440-48; F.W. Gibson (ed.), *Cabinet Formation and Bicultural Relations: Seven Case Studies,* Studies of the Royal Commission on Bilingualism and Biculturalism, No. 6 (Ottawa: Queen's Printer, 1970); K.W.
Knight, "Administrative Secrecy and Ministerial Responsibility,"
Canadian Journal of Economics and Political Science 32 (1966), 77-83;
and Donald Rowat's reply (*Ibid.,* 84-87) as well as his "How Much Administrative Secrecy?" in the same *Journal* 31 (1965), 49-98.

Cabinet organization.   The organization of cabinet reflects the prime
minister's and provincial premiers' prerogative in heading the political
executive. While the following describes the federal cabinet, the same
general principles apply to provincial cabinets. Historically, a federal
cabinet was a small body operating informally with little assistance re-

quired from its secretariat, the Privy Council Office (PCO). The contemporary federal cabinet, however, has an elaborate committee system and secretariat. While prime ministers will organize their cabinets to suit themselves, there is little reason to think that future Governments-of-the-day will revert to a significantly less structured operation. The rules of secrecy apply to the cabinet's organization as well as to its deliberations. Thus, what we know of cabinet organization and structure is what basically a prime minister will permit us to know.

The Treasury Board (committee on expenditure budget and committee on management) is an important exception to the foregoing because it is a statutory committee of cabinet – that is, it exists by an act of Parliament and is formally a committee of the Privy Council. The Treasury Board is chaired by the president, who is a cabinet minister, and includes the minister of finance and four other ministers. With its own secretariat, it is responsible for examining and making recommendations on proposed government expenditures and reviewing approved programmes, and for personnel management in the public service.

When Conservative Prime Minister Joe Clark's short-lived cabinet was organized in 1979, he established an inner cabinet, a group of approximately 12 ministers chaired by the prime minister and responsible for establishing government priorities and limits on spending. In that respect, the inner cabinet did not seem functionally different from Prime Minister Pierre Trudeau's committee on priorities and planning in the Liberal cabinets of the 1970's. The test of a formal inner cabinet would be whether it could assume effective decision-making power on behalf of the entire cabinet. The convention of cabinet solidarity might be weakened if "outer" ministers were compelled to shoulder the burden of a decision, especially one which was in an area of their responsibility, but which was not a decision for which they were personally responsible. The conventions of representation might also weigh upon a prime minister to the extent that the inner cabinet was acknowledged as a decision-making body, unlike Trudeau's committee on priorities and planning. Like the Trudeau cabinet earlier, the Clark cabinet of 1979-1980 also included several policy area committees. Clark's committees were: economic development, economy in government, federal-provincial relations, external affairs and defence, justice and legal affairs, and social and native affairs.

The cabinet secretariat, or Privy Council Office (PCO), the Prime Minister's Office (PMO), and interdepartmental committees of senior civil servants are major influences on cabinet policy-making. In 1940, an order-in-council appointed the clerk of the Privy Council to a new position as secretary to the cabinet. In 1975, the office of secretary to the cabinet for federal-provincial relations was created. Under Trudeau, the PCO organization was congruent with the cabinet committee system. (In 1979, Prime Minister Clark replaced the incumbent clerk of the Privy Council; and the secretary to the cabinet for federal-provincial relations resigned. In 1980, Prime Minister Trudeau transferred the Clark appointee and recalled the earlier clerk.) The PMO, which reports to the prime minister directly, also serves as a source of information and advice to the cabinet. Interdepartmental committees may be established voluntarily or by order-in-council to co-ordinate advice from the administration to relevant cabinet bodies. Consisting of deputy ministers or assistant deputies, these committees are often the site of interdepartmental rivalries and bargaining over competing interests within the public bureaucracy. The elaboration of the PCO and PMO as inputs to cabinet decision-making in the 1970's was, in part, an attempt to develop sources of information and advice in addition to the departmental senior civil service. See *Budgetary process; Cabinet; Inner cabinet; Prime Minister's Office; Privy Council Office; Regulatory agencies (regulations); Treasury Board; Treasury Board Secretariat.*

On the clash between the requisites of "participatory democracy" and cabinet secrecy, see "William Teron vs Walter Rudnicki: How Ottawa Does Its Business," *City Magazine*, November, 1976, 14-24. See also W.E.D. Halliday, "The Privy Council Office and Cabinet Secretariat," in J.E. Hodgetts and D.C. Corbett (eds.), *Canadian Public Administration* (Toronto: Macmillan Co. of Canada Ltd., 1960), 108-19; J.R. Mallory, "The Two Clerks: Parliamentary Discussion of the Role of the Privy Council Office," *Canadian Journal of Political Science* 10 (1977), 3-19; and Mitchell Sharp, "The Bureaucratic Elite and Policy Formation," in W.D.K. Kernaghan (ed.), *Bureaucracy in Canadian Government* (Toronto: Methuen Publications, 1969).

Canada Assistance Plan (CAP), (1966). A major, comprehensive, shared-cost programme between the federal and provincial governments to provide financial assistance for persons in need. Under CAP, the federal government pays the provinces' sharable costs for basic requirements (food, shelter, clothing, fuel, household and personal items, and special items for safety, maintenance, and rehabilitation) and employee costs incurred by agencies providing these requirements. Each provincial government determines eligibility requirements and rates of assistance; the federal government demands only that benefits be based on need, that an appeal procedure exist, and that there be no provincial residence requirement. In the case of Quebec, payments are made through the Department of Finance under the contracting-out provisions of the Established Programmes (Interim Arrangements) Act (Canada, 1965). Thus, CAP is basically a cost-sharing device among governments in a federal system rather than an integrated and uniform welfare programme.

Canada Development Corporation (CDC). A federal mixed public-private corporation created in 1971 to develop Canadian-controlled and -managed private corporations and to give Canadians opportunities to invest through it in the Canadian economy. In 1979, non-government shareholders held approximately one-third of voting rights in the corporation, and the Conservative Government appointed in 1979 intended to reduce government holdings to less than 50 per cent. The Canada Development Corporation Act allows eventually for up to 90 per cent non-government voting rights by Canadian citizens or residents, with each investor restricted to 3 per cent of the total voting shares. In 1979, approximately 18 000 private individuals and institutions held preferred and common shares in the CDC. The company's consolidated assets were more than $2.6 billion.

In its brief history, the CDC has concentrated on equity investments to obtain effective control of corporations in key industries related to resource and high-technology development with potential for international marketing. By 1979, the CDC, its subsidiaries and associated corporations, included 137 companies. In petrochemicals, Polysar, formerly a crown corporation, is now wholly owned by the CDC. In 1979, the CDC owned 30 per cent of Texas Gulf, Inc., one of Canada's leading mineral producers. In oil and gas, the CDC operates through the wholly owned CDC Oil and Gas Ltd.; in health care and pharmaceuticals through wholly owned CDC Life Sciences, Inc.; and in venture capital for small and medium-sized businesses, through CDC Ventures, Inc. Venture capital investments in 1978 involved word processing, aviation, electronic equipment, and chemicals industries.

The creation of the Corporation arose from the debate in the late 1960's and early 1970's over foreign equity (ownership) investment in the economy. The controversy led to considerable debate among political parties and within the Liberal cabinet. The CDC was a limited response to the demand of "economic nationalists" for federal government action to limit further "foreign takeovers" and possibly "buy back" key foreign-owned components of the economy (see Dave Godfrey and Mel Watkins, *Gordon to Watkins to You: A Documentary: The Battle for the Control of Our Economy* [Toronto: New Press, 1970]).

Canada Gazette.   A federal government publication which contains all proclamations issued by the governor general under the authority of the governor-in-council and all government notices such as orders-in-council, regulations, advertisements, or parliamentary matters requiring publication. The *Gazette* is composed of: Part One, which is published weekly and includes certain orders-in-council, proclamations, and other statutory notices; Part Two, which is published biweekly and includes regulations of government departments and agencies as defined by the Statutory Instruments Act (1972); and Part Three, which contains acts of Parliament.

Canada Labour Code.   A federal law, in effect since 1971, which regulates employment practices and standards in enterprises under federal jurisdiction which are not covered by the Public Service Staff Relations Act administered by the Public Service Staff Relations Board. The Labour Code therefore applies in the federal government outside the departmental public service and also in such areas of the private sector of the economy as the banking industry. Because labour legislation involves conditions applied to the rights of employers and employees, and therefore to local works and property and civil rights, the courts have confirmed that otherwise, labour legislation comes under the authority of provincial legislatures (British North America Act, Section 92:10,[13]). The Canada Labour Code also applies to works which Parliament declares to be for "the general Advantage of Canada or . . . Two or more of the Provinces" (Section 92:10[c]). The Code, which consolidated legislation existing in 1971, includes several parts relating to fair employment practices, labour standards, safety of employees, and industrial relations. The Canada Labour Relations Board administers the industrial relations part, which deals with the recognition of bargaining units and their rights. See *Canada Labour Relations Board; Labour Conventions Reference; Public Service Staff Relations Board.*

Canada Labour Relations Board.   A federal body established in 1973 which administers Part V (Industrial Relations) of the Canada Labour Code in industries under federal jurisdiction (otherwise, the provincial governments have jurisdiction in labour relations). The Board exercises statutory and regulatory powers relating to: bargaining rights; the declaration of a single employer and a single bargaining agent; the investigation, conciliation, and disposition of complaints of unfair labour practices; the definition of technological change which would affect the security of employees; and the declaration of illegal strikes and lockouts. The Board consists of a chairman, a vice-chairman (possibly two), and from four to eight members at any time, all appointed by the governor-in-council. See *Canada Labour Code*.

Canada Mortgage and Housing Corporation (CMHC). A federal crown corporation established in 1946 basically to administer the National Housing Act (NHA): that is, to facilitate the flow of capital into mortgages for new and existing owner-occupied, rented, or co-operative-owned housing. However, the CMHC, and its regional officers in particular, are involved through federal-provincial agreements in a variety of endeavours which have had a dramatic impact upon the urban landscape of Canada. The CMHC is involved in servicing new communities by aiding public land assembly and the expansion of sewerage and water supply systems; it is also involved in neighbourhood improvement and planning and in residential rehabilitation in urban centres. The Corporation is involved in the construction and administration of housing. It assists in the construction of senior citizen and native housing projects. In addition, it sets standards of housing construction for the private sector. Finally, funds are provided under the NHA to support the Canadian Housing Design Council, the Community Planning Association of Canada, and the Canadian Council on Urban and Regional Research. The Corporation's policy and research section advises CMHC on its policies, analyzes the housing market, and evaluates relations among the three levels of government (federal, provincial, and municipal) on housing and related policies.

The scope of activity by this federal corporation has extended considerably beyond its original role of increasing the flow of mortgage money in the economy. This is still an important function. But corporation policy has also been responsible for the sprawling, low-density suburbs of single-family dwellings which were constructed in the 1950's and the "bulldozer" urban renewal projects in city centres during the early 1960's, which replaced low-income housing with high-income housing, expensive retail shops, new city halls, art galleries, and concert theatres. Because its activities involve the distribution of hundreds of millions of dollars in a variety of municipality-based programmes and developments in a provincial area of jurisdiction (municipal affairs), the CMHC was the target of provincial representatives in the 1970's who were critical of federal policy, if not of financial involvement, in urban developments. Changes in the scope of the CMHC's activities may follow from a study which the Conservative Government commissioned in 1979.

Canada (Quebec) Pension Plan (CPP, QPP) (1965). A compulsory, earnings-related contributory pension plan which covers most of the work force between 18 and 70 years of age. The federal government introduced the CPP at a time when the provinces were increasingly critical of the centralization of fiscal and social policy. There was considerable opposition, especially from Quebec; this eventually resulted in the Canada Pension Plan and the separate Quebec Pension Plan. Under the CPP, the accumulated funds are at the disposal of the participating nine provinces in proportion to the amount contributed from each of the provinces with which to purchase Canadian and provincial securities. There are differences between the CPP and QPP, but pension credits accumulated under one plan may be transferred to the other.

Canadian Broadcasting Corporation (Radio-Canada) (CBC). A federal crown corporation created in 1936 which provides a national radio and television service, mostly in English and in French. Its parliamentary mandate requires a "balanced service" of information, entertainment, and enlightenment to encourage the expression of a Canadian identity and to enhance national unity. Parliament funds the CBC through annual appropriations and permits limited advertising revenue. The CBC's centre for English services is in Toronto, for French services in Montreal, and for administration in Ottawa. The secretary of state reports to Parliament on behalf of the CBC but is not formally involved in programme decisions. The governor-in-council appoints the CBC president and the board of directors, and the Corporation is subject to the regulatory powers of the Canadian Radio-television and Telecommunications Commission (CRTC).

Because of its public funding and its "nationalizing" political mandate, the CBC is subject to considerable parliamentary, governmental, and public scrutiny and criticism. In the 1970's, apart from standard charges of broadcasting immoral dramatic performances and biased public affairs programmes, the Corporation was subject to a Liberal Government charge that Quebec "separatists" dominated the news and the public affairs programming of Radio-Canada, the French section of the Corporation. Directed by the Government in 1977 to study the matter, the CRTC concluded that there was no evidence of "separatist" infiltration, although it generally criticized the Corporation's handling of the "national unity" question. There has also been dissatisfaction in the western and eastern areas of the country over central-Canadian (that is, Toronto-based) domination of CBC's English programming.

In the 1970's, the Corporation extended French-language radio and television services across the country, in compliance with the Government's bilingualism and biculturalism policy. However, critics maintain that the separate and distinct existence of the two language production centres tends to contribute to a programming schizophrenia in the Corporation, especially in its public affairs programming, and magnifies the bicultural cleavage in Canada. Thus, the suggestion has occasionally been made that the CBC integrate its French and English news and public affairs services. In view of recurring parliamentary and governmental criticisms of the CBC and the inhibitions that these criticisms may create in programme planning, as well as for planning purposes generally, there have also been occasional suggestions for multi-year rather than annual parliamentary financing of the CBC.

For an account of the early years of broadcasting and the CBC, see Frank W. Peers, *The Politics of Canadian Broadcasting, 1920-1951* (Toronto: University of Toronto Press, 1969); and, on broadcasting following the introduction of television, Peers's, *The Public Eye: Television and the Politics of Canadian Broadcasting, 1952-1968* (Toronto: University of Toronto Press, 1979).

Canadian Council of Resource and Environment Ministers. A corporation established and financed by the federal and provincial governments, whose presidency rotates among the particular governments. The Council, which meets annually, was created on the basis of a recommendation from the ministerial Resources for Tomorrow Conference of 1961. The Council possesses a small secretariat which works for the Council rather than particular governments. In the 1960's, the Council was concerned with policy related to such resources as water, forestry, and agricultural land. Since the late 1970's, environmental matters have been more dominant, including the disposal of toxic substances and hazardous wastes, and environmental impact assessments generally.

Canadian Human Rights Commission (Act, Commissioner). A federal commission established in 1977 to investigate and report on cases of alleged discrimination, in areas of federal jurisdiction, on the grounds of race, religion, sex, marital status, physical handicaps, or pardoned criminal offence. The Commission also enforces the principle of equal pay for work of equal value by men and women in the same establishment. Reports submitted to the minister of justice must be tabled in Parliament.

The federal Human Rights Act also provides for a so-called privacy commissioner to regulate the use of personal information contained in federal government data banks; and it allows a person access to the information to correct it and to determine its use. The Act, however, allows ministers to restrict access to certain files on numerous grounds, including national security and the effective operations of the courts or quasi-judicial agencies. Moreover, the ministers are not compelled to give reasons under which access is denied. These provisions may be amended in view of the commitment of all federal parties to "freedom of information." See *Freedom of Information.*

In the first two years as the commissioner of human rights, former Conservative MP Gordon Fairweather encountered both ministerial and administrative objections to the Commission's work, allegedly in areas beyond its jurisdiction.

Canadian Intergovernmental Conference Secretariat (1973-).
Successor to the Secretariat of the Constitutional Conference (itself created in 1968), which was established by the Conference of First Ministers in 1973 and which serves all first ministers' meetings and other federal-provincial or interprovincial meetings of ministers and senior civil servants. Though based in Ottawa, the Secretariat is financed by and is responsible to each government. The Secretariat exists, however, by a federal statutory order and regulation as a department under the Financial Administration Act responsible to the prime minister. Its federal estimates are examined by the House's standing committee on miscellaneous estimates, before which (as well as before other committees) the prime minister, by custom, does not appear. See *Intergovernmental committees.*

Canadian International Development Agency (Board) (CIDA).   The federal agency which is responsible for administering Canada's international development (foreign aid) programme and for recommending aid policy. CIDA's role, originally held by a branch of the Department of Trade and Commerce, was transferred to External Affairs in 1960. CIDA was designated as a department in 1968, with the secretary of state for external affairs as the responsible minister. CIDA is also a forum for interdepartmental and intergovernmental discussions and deals with other national and international public bodies. The Agency maintains contacts with private groups, especially in the recruitment of advisers for foreign assignments. CIDA's president and the Canadian International Development Board which the president chairs direct the Agency. In 1978, the Board included: the undersecretary of state (deputy minister) for external affairs; the deputy ministers of finance and of industry, trade, and commerce; the governor of the Bank of Canada; the secretary (deputy minister) of the Treasury Board Secretariat; and the president of the International Development Research Centre. The latter is a centre established by federal statute and financed by Canada. It includes foreign nationals on its board and conducts research into the problems of developing countries and methods of applying technical and scientific knowledge to their benefit.

CIDA has not been without its critics. In 1978, a report by the Centre for Developing Area Studies at McGill University criticized the Agency for an ambiguous development policy, lack of acceptable evaluation procedures, and financial mismanagement.

Canadian National Railways (CN).   A federal crown corporation created in 1923, CN is the largest public utility in Canada – operating a national railway system, a chain of hotels, a telecommunications company, an express freight company, and steamship ferry services. Since 1977, all rail passenger services have been managed by Via Rail Canada, Inc., a subsidiary of CN which the federal government finances separately and which has its own board of directors. The chairman and president of the board report to the minister of transport. CN is designated a proprietary corporation under the Financial Administration Act. See *Proprietary corporation.*

Canadian Parliamentary Guide.   A publication of the federal government which includes "thumbnail" biographies of current federal MPs and senators, names of officials of Parliament, the membership of the cabinet, and the electoral history of federal constituencies. The *Guide* also contains selective provincial electoral data. Different formats which have been used over the years may lead to some confusion when consulting the *Guide.*

Canadian Radio-television and Telecommunications Commission (CRTC).   A federal agency which regulates broadcasting under the Broadcasting Act of 1968 and certain telecommunications carriers under the CRTC Act of 1976. The Canadian Broadcasting Corporation, itself a major part of the national broadcasting system, regulated broadcasting until the Board of Broadcast Governors assumed the role in 1958 and was in turn succeeded by the CRTC. Authorized to regulate all aspects of the Canadian broadcasting system, the Commission sets standards of broadcast behaviour and considers requests for new licences or renewal of licences in the context of the Commission's standards. The Commission's powers extend, not without opposition from some provinces, to the cable systems which intercept radio and television signals over the air and deliver them by landline (sometimes involving microwave relay transmittors) to subscribers. The CRTC also hears requests for new cable operator's licences or renewal of licences and sets performance standards for these companies. For broadcasters, the most publicly contentious regulations of the Commission pertain to requirements for Canadian content, which the Commission established in 1970 and began to review in 1979. For cable companies, contentious regulations involve priority ranking of broadcast stations and community programming on allocated channels.

In its brief existence, the CRTC, chaired, consecutively, by Pierre Juneau and Harry Boyle, made the Commission an important forum for public debate and an important instrument for "nationalizing" the content of the Canadian broadcasting system. When Boyle was succeeded in 1977 by Pierre Camu, who had until then been a representative for an association of private broadcasters, some observers felt the CRTC might become more "industry-minded." At least by 1979 this did not seem to be the case, as the same public-minded process in the broadcasting sphere was carried over to the Commission's newly acquired responsibility for regulating the telecommunications industry. For example, the CRTC declared in 1978 that companies appearing before it for rate increases would have to start paying costs incurred by certain public interest groups participating in those hearings. At the time, some companies were incurring hearing-related costs of over $1 million, but these were for rate increases involving potential revenue of hundreds of millions of dollars. According to new regulations of the Commission, the companies – including, for example, Bell Canada – would also have to tell their subscribers how to lodge complaints against the companies and receive relevant material which had been supplied to the Commission on rates, service, and other matters. In 1979, John Meisel, a political scientist, succeeded Camu as chairman of the CRTC. See Delegated power; Regulatory agencies (regulations).

For an examination of Canadian broadcasting, including the regulatory changes in the 1950's and 1960's, see Frank W. Peers, The Public Eye: Television and the Politics of Canadian Broadcasting, (Toronto: University of Toronto Press, 1979).

Canadian Transport Commission (CTC). A federal regulatory agency established in 1967 to co-ordinate the activity of transportation carriers, railways, shipping, airlines, extraprovincial trucking, and commodity pipelines. The Commission has several committees to deal with the various types of carriers. The Commission consists of up to 17 members, including its president, whom the governor-in-council appoints for terms up to ten years. The Commission reports to Parliament through the minister of transport. The Commission is a court of record and its rules and procedures, including appeals, are published in the *Canada Gazette*. The decisions of each commissioner are also published.

A controversial decision of the CTC's air transport committee in 1978 illustrates a problem associated with independent regulatory commissions, which is lack of communication between the Government and the regulatory agency designed to implement its policy. In a split decision, the CTC approved Air Canada's purchase of a regional airline. The Commission's hearings did not include any testimony from the Government on competition or on the balance of public and private ownership in the industry, or on the future of regional airlines. The Commission's decision appeared to be based, nonetheless, on the question of competition. Several other regional carriers and the Consumers' Association of Canada appealed either to the CTC or directly to cabinet. The cabinet decided to allow the CTC's decision to stand, but it directed Air Canada to divest itself of the regional carrier within a specified time.

The CTC has also been the object of criticism by interests in the peripheries of Canada. Provincial governments, for example, appear before the federal CTC only as witnesses to request favourable policy, while some critics feel that the CTC should be a joint federal-provincial regulatory commission. See *Delegated power; Regulatory agencies (regulations)*.

See. J. Baldwin, "Transportation Policy and Jurisdictional Issues," *Canadian Public Administration* 18 (1975), 587-600, 630-41, and R. Schultz, "Intergovernmental Co-operation, Regulatory Agencies, and Transportation Regulation in Canada: The Case of Part III of the National Transportation Act," *Canadian Public Administration* 19 (1976), 183-207. See *Delegated power; Regulatory agencies*.

Canadian Wheat Board.   A marketing organization which the federal government established in 1935 to purchase wheat from producers in designated areas and to market it abroad. The federal government asserted control through the use of declaratory power (British North America Act, Section 92:10[c]). Since 1943, the Board has been the sole agency for marketing western Canadian wheat internationally and inter-provincially (oats and barley were added in 1949). Under an open market policy for feed grains, established in 1974, producers may sell to interprovincial markets for feed purposes. The federal agency's headquarters are in Winnipeg. In 1980, the Liberal cabinet included a senator as minister of state with responsibilities for the Canadian Wheat Board.

Capital crime and punishment. Planned and deliberate murder, murder in the course of violent acts, punishable by life imprisonment with eligibility for parole after 15 years served in prison. Although Parliament eliminated the death penalty for murder in 1976, the subject is contentious and Parliament might reinstate it.

See David Chandler, *Capital Punishment in Canada* (Toronto: Macmillan Co. of Canada Ltd., 1976).

Caucus. A regularly held private meeting of all MPs and senators of one political party to discuss parliamentary and electoral matters. Traditionally, a party caucus does not vote on issues before it; instead, it permits discussion to proceed until the party leader articulates a consensus. Theoretically at least, because MPs are bound by party discipline not to express dissenting views in public forums, and because the caucus is held in-camera, the discussions may be frank and critical.

On the Governments's side, the concern of private (that is non-ministerial) members about their role in caucus is particularly strong. Unlike Opposition backbenchers, they seldom criticize the Government in the House or in committees, and they lack the resources comparable to those of a cabinet minister to contest the Government's decisions even in caucus. Between 1968 and 1972, for example, MPs of the governing Liberal party criticized the political role of the Prime Minister's Office as denying them their rightful role in expressing constituency and regional concerns to the cabinet. The Liberal party then attempted to experiment with their caucus. The cabinet was to inform the caucus of measures it intended to introduce in Parliament. Until 1972, the caucus itself was formally divided into functional policy area committees to develop some expertise. In 1972, the caucus reverted to a committee of the whole and *ad hoc* committees. Government parliamentarians also meet in regional or provincial groups. Government caucus meetings themselves are structured events which probably dampen spontaneity and, though seeming to allow for more backbench participation, actually make it easier for the prime minister and cabinet to dominate the group. On the Government caucus in the 1970's, see Mark MacGuigan, in Paul Fox (ed.), *Politics: Canada* (4th ed.; Toronto: McGraw-Hill Ryerson Ltd., 1977), 435-38.

Because opposition parties do not have responsibility for introducing and defending legislative proposals, their caucuses are basically designed to devise parliamentary strategy to criticize the Government. At least theoretically, the decision-making in opposition caucuses can be more collegial and the responsibility more equally distributed, making for a potentially more effective and satisfactory experience in caucus for the backbenchers. Opposition party leaders in Canada have not been inclined to create formal "shadow" cabinets. When he was leader of the Opposition in 1979, Pierre Trudeau indicated that Liberal caucus committee chairmen would be the Opposition Liberal party's designated critics.

Census.   Decennial (since 1871) and quinquennial (since 1956) inventories of Canada's human resources, which the federal government conducts. The main legal reason for the decennial census is to redistribute seats in the House of Commons according to population counts. However, the census, which requires Canadians by law to respond fully and honestly to the census questionnaire, provides information on numerous demographic variables for private and public purposes. The data are used as social indicators to measure socio-economic welfare and to detect socio-economic needs such as improved education facilities, low-income housing, or minority-language service in certain areas of the country. Comparing data across several censuses, observers can plot demographic changes such as urbanization and regional migration patterns, which can result in the alteration of government programmes or the development of new policies to meet projected needs.

Census data are also important to decision-makers in the private sector of the economy and to scholarly researchers. Census data include information, for example, on age, sex, marital status, language, tenure of shelter, level of education, labour force activity, income, migration, urban-rural location, ethnicity, religion, and family size of the population. The census also provides data on household facilities, as well as manufacturing and agricultural statistics. The private sector can obviously use such information to develop products and services. Social scientists can use the data as standards by which to observe and describe human behaviour. Since the late 1970's, the federal government has tried unsuccessfully to persuade the provinces to help finance the census, which they also use for policy-making purposes.

Central agency.   An informal designation of key executive organizations in government, which may be defined narrowly or broadly. The
phrase may specifically refer to non-departmental central agencies in
government finance and administration (for example, the federal Privy
Council Office, Treasury Board Secretariat, and the Public Service
Commission); or it may refer more generally to any group whose terms
of reference extend across all policy areas. The latter definition would
include the Federal-Provincial Relations Office, the Prime Minister's
Office, and the Department of Finance. Such agencies are "central" because they establish policies which other administrative groups must
follow, and they co-ordinate and supervise policy-making by other
groups.

For a descriptive and empirical analysis of central agencies at the
federal level, see Colin Campbell and George J. Szablowski, *The Super-Bureaucrats: Structures and Behaviour in Central Agencies* (Toronto: Macmillan Co. of Canada Ltd., 1979).

Central bank.   The national agency responsible for the country's
monetary policy: that is, the regulation of credit and currency. See
Bank of Canada.

Centralization (decentralization).   Usually a reference in national
politics to the increasing (or decreasing) power of the federal government vis-à-vis the provinces; also, a reference to the location of political power at the centre with attendant antagonism towards the centre
from the alienated population of the periphery, or hinterland. In urban
politics, the phrase often refers to the debate over metropolitan or regional forms of government which involve the creation of a superior
tier of government and the elimination or weakening of long-established area municipalities. On national politics, see *Distribution of
powers; Federalism.*

Chief Electoral Officer (Canada).   The officer responsible for the
conduct of all federal general and by-elections under the Canada Elections Act, and for elections to councils of the Northwest Territories and
the Yukon Territory. The chief electoral officer is appointed by a resolution of the House of Commons and reports through the president of
the Privy Council. Traditionally, the office has been responsible for the
administration of fair and impartial elections, including the training
and appointment of returning officers, the drawing of polling divisions, the enumeration of voters, the preparation and distribution of

ballots, the actual conduct of the poll, and post-election reporting. Since 1974, federal election law includes: an income tax credit system for party and candidate support; limits on campaign expenditures; disclosure of donors' names; and partial reimbursement for campaign expenses. The chief electoral officer is responsible for administering the election-expenses provisions of the Act as well as for supervision of the election.

Civil law.   Private law practised in Quebec and rooted in the French Napoleonic Code and Roman law, as distinct from the uncodified English-based common law which is practised in the other provinces. The legal system of the former French colony was reaffirmed soon after the Conquest, in the British Parliament's Quebec Act of 1774, and finally in Section 92:13 of the British North America Act. The civil law governs personal, family, and property relations in the province. In the 1970's, the civil law was being revised by the Civil Code Revision Office in Quebec.

Civil liberties.   The phrase currently refers to the freedom of individuals to act without legal restrictions, especially in matters which may affect the political governors – for example: freedom of assembly and of speech, of religion, of the right to petition; freedom from detention and from arbitrary arrest; and the right to a fair and public trial with legal representation. In recent years, the list of traditional "freedoms" has been augmented by so-called "positive freedoms," brought about by the interventionist state. Examples are freedom from hunger, illness, and illiteracy, and from discrimination for reasons of sex, religion, or race.

Canada does not have an entrenched bill of rights, but the traditional civil liberties are recognized in the context of the preamble to the British North America Act, which describes Canada's constitution as "similar in Principle to that of the United Kingdom." See *Bill of Rights.*

In Canada, the legislatures are supreme in their areas of jurisdictional competence and are able to modify the common law liberties of individuals by statute. This applies especially at the provincial level, where responsibility rests for "Property and Civil Rights" (BNA Act, Section 92:13). Thus, when legislative breaches of civil liberties occur, they may be effectively challenged only on the basis of jurisdictional non-competence by the offending government. Usually only a minority on the Supreme Court of Canada has been willing at any time to invoke the preamble of the BNA Act as an effective defence of civil liberties against violations by Parliament and the provincial legislatures. See *Canadian Human Rights Commission; Duff Doctrine; Oil, Chemical, and Atomic Workers Case; Padlock Law; Saumur v. Quebec; Supreme Court.*

On the question of civil liberties in Canada, see *University of British Columbia Law Review* 7 (1972), 17-137; F.R. Scott, *Civil Liberties and Canadian Federalism* (Toronto: University of Toronto Press, 1959); and D.A. Schmeiser, *Civil Liberties in Canada* (London: Oxford University Press, 1964). See also reviews and analyses of important cases adjudicated by the Judicial Committee of the Privy Council and the Supreme Court in Peter H. Russell (ed.), *Leading Constitutional Decisions: Cases on the British North America Act* (rev.; Toronto: McClelland and Stewart Ltd., Carleton Library No. 23, 1975).

Civil service.   Body of government employees who carry out the administration of government. See *Public service (administration); Senior civil service.*

Class cleavage.   A social division delineating communities of interest based on the distribution of wealth. Class communities may be defined in subjective terms (that is, self-perception of class) or according to such objective indices as level of education, income, and occupation. Class issues involving the distribution of wealth include such matters as the tax system and business law, or generally the role of government in regulating activities in the private sector of the economy. Policies which would result in more public disclosure of company activities or which would redistribute wealth are said to be "left-wing" policies; policies to the contrary are described as "right-wing."

Unlike the situation in other western industrial societies, the class cleavage in Canada does not apparently generate independently as much public concern as do the traditional loyalties of culture and region. When left-wing class attitudes are expressed, they are often filtered through cultural and regional perspectives. Thus, a Quebec worker may inveigh against "English" business, or a hard-pressed westerner against "Eastern business."

The two major federal political parties, the Liberals and Conservatives, have not fostered clear class perceptions, but have focussed on regional and cultural tensions, adhering to brokerage politics (see *Brokerage politics*). The only major political party in Canada with a decided left-wing image, the moderately left-wing New Democratic party, has consequently not been very strong in federal politics; but it has made a dent in certain provinces, where class consciousness is possibly strengthened by other traditional communities of interest. The fact that labour law is, in large part, a matter of provincial jurisdiction helps to explain apparently stronger class voting in some provincial elections than in federal elections.

Nonetheless, redistributive questions have not been entirely ignored by federal governments. In the 1960's, for example, the national medicare legislation, the Canada Assistance Plan, and the Canada Pension Plan were enacted with redistributive intent. While the tax reform legislation of that decade did not result in the dramatic reforms recommended earlier by the (Carter) Royal Commission on Taxation, a partial capital gains tax was one redistributive measure introduced. Subsequently, the Royal Commission on Corporate Concentration which met during the 1970's recommended abolition of the tax. However, the federal Government shelved the report containing that recommendation immediately upon its publication in 1978, because of the Commission's consistent orientation in favour of "big business."

While the traditional attitude of the two major parties has been to play down class issues, neither wishes at the same time to be perceived as an upper class or "big business" party. The electoral success of the federal Liberals in this century and the concomitant weakness of the federal Conservatives is partly based on the more flexible Liberal approach to class questions and the more sharply defined image of the Conservatives as an upper class or "big business" party. The creation of the Royal Commission on Corporate Concentration in the 1970's was an attempt by the Liberal Government to appear to be acting on this class issue; it bowed to the left in creating the Commission and bowed to the right in appointing a business-oriented panel of commissioners. The Government's silence upon tabling the report in Parliament was also an important political act.

The delicate balance of left and right interests in the class-based strategy of the Liberal and Conservative parties may change in the face of the requirements related to the Election Expenses Act since 1974, which limits and publicizes financial donations to parties and candidates. Historically, the Conservative and Liberal party organizations have been dependent upon the private and legally unlimited largesse of relatively few Montreal- and Toronto-based businesses. However, any alteration would take time. Though the corporate dependence of those parties for finances may diminish, party personnel may still be drawn from upper class and corporate strata and retain the intellectual ambience of the private board room.

See John Porter's classic study of social class in Canada, *The Vertical Mosaic: An Analysis of Social Class and Power in Canada* (Toronto: University of Toronto Press, 1965). For a survey of the literature pertaining to voting and class, see Mildred A. Schwartz, "Canadian Voting Behavior" in Richard Rose (ed.), *Electoral Behavior: A Comparative Handbook* (New York: Free Press, 1974), 543-618. See also M. Janine Brodie and Jane Jenson, *Political Parties and Classes in Canada* (Toronto: Methuen Publications, 1980). For analyses of Canadian politics from a neo-Marxist, political economy perspective, see Leo Panitch (ed.), *The Canadian State: Political Economy and Political Power* (Toronto: University of Toronto Press, 1977). For a study which analyses the relationship of effects of region and class on political attitudes, see Michael D. Ornstein, H. Michael Stevenson, and A. Paul Williams, "Region, Class and Political Culture in Canada," *Canadian Journal of Political Science* 13 (1980), 227–71.

Clerk of the House (of the Senate). The permanent head of the House of Commons (Senate) staff, holding the rank of deputy minister. The clerk of the House is responsible for the records of the House and ensures that the Order Paper is prepared for each parliamentary day's business. The clerk is the recording officer of the House, maintaining minutes and recording divisions. Operating under the direction of the Speaker, the clerk supervises the staff of the House. The clerk of the Senate is likewise the chief administrative officer of that chamber and performs functions comparable to those of the clerk in the House. However, because the Senate is formally the superior body, its clerk is also the clerk of the Parliaments and is the custodian of the original acts of Parliament which have received royal assent. The seal of the clerk of the Parliaments is affixed to the copies of all acts, including those to be produced in the courts.

Clerk of the Privy Council. The person designated as secretary to the federal cabinet in 1940, a position which was established by statute in 1975. The clerk/secretary is the most senior of senior civil servants and heads the cabinet secretariat, which is responsible for co-ordinating the activities of cabinet and cabinet committees. Since 1975, there has also been a secretary to the cabinet for federal-provincial relations and a Federal-Provincial Relations Office which has responsibilities in that specific area. The clerk/secretary holds the position at the prime minister's "pleasure." In 1975, Prime Minister Pierre Trudeau made Michael Pitfield his clerk/secretary; Pitfield was removed by Prime Minister Joe Clark in 1979 and reinstated by Trudeau in 1980.

In a discussion of the estimates of the Privy Council Office in the Commons committee on miscellaneous estimates in 1975, Opposition Conservative MP Joe Clark said: "... from a position where it was simply clerks taking papers and taking notes to a situation where we have an immense government . . . , clearly an expertise has to develop. It would be naïve for anyone to suggest that power does not attach to expertise. Of course it does. The Privy Council Office is the cockpit of the expertise of the Government of Canada and, of course, power attaches to it (*Minutes of Proceedings and Evidence*, May 12, 1975, 33:17). At that time, Clark was objecting to the House committee's not being able to hear from the prime minister or the clerk/secretary on the estimates, but only from the president of the Privy Council, an honorific position for the Government House leader, and also the prime minister's parliamentary secretary. When Clark was prime minister, both he and his clerk of the Privy Council broke with tradition, and appeared before the committee, in 1979, to discuss their office finances and management. See *Privy Council Office*.

For a discussion of the difficulty of parliamentary scrutiny of the central executive agencies, see J.R. Mallory, "The Two Clerks: Parliamentary Discussion of the Role of the Privy Council Office," *Canadian Journal of Political Science* 10 (1977), 3-19.

Closure. Procedural provision for the Government to curtail debate in the legislature. As the legislature's roles are the conflicting ones of criticizing and enacting government legislation, the Government's strategy is to conduct the business of the House expeditiously, while the Opposition's strategy is to create public lack of confidence in the Government. In order to prevent tiresome and possibly politically harmful debate by the Opposition, the procedures of the legislature allow for closure, whereby the Government can unilaterally terminate debate on any matter when no agreement on termination can be reached among the parties' House leaders.

Since the imposition of closure in the so-called pipeline debate in 1956 with attendant negative publicity for the Government, federal Governments have been reluctant to use closure. In 1969, the Government had to use closure in order to introduce changes in the standing orders (procedural rules) of the House of Commons to refashion the rules on limiting debate. Standing order 75(a), (b), and (c) provides for limitation of debate at each stage of a bill's passage through the House. When the Government cannot obtain the agreement of a majority of the parties in setting time limits for debate, the Government may propose an "allocation-of-time" order which is debatable for only two hours.

Coalition government. A Government-of-the-day which includes members from more than one political party. Formal or informal coalitions are required in a parliamentary system when the Government party does not have majority support in the legislature. While formal coalition Governments have been common in provincial politics, there have only been two cases in federal politics: the coalition for Confederation in 1867 and the Union Government from 1917 to 1920. Conservative Prime Minister Robert Borden created the Union Government, which included English-speaking Liberals, in 1917 to expedite conscription and contest a wartime election. The Union Government divided Canada deeply between English and French. Neither the Conservatives nor the Liberal-Unionists appeared to benefit from the coalition experience. Since then, minority Government parties and small groups in the Opposition have preferred to deal with each other on an informal basis, although there are inherent difficulties even here for the junior member. In the federal election of 1974, for example, the opposition New Democratic party appeared to lose, and the governing Liberals to gain, from the two-year informal alliance following the 1972 election. See *Union Government.*

Collective (cabinet) reponsibility. The principle by convention that the cabinet, though composed of many minds, speaks as one and is responsible or accountable as a body to the legislature for the actions and policies of each minister and his or her department. The concept of responsibility which is individual (that is, ministerial), as well as collective, is central to the control of executive power and to parliamentary democracy in Canada. The Government must retain the "confidence" of the legislature (the House of Commons in the bicameral Parliament) in order to remain in office. See *Accountability; Cabinet; Ministerial responsibility; Responsible government.*

See T.M. Denton, "Ministerial Responsibility: A Contemporary Perspective," in Richard Schultz, Orest M. Kruhlak, and John C. Terry, (eds.) *The Canadian Political Process* (3rd ed. rev.; Toronto: Holt, Rinehart, and Winston of Canada, Limited, 1979), 344-62.

Combines (anti-combines legislation). An alliance or close association of private companies which may restrict trade and facilitate price-fixing. Anti-combines legislation declares certain business practices to be illegal, notably those which "unduly" lessen competition at all stages of production, distribution, and retailing in trade and commerce. The director of investigation and research in the bureau of competition policy, in the federal Department of Consumer and Corporate Affairs, is responsible for investigating combines. The director may examine witnesses, search premises, and demand written submissions in the conduct of this office. The Restrictive Trade Practices Commission is responsible for evaluating the evidence before making a recommendation to the minister. Regardless of the minister's decision, it is required by law that each report of the Commission be published.

Prosecutions, especially successful ones, under anti-combines laws are rare. Some critics charge that the legislation is designed to give the appearance of government supervision without excessively disturbing large-scale business with the reality of supervision. Because prosecutions are judicial rather than administrative in nature, judicial rules of evidence apply, involving costly gathering of admissable evidence and court proceedings with the usual provisions for appeals.

Commissioner of Official Languages (language ombudsman). The federal officer responsible for ensuring the recognition of equal status for French and English in the operations of the government of Canada. This officer advises the public of the requirements of the Official Languages Act of 1969, receives complaints, and conducts investigations of alleged violations. Parliament appoints the commissioner, according to the Official Languages Act, for seven years, renewable until 65 years of age.

The first Commissioner, Keith Spicer, and his successor in 1977, Max Yalden, have stressed the importance of making French a language of work in the federal civil service. However, they disagree on the value of the in-service language training programme. Spicer suggested in 1977 that the costly programme had not been very successful but had probably achieved what it could. He recommended greater provincial commitment to second-language training in the schools. Yalden, however, with respect to the Government's decision to phase out in-service training after 1983, reported to Parliament in 1978: "It is sheer foolishness to assume that future public servants, now 16 years old and in secondary schools in British Columbia, Nova Scotia, for that matter in parts of Quebec, will show up by 1983 fully bilingual and ready for service in English and French." See *Bilingualism; Official Languages Act.*

Committee of the Whole (Supply; Ways and Means). Until 1969, the House of Commons committee which examined bills after second reading. Supply bills were dealt with in committee of supply; revenue bills in committee of ways and means. Since then, departmental estimates have gone to the relevant standing committee of the House.

The committee of the whole includes all the members of the Commons, meeting in the chamber as a committee chaired by the deputy speaker. The Commons used to meet as committee of the whole to consider legislation clause by clause after second reading of the bill when approval in principle was granted. Now, clause-by-clause study of legislation is performed in the relevant standing committee.

The objective of this change from the committee of the whole to policy area-designated standing committees was to involve more MPs in the legislative process and to allow for specialization. The change has not been a complete success, especially for members of the Opposition, whose criticism of the Government is now diffused in committees which do not receive much attention from the mass media. However, a complete reversion to the pre-1969 practice is unlikely. In 1979, the federal Conservative Government proposed in a White Paper on the reform of Parliament that, each spring, the leader of the Opposition designate two departments whose estimates would be debated in committee of the whole rather than in standing committees. See *Standing (select, special) committees.*

Common Law. The unwritten law based on custom, as opposed to statutory law; it is found in many English-speaking parts of the world. The common law has been very important in the development of Canadian government. For example, the discretionary, or prerogative, powers of the Crown derive in part from common law, restricted from time to time by statutory instruments. Civil liberties such as freedom of speech and of religion are also rooted in the common law. However, under Section 92:13 of the British North America Act, the provinces have the power to modify common law rights by statute. At the federal level, a Government may propose amendments to the criminal law to modify common law rights (Section 91:27). Consequently, there has always been a body of opinion in Canada favouring an entrenched bill of rights. See *Bill of Rights; Civil liberties.*

Commonwealth (The British . . . of Nations). An association of approximately 35 independent nations and some associated states which were former colonies or trusts of the United Kingdom. The Commonwealth has a secretariat in London reponsible for conferences pertaining to both governmental and non-governmental programmes in trade, technical co-operation, youth, science, and athletics. The Commonwealth originated in imperial conferences held in the early decades of the twentieth century, but it constitutionally dates from the Statute of Westminster of 1931 (see *Statute of Westminster*).

The British monarch, who is also the monarch of Canada and of several other Commonwealth countries, serves as head of the Commonwealth. The main body of the association consists of the heads of government who hold an informal meeting every two years.

Communist party of Canada.   Founded as a Marxist-Leninist party in 1921, the Communist party of Canada was an illegal organization, operating underground or under another label for some of its history. Otherwise, it has competed for electoral office legally under its official name. The Communist party has supported the policies of the Communist Party of the Soviet Union.

Generally unimportant as an electoral force, the Communist party experienced its greatest success during the depression of the 1930's, when it participated actively and prominently in the organization of some trade unions. During the short-lived Soviet-German defence pact at the outbreak of World War Two, the party sought to undermine the industrial labour movement. Styled the Labour Progressive party from 1943 to 1959, it was courted unofficially by the Liberal party in 1945 in an effort to ward off the growing strength of the socialist CCF. The party managed to elect an MP, who was later convicted of conspiracy in a Soviet espionage operation in the late 1940's.

The Soviet party's denunciation of Stalin, the Soviet invasion of several European countries, and the Sino-Soviet schism in the 1950's and 1960's were severe blows to a party which even then was of little electoral significance. The Communist party of Canada (Marxist-Leninist), a small group which is loyal to the ideas of Mao Tse-Tung, and which is a splinter from the Communist party itself, has become more prominent in elections and political activity generally than the Communist party.

See Ivan Avakumovic, *Communism in Canada: A History* (Toronto: McClelland and Stewart Ltd., 1975); William Rodney, *Soldiers of the International: A History of the Communist Party of Canada, 1919–1929* (Toronto: University of Toronto Press, 1968); and I.M. Abella, *Nationalism, Communism, and Canadian Labour: The C.I.O., The Communist Party, and the Canadian Congress of Labour, 1935-36* (Toronto: University of Toronto Press, 1972).

Community (the Francophone) (la Francophonie).   An association of
French-speaking or partly French-speaking states and associated states
founded in the early 1960's. The term *"la Francophonie"* also refers
more generally to relations among French-speaking states. Initially ill-
disposed to the idea when a spirit of independence took hold in most
French colonies in Africa in the early 1960's, President Charles De
Gaulle later came to appreciate the positive foreign policy implication
for France of such an association. Thus, France has sought to use the
community and other *"Francophonie"* endeavours to enhance the position of France as the central force in *"la Francophonie."*

For its part, the Canadian government has sought to demonstrate
abroad the bilingual and bicultural aspect of Canadian society by associating itself with *"la Francophonie."* By France, however, particularly
under De Gaulle, Canada has been perceived as a challenger to a
France-centred *"Francophonie,"* and a challenger with a predominantly English-speaking cast as well. Consequently, French reaction
has ranged from outright support in the 1960's for the Quebec independence movement to a recent structuring of *"Francophonie"* conferences in order to reduce the impact of Canada's association.

As a member of the Community, Canada is involved in multilateral
and bilateral trade, as well as technical, youth, education, and athletic
endeavours through the Agency for Cultural and Technical Co-operation and in various conferences of ministers (education and youth, for
example). The Canadian government has also approved the participation of notably Quebec, but also Manitoba, New Brunswick, and Ontario in agency and conference activities. For example, a Quebec official occupies one of Canada's two positions on the Agency's board of
directors.

Compact Theory of Confederation.   An interpretation that treats the
British North America Act of 1867 as the outcome of a treaty, or compact, among colonial participants. The provinces are understood to be
the successors of the colonial elites, and all provincial governments
therefore heirs to a negotiating role in Confederation. Thus, all provinces, according to this theory, must consent to proposed amendments
to the Act.

The theory, however, has no legal foundation, and the Act on occasion has been amended without consultation with the provinces. The
federal government has also used the theory as an excuse for inaction,
to avoid a constitutional controversy. Indeed, Prime Minister William
Lyon Mackenzie King managed to take both positions within a three-

year period. The "unemployment insurance" amendment of 1940 was postponed until the approval of all provinces was received. "We have avoided," King told the Commons, "a very critical constitutional question... whether... in amending the British North America Act it is absolutely necessary to secure the consent of all provinces ... " (Canada, House of Commons, *Debates*, June 21, 1949, 1117–18). In the case in 1943 of the postponement of the redistribution of seats in the Commons, King did not consult the provinces and refused to relay the Quebec premier's request that the British Parliament reject the federal amendment. Then, it was King's opinion that "the [compact] theory ... does not appear to be supported either in history or in law" (*Montreal Gazette*, July 16, 1943).

Comptroller-General (of Canada).   Appointed by the federal government at deputy minister rank, the comptroller-general presents to the president of the Treasury Board an evaluation of financial controls, reporting systems, and programme objectives of government departments. The government created the position in 1977 and appointed the first comptroller-general in 1978. The creation of the office was a response to criticism in 1976 by the auditor general that the Government had in effect lost control of the treasury.

The first comptroller-general was Harry Rogers, a former vice-president of a Canadian subsidiary of a U.S.-based multinational corporation. Rogers accepted the position when he was satisfied that he could establish "effective relationships" with senior public officials and establish an agreement with the Government on resources and organizational needs to develop systems of financial management in the departments. The comptroller-general has to contend with a public system in which department heads traditionally tend to spend money in order to claim comparable or increased funding from the Treasury Board; in which salaries and ranks of senior officials depend in part on the number of people beneath them; and in which appointments to senior rank are often a result of skill in policy counsel and personnel management, rather than in financial management.

In 1978, the comptroller-general took over two branches of the Treasury Board which were responsible for financial administration and the development of guidelines for measuring economy, efficiency, and effectiveness in the civil service. In 1979, the comptroller-general prepared status reports on the 20 largest departments as a basis for future action in accounting controls and reporting, internal financial audits, programme assessment systems, forecasting, and budgeting. These studies (Improvement in Management Practices and Control [IMPAC]) were not to be made public, although the "action plans" based on them would be presented to Parliament.

Unlike the auditor general, the comptroller-general has no direct access to Parliament. However, the auditor general will still be able to report to Parliament on the progress of the comptroller-general. See *Auditor General; Treasury Board Secretariat*.

On the Office of comptroller-general, see Sonja Sinclair, *Cordial but Not Cozy: A History of the Office of the Auditor General* (Toronto: McClelland and Stewart Ltd., 1979).

Concurrent powers.   Under Section 95 of the British North America Act, agriculture and immigration are designated as areas of jurisdictional competence held by both federal and provincial levels of government. The Act was amended in 1951 (Section 94[a]) to add old age pensions as an area of concurrent power. In the case of conflicting legislation, the Act provides for federal superiority in agriculture and immigration, but no federal legislation on pensions can "affect the operations" of any provincial legislation on that subject.

Conditional grants (special-purpose transfer payments).   Also referred to as grants-in-aid, federal monies transferred to provincial treasuries for agreed upon, shared-cost programmes. Such grants, or transfer payments, involve hundreds of millions of dollars annually. At the close of World War One, conditional grants were experimental and involved programmes with fixed terms. By the mid-1970's, the federal government was moving to extricate itself from expensive shared-cost programmes in such provincial fields as social welfare, hospital and medical care, and post-secondary education. Through joint federal-provincial efforts, minimum national standards of service could be established without having to amend the constitution. However, the federal government was committing itself in uncontrollable, or statutory, expenditures to subsidizing escalating costs of provincial programmes; and the provinces were increasingly opposed to the federal government setting their policy priorities. For example, the federal Medical Care Act (1968) allowed the federal government to pay 50 per cent of the national average per capita costs of insured medical services in provinces which established plans meeting federal requirements – that is, which were comprehensive, universal, portable, and publicly administered.

The initial federal response to provincial criticisms and rising costs came in 1965. Under the Established Programmes (Interim Arrangements) Act of 1965, the provinces were given the option of contracting or opting out of shared-cost programmes. Only Quebec took up the offer to assume all administrative and financial responsibilities for programmes in return for a specified percentage of the individual income tax on the income of the province's residents (tax abatement) and, in certain programmes, an associated equalization and operating cost adjustment grant.

Since 1965, the federal government has been putting limits on federal payments in shared-cost programmes. Under the Established Programmes and Fiscal Arrangements Acts of 1977, the federal government replaced conditional grants for medical and hospital insurance and for post-secondary education with unconditional grants and abatement of tax points. Since then, the provinces have met rising costs by increasing revenue, shifting funds from one programme to another, or reducing services through a programme. See *Equalization grants; Established Programmes (Interim Arrangements) Act; Federal-provincial tax-sharing agreements.*

Confederation. The act of creating Canada as a federal union with a constitution otherwise similar to that of the United Kingdom, embodied in the British North America Act (U.K.), July 1, 1867, through the union of Canada, New Brunswick, and Nova Scotia.

Confederation represented a response of several colonial elites to American expansion, the changing nature of imperial needs, and their domestic self-interest. The internal impetus came from the Province of Canada, where political and ethnic conflict had immobilized the political forces of Canada East (known earlier as Lower Canada) and Canada West (Upper Canada). Initially well-disposed to Maritime union because of the smallness and isolation of their colonies, politicians from New Brunswick, Nova Scotia, and Prince Edward Island met in Charlottetown in 1864 to discuss their problems. Canadian politicians, who had by then formed a grand coalition to pursue the project of a larger union, attended the Maritime conference to advance their proposition. The conference at Charlottetown was followed by one at Quebec City to consider formally a federal union. The Quebec conference adopted 72 resolutions, including one to seek "the sanction of the Imperial and Local Parliaments...for the union...."

Only the Province of Canada, however, had much enthusiasm for the union. Newfoundland and Prince Edward Island refused to participate. The Government of New Brunswick was defeated in an election on the issue, and the Nova Scotia Government simply reaffirmed its support for a Maritime union. The Canadian Government then lobbied the British government, which put considerable pressure on the Maritimes. In a conference in London begun late in 1866, representatives from Canada, Nova Scotia, and New Brunswick agreed to 69 resolutions which became the basis of the British North America Act.

Under the Act, Canada was created as a federation with a strong central government and a constitution similar in principle to that of the United Kingdom. French and English were made the official languages of Parliament, the federal courts, and the Legislature and courts of Quebec; minority rights in education were guaranteed in all provinces, which now included Ontario and Quebec as well as New Brunswick and Nova Scotia. The bicameral Parliament included an elected lower house and an appointed upper house based on regional representation. Recognizing the weak financial basis of the provinces, the principle of federal statutory subsidies was established. The western British North American territories known as Rupert's Land and the Northwest Territory were later annexed to Canada and administered by the Canadian government. In 1870, Manitoba was created as a province on the same bilingual basis as Quebec, though that was changed later. British Columbia "entered" Confederation in 1871, followed by Prince Edward Island two years later. In 1905, Alberta and Saskatchewan were created out of the western territory by federal statute; in 1949, Newfoundland "joined" Confederation.

The legislative responsibilities of the Parliament and provincial legislatures were outlined in several sections of the BNA Act, notably 91 and 92. The preamble to Section 91, which described Parliament's general responsibility for the "Peace, Order and good Government of Canada" in matters not exclusively assigned to the provinces, indicates the intention of the "fathers" of Confederation to have a dominant central government. See *British North America Act* and other relevant items.

Confederation for Tomorrow Conference (1967).   A meeting in Toronto of provincial premiers with federal officials as observers to discuss the future of Canadian federalism. Initiated by Premier John Robarts of Ontario, the conference was held during the centennial year of Confederation and one year after the election in Quebec of the *Union nationale* Government, which was committed to constitutional reform along binational lines. In Ottawa, the federal Liberal Government, which included the influential Minister of Justice Pierre Trudeau, had articulated a "hard line" against such a constitutional change. The federal Government was annoyed by the provincial initiation of such a conference, despite assurances that there would be no decisions or drafting of proposals for constitutional reform. Not surprisingly, the conference identified constitutional change, regional disparity, and language rights as subjects for future consideration. Otherwise, the conference was notable for being the first meeting of heads of Government held in public and televised nationally. See *Conference of First Ministers.*

Conference of First Ministers. Meetings of the heads of the eleven provincial and federal governments, usually held annually but occasionally twice a year. Styled earlier as dominion-provincial and federal-provincial conferences, these meetings have been held more regularly since the 1960's. The conferences are usually convened in Ottawa and chaired by the prime minister; they seek to establish agreement on policies of federal and provincial concern. The "summits" receive extensive coverage by the mass media, and the formal sessions are usually broadcast nationally on radio and television. The public meetings largely involve formal statements of government views by the heads or appropriate ministers, as well as occasional exchanges among the politicians conscious of their "viewing audience." Effective bargaining and negotiation therefore usually take place in private meetings. The Conference of First Ministers is the most visible and formalized aspect of federal-provincial relations. See *Dominion-provincial conferences; Intergovernmental committees.*

See Richard Simeon, *Federal-Provincial Diplomacy: The Making of Recent Policy in Canada* (Toronto: University of Toronto Press, 1972).

Conference of Ministers (of Welfare, Education, etc.). Councils of ministers which meet annually to discuss and co-ordinate various federal-provincial policies and programmes relevant to their portfolios. See *Intergovernmental committees.*

Conference of Provincial First Ministers. A meeting of provincial premiers held on an annual basis since the 1960's. The first interprovincial heads-of-government meeting took place in 1887, but did not become a permanent feature of Canadian federalism at that time. In the 1970's, the annual meeting has taken on more political significance as "federal-provincial diplomacy" has expanded. Scores of federal-provincial conferences are held and often, in the views of the provinces, they work to the advantage of the federal government. See *Intergovernmental committees.*

See Richard Simeon, *Federal-Provincial Diplomacy: The Making of Recent Policy in Canada* (Toronto: University of Toronto Press, 1972).

Conflict of Interest.   A personal pecuniary interest sufficient either to influence or to appear to influence the exercise of a legislator's or civil servant's public duties.

At the federal level, provisions of the Senate and House of Commons Act dealing with conflict of interest are acknowledged to be ineffective. Proposals for an Independence of Parliament Act have been put forward since the mid-1970's. By their rules, senators are forbidden to vote on a question in which they have "any pecuniary interest whatsoever, not held in common with the rest of the Canadian subjects of the Crown." The only penalty for infraction of the rule is the disallowance of the disputed vote. Senators are not effectively prevented from acting as lobbyists or as lawyers for clients who deal with the government or from participating in committee or Senate debates on matters in which they have a pecuniary interest. (See Colin Campbell, *The Canadian Senate: A Lobby from Within* [Toronto: Macmillan Co. of Canada Ltd., 1978]; and John McMenemy, "Influence and Party Activity in the Senate: A Matter of Conflict of Interest?" in Paul Fox [ed.], *Politics: Canada* [4th ed.; Toronto: McGraw-Hill Ryerson Ltd., 1977], 454-61.)

In the House of Commons, there are likewise no effective restrictions on the behaviour of MPs. Since 1974, however, there have been ministerial guidelines which are "conditions of employment" but do not have the force of law. Prime Minister Joe Clark's conflict-of-interest guidelines for cabinet ministers in 1979-1980 were somewhat stronger than the earlier ones of Prime Minister Pierre Trudeau. The Clark guidelines required ministers, their wives and children, and senior staff to sell publicly traded shares and speculative investments or to place them in a blind trust which they could not control, and to disclose publicly their financial interests. There was, for the first time, a $10 000 limit on holdings of foreign currency. Deposits in foreign banks over $10 000 were be in a blind trust. Also, ministers had to disclose personal gifts worth more than $100 that were received from anyone outside their family. Ministers were also prohibited from giving preferential treatment to a relative, friend, or organization in which they have an interest; from practising a profession; from serving as a paid consultant, director of a company or of a union, and from acting as a lobbyist or doing business with their previous department for two years after leaving the cabinet.

In 1975, a House of Commons committee which studied a green paper on conflict of interest recommended that all MPs be required to register annually a confidential (that is, not publicly available) copy of their income tax returns and details of their families' financial interests. One year later, the Senate published a less than enthusiastic report on the green paper. In 1978, the Liberal Government introduced conflict-of-interest legislation (the Independence of Parliament Act), which died on the Order Paper in 1979. The Conservative and New Democratic parties also favour such legislation.

In 1973, an order-in-council established "Public Servants Conflict of Interest Guidelines," warning civil servants against questionable behaviour or the appearance of it when in the employ of the government. The guidelines made no reference to the activities of such officials once they had left the public service. Senior civil servants in "retirement" have been known to establish themselves as management consultants to firms dealing with the federal government. Some officials in the Prime Minister's Office also established themselves as consultants following their departure from Prime Minister Trudeau's service.

Conscription.   The popular term in Canada for compulsory military service. The issue has always been a divisive one in Canada, particularly during the two world wars, dividing the francophone and anglophone communities. In 1917, there was considerable strife in Quebec when the Union Government introduced conscription, manipulated the franchise, and won a general election. This was one of the few instances when French Canadians were not represented on the Government side of the House. The issue was raised again in 1940-1944. Liberal Prime Minister William Lyon Mackenzie King, who had pledged opposition to conscription, in 1942 conducted a referendum to release the Government from its pledge. Late in 1944, King sent conscripts overseas, but none were used in battle. King's peregrinations on conscription are remembered in the phrase "conscription if necessary, but not necessarily conscription."

On the "crisis" during World War Two, see R. MacGregor Dawson, *The Conscription Crisis of 1944* (Toronto: University of Toronto Press, 1961).

Conservatism.   Historically, a term used in Canada with reference to British Toryism or to European conservative political thought generally. Since the 1960's, the use of the term has been confused with the contemporary use of the phrase in the United States. In the American sense, conservatism is a manifestation of early liberalism in which individualism, self-reliance, and antipathy to the state are stressed, and in which progress or the improvement of the human condition is viewed as the inevitable outcome of unrestricted interaction among rational and self-interested individuals. By contrast, conservatism in the European and British tradition ranks order above individual freedom. It is based on the "right of the community to restrain freedom in the name of the common good" (George P. Grant, *Lament for a Nation: The Defeat of Canadian Nationalism* [Toronto: McCelland and Stewart Ltd., 1965], 64).

Conservative (Progressive Conservative) party.   Begun in the 1850's as a Liberal-Conservative coalition in the Province of Canada, the Conservative party took form as the "Confederation party" in the 1860's. At that time, ministerialism, or attachment to the partronage-dispensing Government rather than to a party organization, determined the loyalty of legislators. Under the leadership of Sir John A. Macdonald, the Conservative party was dominant until the 1890's. Since 1896, the party has seldom been in power federally.

The party's lack of success nationally may be understood with reference to its nineteenth-century success and to contemporary Liberal party success. The Conservative party then included an English-Canadian elite conscious of and sympathetic to French-Canadian aspirations and a Quebec leadership which had the confidence of the French-Canadian population in that province. The Conservative party then had a business orientation which was tempered by a progressive image of "the working man's party." At the level of political symbolism, the Conservative party was readily identified with Canadian nationalism.

The federal Conservative party has never had a French-Canadian leader and, in the 1970's, had fewer than five French-Canadian MPs. Following the election of 1979, the Conservatives formed a minority Government with only two MPs from Quebec elected as Conservatives, and only one of them a francophone. In the election defeat of 1980, the party elected only one MP from Quebec and gained 13 per cent of the provincial popular vote. The party also has a business image particularly inappropriate to the relative egalitarianism and collectivism of the twentieth century, and, holding power in many provinces, argues at the federal level for enhanced consultation with the provincial governments and provincial roles in the decision-making of federal government bodies.

Academic works on the federal Conservative party in this century include: John English, *The Decline of Politics: The Conservatives and* the Party System, 1901-1920 (Toronto: University of Toronto Press, 1977), J. L. Granatstein, The Politics of Survival: The Conservative Party of Canada, 1939-1945 (Toronto: University of Toronto Press, 1967); and J. R. Williams, The Conservative Party of Canada, 1920-1949 (Durham: Duke University Press, 1956). See also the biography of the party's leader from 1942 to 1948, in whose time the name "Progressive Conservative" originated: John Kendle, John Bracken: A Political Biography (Toronto: University of Toronto Press, 1979). The literature on the party since 1956 has been more controversial. See for example, John Diefenbaker's three volumes of memoirs, One Canada: Memoirs of the Right Honourable J. G. Diefenbaker: The Crusading Years, 1891-1956; The Years of Achievement, 1956-1962; and The Tumultuous Years, 1962-67 (Toronto: Macmillan Co. of Canada Ltd., 1976, 1976, 1977); and Peter Stursberg's two volumes, Diefenbaker: Leadership Gained, 1956-1962 and Leadership Lost, 1962-1967 (Toronto: University of Toronto Press, 1975, 1976). See also Peter Newman, Renegade in Power: The Diefenbaker Years (Toronto: McClelland and Stewart Ltd., 1963); and Peter Regenstreif, The Diefenbaker Interlude: Parties and Voting in Canada (Toronto: Longman Canada Ltd., 1965). On the minority status of the federal party, see George C. Perlin, The Tory Syndrome: Politics in the Progressive Conservative Party (Montreal: McGill-Queen's University Press, 1980). There are no scholarly biographies of Diefenbaker's successors, Robert Stanfield and Joe Clark.

Consociational democracy. A concept originating with Arend Lijphart, who seeks to explain why some countries which possess fragmented political cultures are nonetheless stable democracies. At the core of such a "democracy" is a set of leaders of important groups or sub-elites who choose to govern in mutually supportive ways rather than through basically competitive and stressful relationships. See his "Cultural Diversity and Theories of Political Integration," Canadian Journal of Political Science 4 (1971), 1-14.

In Democracy in Plural Societies: A Comparative Exploration (New Haven: Yale University Press, 1977), Lijphart described Canada as a semi-consociational democracy. In this case, the fragmentation of the political culture on ethnic grounds between English- and French-speaking Canadians is institutionalized in the federal system of government. Federal-provincial and interprovincial relationships, rather than electoral and legislature-based conflicts among political parties, mark the location of major consociational activity among the elite. Lijphart concluded that the Canadian political system would move either "in the direction of greater consociationalism – or in the direction of a more centrifugal régime with a partition of the country as its more likely outcome" (129). See *Federalism*.

Consociationalism has been examined with respect to Canada by S.J.R. Noel ("Consociational Democracy and Canadian Federalism," *Canadian Journal of Political Science* 4 [1971], 15-18) and by Kenneth McRae ("Consociationalism and the Canadian Political System," in Kenneth McRae [ed.], *Consociational Democracy* [Toronto: McClelland and Stewart Ltd., 1974], 238-61). See also Lijphart's "Consociation and Federation: Conceptual and Empirical Links," and McRae's comment, "Federation, Consociation, Corporatism: An Addendum to Arend Lijphart," in *Canadian Journal of Political Science* 12 (1979), 499-522. Finally, see Robert Presthus, *Elite Accommodation in Canadian Politics* (Toronto: Macmillan Co. of Canada Ltd., 1974).

Consolidated Revenue Fund. Money accumulated by the government of Canada which the cabinet allocates to departments and to certain public corporations with parliamentary approval. The Financial Administration Act contains procedures governing revenues and expenditures. This aggregate of public money is credited to the receiver general of Canada, who is also the minister of supply and services. The Bank of Canada and chartered banks are the actual holders of the money on a basis agreed to by the banks, taking into account the cash needs of the government and its monetary policy.

Constituency (riding). A legislative district. In the appointed federal upper house (the Senate), the constituencies are the provinces – except for Quebec, where a senator is appointed in each of the 24 electoral divisions of Lower Canada – the Yukon Territory and the Northwest Territories. In the popularly elected lower house (the House of Commons), the constituencies are determined when their boundaries are readjusted following each decennial census (British North America Act, Section 51). As a result of the readjustment of boundaries in 1974, there are 282 constituencies, from each of which one MP is elected. The provincial and territorial representation in the House since 1979 is: Ontario 95, Quebec 75, British Columbia 28, Alberta 21, Manitoba 14, Saskatchewan 14, Nova Scotia 11, New Brunswick 10, Newfoundland 7, Prince Edward Island 4, Northwest Territories 2, Yukon Territory 1.

Constituency (riding) association. The party organization in the constituencies of the elected legislatures. The purpose of the constituency association is to nominate a candidate and conduct an election campaign. All parties do not have constituency associations in all ridings, and some associations may exist only on paper. In such cases, senior party officials select the candidates. Particularly in the urban areas, the associations' executives may attempt to maintain social and political activities between elections in alliance with area associations of the same party.

Constitution. A basic statement of the functions and relationships of institutions and of individual rights in a political community. Constitutions may be "written" documents, but they may also include "unwritten" rules based on generally accepted, cumulative patterns of behaviour.

The Canadian constitution is drawn from several sources: the British North America Act and certain other British statutes; certain Canadian and provincial statutes; certain British, Canadian, and provincial orders-in-council; certain informal practices based on custom, usage, and convention; and judicial interpretation of written and common law aspects of the constitution. See *British North America Act; Custom, usage, and convention; Distribution (division) of powers; Judicial Committee of the Privy Council; Supreme Court.*

On the Canadian constitution, see J. Noel Lyon and Ronald G. Atkey, *Canadian Constitutional Law in a Modern Perspective* (Toronto: University of Toronto Press, 1970).

Constitutional Act (U.K., 1791). An act which superseded the Quebec Act of 1774 and by which Quebec was divided into Upper and Lower Canada, each colony having a governor, advised by an appointed Executive Council, and an elected Legislative Assembly and an appointed Legislative Council. Several factors were involved in dividing Quebec and introducing representative government. One was the influx of Loyalist settlers, following the American Revolution, who demanded political rights which they had enjoyed in the American colonies. The Constitutional Act enhanced the prospects for the survival of French culture by the establishment of Lower Canada. One of the earliest acts of Upper Canada was the replacement of civil law imposed by the Quebec Act (subject to local modification) with English common law. However, the civil law was maintained in Lower Canada.

Consumer Price Index (CPI). A measure of change in the retail prices of goods and services bought by a representative cross-section of the urban population. The CPI is published monthly by Statistics Canada. There is also an inter-city consumer price index, which compares price levels among major cities. In 1978, the calculation of the CPI was revised. The CPI is based on 1974 spending patterns for everyone on a weighted fixed list of 400 items. The weights reflect the percentage spent by the targeted group on average during the selected year. Since 1975, the index has been reported using a 1971 = 100 time reference base. Thus, the CPI is a measure of inflation and the purchasing power of the Canadian dollar.

The CPI has considerable significance beyond that of an economic monitor. Pensions, family allowances, and many labour contracts are based on fluctuations of the CPI. Since the new CPI calculations might result in a figure lower than the old calculation, and thus represent loss of income to pensioners and union members, for example, the federal government yielded to pressure to make calculations available on a modified old index as well as the new index.

Continentalism. A term used pejoratively by Canadian nationalists to describe Canadian-U.S. relations in terms of a continental region, the result of which, particularly since 1945, is for Canada "to be absorbed increasingly into the American empire [and] to be dominated ... by giant American-based corporations" (Mel Watkins in James Laxer, *The Energy Poker Game* [Toronto: New Press, 1970], 1). While the impact of continentalism can be observed in cultural terms (in the book publishing, film, and television industries) the debate over Canada-U.S. relations has more often focussed on the large amount of U.S. equity (ownership) capital invested in Canada, as well as on energy, resource, and defence policies.

The debate on continentalism in the late 1960's and 1970's gave rise to the left-nationalist "Waffle" movement within the New Democratic party, to the centrist Committee for an Independent Canada, and to debate within the federal Liberal Government. One legislative outcome of the debate was the Foreign Investment Review Agency, which the federal government established in 1973. Non-Canadians may not purchase established Canadian businesses or create businesses in Canada without the approval of FIRA, which advises the minister of economic development and trade on the significant benefit of further proposed non-Canadian ownership of Canadian businesses. See *Foreign Investment Review Agency; Waffle, the.*

See Andrew Axline *et al.* (eds.), *Continental Community? Independence and Integration in North America* (Toronto: McClelland and Stewart Ltd., 1974); Annette Baker Fox *et al.*, "Canada and the United States: Transactional and Transgovernmental Relations," *International Organization* 28 (1974), *passim*; Dave Godfrey and Mel Watkins (eds.), *Gordon to Watkins to You: A Documentary: The Battle for Control of Our Economy* (Toronto: New Press, 1970); and Kari Levitt, *Silent Surrender: The Multinational Corporation in Canada* (Toronto: Macmillan Co. of Canada Ltd., 1970). See also Elizabeth Smythe, "International Relations Theory and the Study of Canadian-American Relations" *Canadian Journal of Political Science* 13 (1980), 121-47.

Continuing Committee of Ministers of Finance and Provincial Treasurers.   Regular meetings of ministers of finance and provincial treasurers to discuss and attempt to co-ordinate their governments' policies in fiscal and economic matters. See *Intergovernmental committees.*

Continuing Committee on Fiscal and Economic Matters.   Established in the 1950's, originally to advise the first ministers on the co-ordination of federal-provincial fiscal arrangements. The committee includes senior finance and treasury officials of the eleven governments and now advises the Continuing Committee of Ministers of Finance and Provincial Treasurers. See *Intergovernmental committees.*

Contracting out (opting out).   A provision under the federal Established Programmes (Interim Arrangements) Act of 1965 by which provinces could withdraw from and receive financial compensation for, several major federal-provincial shared-cost programmes: hospital insurance; old-age assistance; allowances for blind and disabled persons; the welfare portion of unemployment assistance; technical and vocational training for young people; and the health grant programme. The Act also allowed for withdrawal from several smaller and temporary programmes, and was later amended to include the Canada Assistance Plan. The formula was proposed in response to objections by Quebec and other provinces to federal conditional grants in areas of provincial jurisdiction. As compensation for not receiving federal monies, the federal government would lower federal personal income tax rates up to 20 per cent in the provinces which were contracting out, with cash transfers to make up any difference between the yield of the taxes and the amount of the conditional grant which the provinces would have received.

Only Quebec exercised the option to contract out of certain programmes. See *Conditional grants.*

Contractual Link.   An agreement between Canada and the Council of European Communities, signed in 1976. It represents a framework for commercial and economic relations, developed as part of Canada's so-called "third option" in international trade (the first traditionally having been relations with the United Kingdom and the Commonwealth; and the second, relations with the United States). The link, formally the Framework Agreement for Commercial and Economic Co-operation between Canada and the European Communities, represents the federal Liberal Government's attempts to offset the considerable preponderance of the United States in the Canadian economy. The object of this relatively low-status formal link with the EEC was thus to increase trade and investment opportunities for Canada in Europe. As a framework agreement, both parties are committed only to semi-annual consultations. By 1979, however, only 2.5 per cent of imports to the nine countries of the European Economic Community came from Canada, a decrease from the 1960's.

Controverted election.   A constituency election challenged because of alleged irregularities or corrupt and illegal practices. Controverted federal elections are investigated by two superior court justices for the province in which the disputed election took place. The judicial report is transmitted to the Speaker of the House of Commons and may result in the election being declared void and the seat vacant. The decision may be appealed both in law and in fact to the Supreme Court.

Co-operative Commonwealth Federation (CCF).   A grassroots socialist party, founded in 1933 and reconstituted as the New Democratic party in 1961. The CCF programme was based on the Regina Manifesto, which called for "genuine democratic self-government, based on economic equality" through public ownership of major industries and government planning. In contrast to the Conservative and Liberal parties, the CCF stressed membership participation in policy-making and in party finance.

The party achieved its greatest success in the mid-1940's. In September 1943, a Gallup poll showed a slight lead for the CCF over the Liberals and Conservatives in national popularity. The party formed the official Opposition in Ontario in the same year and won an election in Saskatchewan in 1944. However, the victory in Saskatchewan, which was repeated several times until 1964, was the only electoral break-through for the party. The CCF fell to third place in Ontario through the 1940's and 1950's, although it formed the official Opposition in British Columbia throughout the 1950's.

Consistent with changes which took place in socialist movements throughout western Europe, the CCF modified its socialist principles in the Winnipeg Declaration of 1956. Planning and regulation took priority over public ownership as a means to achieve social equality. From 1958 to 1961, the CCF leadership transformed the party structure to allow for greater participation of trade unions, and generally to create an image which would be more appealing to a youthful, urban, self-perceived socially mobile, and central Canadian population. See *Agrarian socialism; League for Social Reconstruction; Movement parties; New Democratic party; Regina Manifesto; Socialism.*

On the CCF, see Walter D. Young, *The Anatomy of a Party: The National CCF, 1932-1961* (Toronto: University of Toronto Press, 1969), Leo Zakuta, *A Protest Movement Becalmed: A Study of Change in the CCF* (Toronto: University of Toronto Press, 1964); and Ivan Avakumovic, *Socialism in Canada: A Study of the CCF-NDP in Federal and Provincial Politics* (Toronto: McClelland and Stewart Ltd., 1978). On the CCF in Saskatchewan, see S.M. Lipset, *Agrarian Socialism: The Co-operative Commonwealth Federation in Saskatchewan* (Berkeley: University of California Press, 1959).

Co-operative federalism.   A political slogan associated with the federal Liberal Governments under Lester Pearson's leadership in the 1960's. The slogan described a trend under Pearson to settle federal-provincial jurisdictional disputes through accommodative intergovernmental bargaining. Phrases used to describe federal-provincial diplomacy since then are "administrative" or "executive" federalism. See *Federalism.*

Corporation and Labour Unions Returns Act (CALURA).   Federal legislation enacted in 1963 which requires large private corporations and labour unions in Canada to submit operational information and statistics to the government, some of which are published annually. The Act was a response to concerns voiced by "economic nationalists" about the extent and implications of non-resident direction of the Canadian economy – concerns which became more vocal later in the 1960's.

The non-confidential CALURA statistics on corporations include information on the incorporation, officers and directors, and ownership of the corporations' issued share capital. The confidential section includes financial statements of the corporations and a schedule of selected payments to non-residents. Published data on labour unions concern constitutions, officers, membership, locals, trusteeships, and collective agreements, while the confidential information concerns financial statements.

CALURA represents an important source of data for examination of the corporate structure of the Canadian economy. See, for example, Wallace Clement, *The Canadian Corporate Elite: An Analysis of Economic Power* (Toronto: McClelland and Stewart Ltd., 1975) and *Continental Corporate Power: Economic Elite Linkages between Canada and the United States* (Toronto: McClelland and Stewart Ltd., 1977).

Council of Maritime Premiers.   A body comprising the heads of government of New Brunswick, Nova Scotia, and Prince Edward Island. It was created in 1971, and under it various official interprovincial consultations and co-ordination of policy and policy proposals take place. Each of the Maritime legislatures has passed legislation giving the Council legal status as an agent in specific administrative matters. The Council has its own secretariat. See *Intergovernmental committees.*

Count (election), official and unofficial.   The tabulation of votes cast in general and by-elections. The deputy returning officer in each polling station conducts the unofficial count on election night, immediately after the closing of the polls. All candidates are permitted to have a representative (scrutineer) at the polling station throughout the day and during the unofficial count. After the unofficial count, the ballots in each station are returned to the ballot box, which is delivered to the returning officer of the constituency. The returning officer is responsible for safeguarding the boxes and ballots until conducting the official count. In federal elections, only the vote total from each polling station is counted in the official count, at which time ballots cast by military personnel and other non-resident electors are counted. Following the official count, the returning officer certifies the name of the winning candidate, the total number of votes cast for each candidate, and the number of rejected or spoiled ballots.

Criminal Code of Canada.   Law pertaining to crimes against society; it is rooted in large part in English criminal jurisprudence and is ap-

plied uniformly across Canada. The Criminal Code is applicable
throughout the country, in contrast to private law, which is based on
civil law in Quebec and on common law elsewhere. Under the British
North America Act, Parliament is responsible for criminal law (Section
92:14).

The ability of Parliament to declare action to be criminal is tempered
by the distribution of powers under the BNA Act, in particular with respect to the "Property and Civil Rights" power allocated to the provinces (92:13). In the 1930's, the Judicial Committee of the Privy Council declared that "Parliament shall not in the guise of enacting criminal
legislation . . . encroach on any classes of subjects enumerated in Section 92" (quoted in Bora Laskin, *Canadian Constitutional Law* [2nd
ed., Toronto: Carswell Co. Ltd., 1969], 284). To put it positively, Parliament may exercise criminal law power in an area of provincial jurisdiction for federal purposes.

Recent changes to the Criminal Code include amendments relating
to homosexuality (1969), abortion (1969), bail reform (1971), the jury
system (1972), eavesdropping on or recording of private conversations
(1974), restriction on the application of the death penalty for capital
murder (1976), and rules regarding evidence in cases of alleged sexual
offence such as rape (1978).

In 1970, the Law Reform Commission of Canada was established as a
permanent body to report to Parliament through the minister of justice
on recommendations for the "improvement, modernization, and reform" of Canadian law (Law Reform Commission Act). See *Law Reform Commission of Canada*.

Crossing the floor. An act by which a legislator leaves his or her
party and sits "across the floor" from former colleagues as an Independent member or as a member of another party. This action results
from an irreconcilable difference between the member and his or her
former party leadership, and it is usually preceded by obvious signs of
disaffection. It is a rare event for a member to become an Independent,
because elections and House procedure – including recognition by the
Speaker to address the House – are based on party affiliation. It is un-
common for an Independent candidate to win against party-affiliated
candidates. It is also rare for a member to change parties because,
though the person may be welcomed to another party, he or she might
not be re-elected as a candidate of the new party.

Crown. The supreme executive authority in Canada which derives from the monarchy of the United Kingdom and therefore bears constitutional likeness to it. In fact, the Canadian monarch, sovereign, or head of state is the same person as the British monarch and is represented in Canada by the governor general. Section 9 of the British North America Act (1867) declares the "Executive Government and Authority of and over Canada . . . to continue and be vested in the Queen" and, by implication, her successors. British constitutional development involved the wresting of prerogative powers from the monarch by Parliament. This occurred, not through the seizure of the power of the state, but by the supply of advice and the maintenance of royal legitimacy. Today, the monarch herself, or the governor general in her place, does virtually nothing without the "advice" of her constitutional advisors, "the Queen's Privy Council for Canada" (Section 11). The effective part of the Privy Council is the cabinet, the Government-of-the-day, formed largely from and with the continued confidence of the House of Commons. See *Crown prerogatives; Governor General.*

Executive power is held by the Crown; but, as Canada has a federal system of government, the Crown is represented in each provincial government as well as in the federal government. In the provinces, the lieutenant-governors act virtually always on the advice of their respective Executive Councils or provincial cabinets. An important exception is that, as the office of lieutenant-governor is a federal office, the governor-in-council, or federal cabinet, may direct a lieutenant-governor with respect to provincial legislation. See *Disallowance; Reservation.*

The Canadian monarch "reigns, but does not rule." Similarly, the political executive or cabinet rules, but formally has no authority in its own right – only as advisors to the Crown. Supporters of the monarchy make much of this distinction. Frank MacKinnon, for example, feels that the dual executive, which distinguishes the custodial function of possessing power from the practical function of wielding power, is crucial to a democratic government (*The Crown in Canada* [Calgary: Glenbow-Alberta Institute, 1976]). See *Crown prerogatives.*

Crown corporation. An organization with the structure of a private or independent enterprise, but which is established by specific acts or pursuant to enabling legislation of a federal or provincial legislature and which usually reports to the legislature through a designated minister. At the federal level, the Financial Administration Act prescribes a system of financial control and establishes three classes of crown corporations: departmental, agency, and proprietary corporations. Departmental corporations – such as the Economic Council of Canada, the Fisheries Prices Support Board, or the Unemployment Insurance Commission – concern administrative, supervisory, or regulatory services of the government. Agency corporations – such as Atomic Energy of Canada Limited, the Canadian Dairy Commission, or the Canadian Film Development Corporation – involve quasi-commercial trading or service operations or the management of procurement, construction, or disposal activities of the government. Proprietary corporations – such as Air Canada, the Canadian Broadcasting Corporation, or the Canada Mortgage and Housing Corporation – involve the management of lending or financial and of commercial or industrial operations supplying goods and services to the public. There are also crown corporations – such as the Bank of Canada and the Canadian Wheat Board – which are audited under the Financial Administration Act, but which otherwise are governed by their own acts of incorporation. Finally, Parliament has established such crown corporations as the Canada Development Corporation and Panarctic Oil Limited, which are not subject to the provisions of the Financial Administration Act and which do not report to Parliament.

Unlike government departments, crown corporations are not supervised directly by a minister. They are managed by independent boards whose members are appointed for fixed terms by the Government. The boards usually include a full-time chairman or president as chief executive officer and members who are involved on a part-time basis. Some corporations, such as the Bank of Canada, have senior civil servants on their boards. In departmental corporations, the employees are civil servants, whose recruitment and working conditions are regulated by the Public Service Commission. Personnel management of other corporations is generally a matter internal to those corporations.

While the ministers designated responsible for the corporations do not direct activities of the corporations on an overt or on-going basis, they must defend the corporations in the House and guide their estimates through the legislature. Thus, the designated ministers do have a basis on which to influence the boards of the corporations. Activities of corporations may also be affected by subsequent legislative amendments or repeal of their statutory basis of existence. See *Agency corporations; Departmental corporations; Proprietary corporations.*

On crown corporations, see R.A. Ashley and R.G.H. Smails, *Canadian Crown Corporations* (Toronto: Macmillan Co. of Canada Ltd., 1965).

Crown prerogatives.   Under common law, unrestricted by statute, a residue of discretionary authority which is delegated to the governor general through Letters Patent, the Instrument, and the Commission of Appointment. Otherwise, the Crown and its representatives act entirely on the advice of their councils (cabinets), which are themselves accountable to their respective legislatures.

The discretionary powers, or crown prerogatives, are historically shrinking. The most important of the prerogatives remaining in Canada pertain to the Crown's role in dissolving Parliament and provincial legislatures and appointing a prime minister or premier. In the twentieth century, there has been only one instance of such discretionary power being exercised by the governor general. In 1926, the governor general refused to grant dissolution on the "advice" of a Government which had won only the second largest number of seats in an election eight months earlier; it was then undergoing a debate on a censure motion which it was likely to lose; and there appeared to be a possibility for an alternative Government to be formed – although the largest group, the Conservatives, did not have a majority (see *King-Byng Crisis*).

There appear, however, to be two conditions necessary before the governor general or a lieutenant-governor exercises such prerogatives on behalf of the Crown: the situation would have to occasion a state of affairs which was clearly a violation of the intent of the constitution; and there should be no reasonable doubt about the judgment and justice of the independent action. See *Crown; Governor General; Letters Patent.*

In R. MacGregor Dawson's view, the residue of discretionary crown power "is an emergency device invoked to re-establish genuine democratic control at a time when the normal constitutional procedures have faltered and are in danger of being improperly and unscrupulously employed" *(The Government of Canada* [5th ed., rev. by Norman Ward; Toronto: University of Toronto Press, 1970], 163). On the Crown and its prerogatives, see also Dawson, *Constitutional Issues in Canada, 1900-1931* (Toronto: University of Toronto Press, 1933); and Eugene A. Forsey, *The Royal Power of Dissolution of Parliament in the British Commonwealth* (Toronto: University of Toronto Press, 1943).

Crows Nest Pass Agreement (Rates).   An agreement made between the Canadian Pacific Railway and the federal government in 1897 and subsequently amended, by which the railway reduced its freight rates on goods coming into the prairie West and on grain leaving the Prairies for world markets. In return, the CPR obtained a government subsidy in 1898 to construct a branch line through the Crows Nest Pass in the Rocky Mountains. The object from the government's perspective was to reduce the cost of bringing goods into the Prairies and the cost of exporting western grain. The renegotiated subsidized freight rates, similar to agreements under the federal Maritime Freight Rate Act for eastern Canada, are defended as necessary for regional welfare. Generally, the railways criticize the subsidies as inadequate to meet real costs. In 1979, the governments of British Columbia, Alberta, and Manitoba proposed that the benefit – the difference between the statutory rates and the actual cost of hauling grain – be paid directly to grain farmers, and that the railways apply to the Canadian Transport Commission for new rates which would reflect actual cost. Saskatchewan, which produces 60 per cent of the export grain, preferred the traditional arrangement of subsidies to the railways.

Cultural duality.   The division of Canadian society into anglophone and francophone communities, which has been fundamental to Canadian history and constitutional development since the Conquest of 1759-60. The Quebec Act of 1774, which allowed Roman Catholics freedom of worship and allowed Catholics to hold public office, and retained civil law in the colony, represented the earliest constitutional recognition of cultural duality. The Constitutional Act of 1791 divided Quebec into Upper and Lower Canada and granted representative government to each colony. Civil law was retained in Lower Canada; and by 1840, when the British enacted the assimilative Act of Union, bringing the two colonies together again, French-Canadian society was firmly entrenched in British North America. The outcome of the union was not assimilation, but the creation of a number of political devices recognizing the cultural duality of the Province of Canada. The new federal state in 1867 recognized the duality of the country through various constitutional provisions. For example: the British North America Act allocated matters of cultural significance such as education, property, and civil rights to the provinces, which now included Quebec; the Act established rights for the French and English languages in Parliament, in the Quebec Legislature, and in the federal and Quebec courts; and it protected minority education rights.

French Canada's political leadership generally accepted the Confederation agreement until the 1960's. Since the so-called Quiet Revolution in Quebec, the provincial political leadership has argued for a recognition of Quebec as a peculiar jurisdiction based on the predominance of French Canadians in its population. Demands by

French-speaking Quebeckers to become "maîtres chez nous" (masters in our own house), have ranged from various forms of formal recognition of special status for Quebec within a federal union to a new constitution based on an independent and sovereign Quebec associated economically with the rest of Canada. The response of successive federal Liberal Governments from 1963 to 1979, supported by the leadership of all federal parties, was to enhance the cultural duality of Canada at the federal level, primarily through the Official Languages Act (1969). In 1978, the federal Liberal Government proposed constitutional changes which would have enhanced the cultural duality of such federal institutions as the Senate and the Supreme Court of Canada, and would have created an entrenched Charter of Human Rights which would include language rights. The constitutional amendment bill died on the Order Paper in 1979. See *Bicultural cleavage; Bilingualism and biculturalism; Quiet Revolution; Sovereignty-association; Two nations.*

Custom, convention, and usage.   Constitutional requirements which do not have explicit statutory sanction, but which are based on long-established observance. Customs are sanctioned by the courts; conventions are obligatory practices; usage denotes long-established unwritten practices. In Canada, many such constitutional elements actually modify or oppose statutory requirements. They determine, for example, executive behaviour far more than the provisions of the British North America Act: the governor general chooses a party-designated leader as prime minister; the governor general acts virtually always on the advice of the prime minister; the prime minister selects the cabinet; and the cabinet is the effective executive. Custom, convention, and usage also determine the relations between the executive and the legislature. For example: cabinet members must have seats in the House of Commons, with some tolerance allowed for Senate membership; the cabinet remains in office only as long as it has the support of the House; that support is based on strict party discipline and is almost always assured in majority governments; effectively, the prime minister determines the date for the dissolution of Parliament and therefore the date of the next election.

Practices become constitutional custom through constant use or disuse. The power of federal disallowance of provincial legislation, for example, is permitted under the British North America Act; but it has fallen into disuse, and it is therefore a convention that such action not take place. Of course, a federal Government could assert its power under the BNA Act and begin a reversal of such practice. See *British North America Act.*

D

Declaratory power. The authority of Parliament to take control of "Local Works and Undertakings" which would normally be a provincial responsibility, by declaring them to be "for the general Advantage of Canada or for the Advantage of Two or more of the Provinces" (British North America Act, Section 92:10[c] and Section 91:29). Such federal control could be assumed before or after the work or undertaking was completed. The courts have interpreted "Works" broadly, to include "integrated activities" as well as "things" or "facility." The imposition of federal control over the uranium industry during and after World War Two is a case of the broad use of declaratory power. This constitutional provision illustrates the intention of the "fathers" of Confederation to create a centralized federation.

In discussions in the 1970's on a revised constitution, several provincial governments expressed concern about federal declaratory power. In 1976, for example, Alberta voiced apprehension about the potential use of declaratory power with respect to the petroleum industry. All provincial governments agree that, in a new constitution, a veto over federal use of declaratory power should be held by the provinces concerned.

Delegate theory of representation. A view that legislators should represent faithfully the views or the general will of their constituents. The delegate theory is a populist notion which would keep elected members in a distant capital more than mindful of local grassroots opinion. The theory found support in western Canada in the early part of the twentieth century as part of a deliberate attempt to undermine the disciplined party system by which a legislator's vote, particularly on the Government side, was really determined by the party leadership. Western populists contended, not without reason, that the two major federal parties, the Liberals and Conservatives, were dominated by central Canadian financial and commercial interests. Around 1920, the United Farmers parties required their candidates to commit themselves to this theory prior to their nomination. Indeed, Alberta had a provincial Recall Act until 1937.

The theory is in contrast to the representative theory, according to which legislators are elected as parliamentarians to reflect on and articulate policy in the national interest, based on their own good judgment. As mentioned above, the disciplined party system usually determines the votes of most MPs. The Canada Elections Act makes it illegal for any candidate for the House of Commons to commit himself "to follow any course of action that will prevent him from exercising freedom of action in Parliament . . . or to resign . . . if called upon to do so by any person, persons, or association of persons."

Delegated power. Legislative, judicial, and quasi-judicial power delegated by acts of Parliament (or a provincial Legislature) to the governor-in-council (or lieutenant-governor-in-council) (cabinet) to departments, boards, commissions, and other government bodies. In a federal system, delegation of power may be horizontal (from one jurisdiction to another), as well as vertical (within a jurisdiction). Delegated legislative power is power to enact subordinate legislation by order-in-council or by regulation; while delegated judicial and quasi-judicial powers are powers to adjudicate on administrative disputes with possibly no appeal to the courts.

In Canada, the British North America Act does not permit horizontal delegation (interdelegation) of powers between Parliament and the provincial legislatures. The Supreme Court has allowed Parliament to delegate power to an administrative agency established by a provincial legislature. The Fulton-Favreau constitutional proposals of 1964 included provision for horizontal delegation of power. Some provinces continue to support such interdelegation of power, but later proposals by the federal government have not included the procedure. See *Fulton-Favreau Formula; Interdelegation Reference.*

Power delegated vertically through enabling legislation is so common that the law is effectively formed by these executive and administrative bodies, rather than by the legislature. The legislature's role is to pass the initial legislation authorizing certain agencies to devise, promulgate, and supervise regulations "as may be deemed necessary for giving full effect" to the particular act. At the federal level, regulations flowing from enabling legislation must be published in the *Canada Gazette.*

The most extreme example of delegated legislative power is the War Measures Act, which represents Canada's "emergency legislation." The Act, passed by Parliament during World War One, gives the governor-in-council power to make regulations which it deems "necessary or advisable for the security, defence, peace, order and welfare" of Canada. The Act thus transfers from Parliament to the cabinet the emergency powers which were granted Parliament under the "Peace,

Order and good government" clause in Section 91 of the British North America Act.

The legislatures also delegate judicial and quasi-judicial powers. Some executive and administrative decisions are judicial. Other administrative tribunals, however, have discretionary, quasi-judicial powers. A quasi-judicial tribunal makes regulations which are a mixture of law and policy, recognizing extenuating circumstances in particular cases.

While the denial of judicial review in the administrative process is based on a desire for a more flexible process, there is considerable scope for abuse of power by ministers, civil servants, and members of regulatory bodies. To deal with potential abuse, the procedures of such tribunals should be accessible to all concerned, with efficient and wide distribution of information prior to and following public hearings. Decisions of many regulatory agencies may be appealed to the cabinet; but procedures there are informal, and deliberations are secret.

Having "enabled" the growth of the administrative process, Parliament has been slow to supervise it. Only in 1971 did Parliament pass the Statutory Instruments Act and establish a joint Senate and House committee on regulations and other statutory instruments. The purpose of this joint parliamentary committee is to scrutinize subordinate legislation. However, such legislation is so extensive that Parliament can do little other than conduct random checks and investigate only some apparent abuses. Finally, the creation of the office of ombudsman in several Canadian jurisdictions during the 1970's is, in part, recognition by legislators that they are incapable of dealing effectively with alleged abuses by administrative tribunals exercising delegated legislative, judicial, and quasi-judicial power under enabling legislation. See *Ombudsman; Regulatory agencies (regulations)*.

Department (of government). An administrative unit, sometimes called a ministry, which is headed by a cabinet minister and staffed by civil servants; in this unit, government policy in a particular area is formulated and carried out. The minister is the political head of the department, its representative and defender in the cabinet and in the legislature. The deputy minister is the administrative head and holds that position at the pleasure of the Government. A federal department, for example, will have one or more assistant deputy ministers, whose positions are staffed in accordance with the Public Service Employment Act. The deputy and the assistant deputy ministers, and directors of various departmental sections or branches, constitute the senior departmental civil service. As the financial operations of departments are subject to the estimates procedure, there is considerable importance attached to interdepartmental co-ordination of policy planning and administration. See *Budgetary process; Deputy minister.*

The federal departments, for example, are based on a combination of policy, function, and clientele. The Department of Energy, Mines, and Resources, and the Department of Finance deal with distinct policy areas. The title of the Department of Employment and Immigration suggests the relationship, from the government's point of view, between national immigration policy and the possession of suitable work skills by individuals. Some departments – such as Agriculture, Labour, and Veterans Affairs – seem to be based on a policy area and a particular clientele. For some, such as the Department of Regional Economic Expansion, the clientele is territorial rather than occupationally defined.

Departmental organization is usually in a state of change. Some departments, such as National Defence, are integrated vertical organizations in which a hierarchical structure up to the deputy ministers includes most of the staff and administrative units. Others may be placed along an organizational continuum which leads to horizontal departments, such as Transport, which are frameworks for a variety of autonomous agencies and crown corporations.

A few departments have remained distinct over the years, while a number have operated under different names or been amalgamated with others. Customs and Internal Revenue, for example, operated as separate departments in the early decades of Confederation and became the Department of National Revenue in 1927; Justice and Finance are two of the oldest and most senior of departments, indicating a long-term interest of the federal government; External Affairs, not established until 1909, has also had high status in the civil service; the large Health and Welfare portfolio illustrates epochal change in the scope of government policy interests; Consumer and Corporate Affairs represents a response to timely interests; Secretary of State represents a variety of interests (ceremonial, archival, and cultural) which are considered worthy of government attention, but which do not warrant separate departments; Supply and Services serves other government departments. Other federal departments in 1979, which are not mentioned above, include Communications, Environment, Fisheries and Oceans, Indian Affairs and Northern Development, Industry, Trade and Commerce, National Revenue, Public Works, Solicitor General, and Post Office.

Department of Regional Economic Expansion (DREE). A federal department created in 1969 to consolidate existing programmes dealing with regional economic disparities and develop proposals to deal with social adjustment and economic expansion in hard-pressed regions, in concert with the provincial governments. The Department's major innovation is its regional development incentives programme which is carried out under General Development Agreements and Subsidiary Agreements with the provinces. For example, in 1978, the DREE minister and his counterpart in Manitoba announced a five-year, $44 million shared-cost programme (federal share 60 per cent) to expand the province's industrial base. The programme, Enterprise Manitoba, consisted of several parts – including a rural incentive programme offering forgivable loans, research assistance, counselling, and other services to manufacturers who established or expanded facilities outside Winnipeg.

DREE is also responsible for administering such established programmes as the Agricultural and Rural Development Act (ARDA), the Fund for Rural Economic Development (FRED), and the Prairie Farm Rehabilitation Act (PFRA), programmes which provide funds to facilitate economic and social development in economically depressed areas.

DREE is a major federal department, not only in terms of its mandate but also because of its centrality in federal-provincial relations, as well as the large sums of money involved in its programmes. While the goal of eliminating regional disparities is not questioned, the Department's strategy of subsidizing economic developments which might otherwise be inefficient is much debated. See *Agricultural and Rural Development Act; Fund for Rural Economic Development; Prairie Farm Rehabilitation Act; Regional disparity.*

Departmental corporation. A type of federal crown corporation which is responsible for administrative, supervisory, or regulatory services of a governmental nature. A departmental corporation buys, sells, and owns assets in the name of the Crown; and, as with a regular department of government, its financial operations are subject to the estimates procedure of the government (see *Budgetary process*). Its estimates are usually included in those of the department of the minister who is designated responsible for the corporation. The governor-in-council appoints the boards of departmental corporations either for a fixed term or "at the pleasure of Her Majesty," that is, of the Government. The employees of most departmental corporations are civil servants subject to the Public Service Employment Act. Some departmental corporations, however, have internal responsibility for personnel management. All departmental corporations make annual reports to the ministers which are tabled in the House. See *Crown corporation.*

On departmental corporations and crown corporations generally, see C.A. Ashley and R.G.H. Smails, *Canadian Crown Corporations* (Toronto: Macmillan of Canada Ltd., 1965).

Deputy minister. The appointed head of a department of government. A person may have deputy minister status as a chief executive officer of a branch of government other than a department, but which also reports to Parliament through a minister. Deputy ministers of departments hold office at the pleasure of the Government and must therefore have its confidence.

The functions of a deputy minister are both managerial and advisory. A deputy minister faces the department as a manager, directing its affairs, but also recommends new policy and serves as the important adviser to the minister, the political head of the department. The deputy is particularly influential in relation to the minister because, unlike the minister who has several political roles and for whom the portfolio is probably a short-term responsibility, the deputy is a full-time and potentially longer-term department head. The deputy minister is also responsible for liaison with other departments in related policy and programme areas. Increasingly in the 1970's, the deputy was also involved in a diplomatic function with counterparts in other jurisdictions. The committee system of deputy ministers is one of the most important strata of intergovernmental committees. For example, the continuing committee on fiscal and economic matters, which is composed of deputy ministers of finance and deputy provincial treasurers, is a key bureaucratic committee. The committees of deputy ministers support the political committees of ministers and usually meet more often than the intergovernmental ministerial committees or councils.

Thus, while the role of deputy minister may seem largely administrative and managerial, the deputy ministers' political role is often more important in the political system. Administrative and managerial tasks may be delegated to the ranks of permanent assistant deputy ministers and directors, while the deputy pays greater attention to the political role of that office both within and in its relationship to other jurisdictions.

Since the 1960's, the rank of federal deputy minister has not been as monopolistically high-status in Canadian politics as it was earlier (though it retains high status), especially given the rise in prominence of provincial public bureaucracies. The senior federal civil service has become more fluid, larger, and more competitive as well, although the rank of deputy minister still includes only several dozen people. While deputy ministers hold office at the pleasure of the Government, their importance to a new Government was illustrated by Conservative Prime Minister Joe Clark's decision in 1979 not to ask for letters of resignation from most deputy ministers who were appointed by the previous Liberal Government.

Direct (indirect) taxation.   Under the British North America Act, direct taxation is the source of provincial revenue (92:2), including such taxes as personal and corporate income tax, property tax, sales tax, and succession duty. Defined by the Judicial Committee of the Privy Council in the manner of John Stuart Mill, a direct tax is a tax "demanded from the very persons who it is intended or desired should pay it" *(Bank of Toronto v. Lambe, 1887)*. This power, however, has not been interpreted as exclusive to the provinces. Under Section 91:3 of the BNA Act ("The Raising of Money by any Mode or System of Taxation"), the courts have agreed that the federal government has the power to impose direct and indirect taxes. Thus, the provincial governments have access only to direct taxation, while the federal government has access to both direct and indirect taxation. Section 121 of the BNA Act prohibits provincial tariff barriers and Section 125 exempts public land or property belonging to "Canada or any Province" from taxation.

   The revenue needs of the provinces have increased significantly in the twentieth century, but not their access to taxation. Thus, since World War One, the federal government has made transfer payments to the provinces in the form of conditional grants. Prior to World War Two, the provinces were responsible for such areas as education, roads, and unemployment relief, yet were clearly incapable of funding the necessary programmes. The federal Government appointed the Royal Commission on Dominion-Provincial Relations (Rowell-Sirois) in 1937. In 1940, the Commission recommended a shift of government functions and powers of taxation to the federal government and the introduction of a programme of equalization payments. The report was not received enthusiastically by the provinces. However, it represented a departure point from the years of the fiscal straightjacket of the judicial interpretations of the BNA Act (which gave the level of government with the least access to revenue some of the most costly legislative obligations) and a move toward the era of administrative, or executive, federalism. See *Federal-provincial tax-sharing agreements; Rowell-Sirois Royal Commission on Dominion-Provincial Relations.*

Disallowance. The voiding of provincial legislation by the governor-in-council (that is, the federal cabinet) on the recommendation of the minister of justice within one year of the receipt of the provincial act. The power of disallowance is based in the federal appointment and control over the office of lieutenant-governor. It represents the existing function of the imperial government in 1867 which was transferred to the federal government in Canada (British North America Act, Sections 56, 58, 60, 61).

The power of disallowance illustrates the intention of the "fathers" of Confederation that Canada be a centralized, federal state. Common in the early years of Confederation, federal disallowance fell into disuse in the early twentieth century. In the late 1930's, however, the federal government disallowed 16 statutes dealing with federal matters which had been enacted under the Social Credit Government in Alberta. Asked by the federal government for a reference on such powers, the Supreme Court declared the powers of disallowance and reservation to be unimpaired (Disallowance and Reservation Case [1938]).

The notion of the federal government as a paternalistic watchdog of the provinces is now out of fashion. The power of disallowance has not been exercised since 1943. By the 1970's, the federal government was willing to abandon both disallowance and reservation in a new constitution (the Victoria Charter [1971]). In 1977, the federal Liberal Government rejected suggestions that it disallow the Official Language Act of Quebec, Prime Minister Pierre Trudeau preferring to leave the matter to the courts and to the electoral process. See *Reservation.*

On the disallowance of Social Credit legislation, see J.R. Mallory, *Social Credit and the Federal Power in Canada* (Toronto: University of Toronto Press, 1955).

Discretionary power. Power to act on the basis of one's own judgment. Discretionary power is found in the Canadian political system in the office of governor general in the form of crown prerogatives (the residue of authority unrestricted by statute) and in the quasi-judicial powers granted ministers and administrative tribunals under enabling legislation. See *Crown; Delegated power; Regulatory agencies (regulations).*

Dissolution of Parliament (the Legislature). The termination of a current Parliament (that is, the House of Commons) or provincial Legislature, with the issuance of writs for a general election. Dissolution occurs automatically five years from the date of the return of the writs for choosing the House, or sooner on action by the governor general (provincial lieutenant-governor), usually on the advice of the prime minister (premier). Only once in this century has the governor general refused a request of a prime minister to dissolve Parliament and instead appointed another Government from the same House. See *Crown prerogatives; King-Byng Dispute.*

Distribution (division) of powers. The legislative competence of the federal and provincial levels of government as outlined in the British North America Act and interpreted by the Judicial Committee of the Privy Council until 1949, and the Supreme Court of Canada.

The distribution of legislative powers, which is fundamental to any federal system, is the source of much political dispute and controversy. The BNA Act grants broad powers to the federal government to make laws for "the Peace, Order and good Government of Canada in relation to all Matters not coming within the Claims of Subjects by this Act assigned exclusively to the Legislatures of the Provinces" (Section 91). The Act then enumerates matters of federal competence – "but not so as to restrict the Generality of the foregoing" – including the regulation of trade and commerce (:2), the raising of money by any mode or system of taxation (:3), currency (:14), banking (:15), and the criminal law (:27).

The enumerated legislative powers of the provinces (Section 92) are not preceded by such a comprehensive phrase as the "Peace, Order and good Government" clause mentioned above. The powers of the provinces include: direct taxation within the province for provincial purposes (:2), the amendment of provincial constitutions, except the office of lieutenant-governor (:1); property and civil rights (:13); the administration of justice (:14); municipal government (:8); and most hospitals (:7). In Section 93, the BNA Act refers to provincial rights and obligations in education.

Section 95 establishes agriculture and immigration as powers to be held concurrently by both levels of government. An amendment in 1951 added old age pensions to concurrent powers. In disputed cases, the federal legislation takes precedence in agriculture and immigration, while the provincial legislation takes precedence in the matter of pensions. Section 132 refers to the treaty-making powers of the federal government, which have been modified by the Court in consideration of the enumerated powers in Sections 91 and 92.

In 1951, the Supreme Court declared that neither Parliament nor any provincial Legislature could directly delegate its power to the other level (*Nova Scotia Delegation Reference* [1951]), although indirect delegation has been allowed from a legislature at one level to an administrative agency at the other level (*P.E.I. Potato Marketing Board v. H.B. Willis Inc. and A.G. of Canada*, 1952).

Section 56 allows the governor-in-council (federal government) to disallow provincial legislation, and Sections 58 to 61 create the "federal" office of lieutenant-governor in each province. The lieutenant-governor has the power to reserve any provincial bill for consideration by the governor-in-council. These federal veto powers, however, have fallen into disuse and would likely disappear in any rewriting of the constitution. See *Disallowance; Reservation*.

The history of Canadian federalism is basically an account of disputes over the distribution of powers. Generally, from the 1880's to the 1930's, federal powers waned. This was because of the weakening of the "Peace, Order and good Government" clause, the strengthening of the "Property and Civil Rights" clause, and the disputes over the criminal law and treaty-making powers of the federal government. Indeed, it may be argued that the Judicial Committee of the Privy Council rewrote the British North America Act, interpreting the Act literally and ignoring the centralist intentions of its framers. See *Judicial Committee of the Privy Council; Supreme Court.*

In the latter part of the twentieth century, the federal and provincial governments have devised ways other than legal confrontation to deal with situations in which the provinces have legislative competence in costly policy areas, while the federal government has greater access to revenue. Attempts to rewrite the constitution have usually failed, as in the case of the Victoria Charter (1971), on the question of the procedure for amending the distribution of powers. See *Federal-provincial tax-sharing agreements; Spending power.*

Nonetheless, the provinces are always conscious of federal incursions into their areas of jurisdiction. At the conclusion of a meeting of provincial attorneys-general in 1978, for example, the ministers declared they were prepared to consider court challenges to "resist the growing trend of the federal authorities ... to move into areas constitutionally under provincial jurisdiction." Pointedly, the provinces had refused the requests of interested federal ministers to attend. Federal actions which the provincial attorneys-general defined as intrusions were: the proposed Canadian Transportation Accident Investigation Commission, which would permit the federal government to conduct investigations of accidents involving federally regulated modes of transport (which the provinces viewed as a responsibility of provincial coroners and provincial criminal investigation authorities); the proposed Canada Ports Act, which provided for the establishment of a federal harbour police force (which the provinces viewed as an interference with provincial police responsibilities); the Human Rights Act, which would establish a federal agency for the handling of criminal intelligence gathered by provincial police forces; and the Young Offenders Act, which would have restricted provincial discretion in charging individuals with offences. Some authorities had already intervened before the Supreme Court in 1978, in a case challenging amendments to the Criminal Code in 1969 which gave the federal government some authority in criminal prosecutions. The provinces interpreted the amendments as interference with their power to administer justice. See *Declaratory power*.

Division of the House.   The taking of votes in a legislature. Upon a call for division of the House, bells summon members for the vote. The division in the House of Commons, for example, is a standing vote. Members are required to stand for identification when their votes are recorded and may then resume their seats. The results of the division are predictable, as almost all divisions take place on party lines and are usually won by the Government.

Members who expect to be absent during a vote may, with the approval of the party whips, "pair" with an MP on the other side of the House. In such a case, neither MP votes; thus, the Government's and Opposition's relative strength remains unaffected. After a division is recorded and announced, some members may declare their pairing and how they would have voted if they had not been paired. These announcements are made for the record in Hansard.

Dominion (of Canada; government; status).   A now seldom-used term with reference to the country as the Dominion of Canada (British North America Act, preamble) or to the national, federal, or central government, or Parliament. Created as a dominion within the British Empire, Canada's dominion status refers to the relative autonomy possessed by Canada with respect to the imperial government or Parliament at a given time (see *Statute of Westminster*).

Because of its pejorative overtones, both externally with respect to the United Kingdom and internally with respect to the provincial governments, the term has been largely abandoned since the 1960's. The country is simply known as Canada; the dominion government is commonly referred to as the federal government, and dominion-provincial conferences as federal-provincial conferences.

Dominion-provincial conferences. Referred to subsequently as federal-provincial conferences and the Conference of First Ministers, meetings involving the prime minister and provincial premiers or their representatives, held in 1927, 1935, 1945-1946, 1957, and 1960-1961. The term federal-provincial conference now also refers to innumerable meetings involving not only the heads of government but also ministers with particular portfolios, or senior civil servants of particular departments or with particular policy responsibilities. Most of the conferences which were styled "dominion-provincial" concerned the distribution of legislative powers and a "domestic" amending formula for the British North America Act. For example, the Dominion-Provincial Conference on Reconstruction of 1945-1946 concerned the report of the (Rowell-Sirois) Royal Commission on Dominion-Provincial Relations, which was established unilaterally by the dominion (federal) government in 1937 and which recommended in 1940 wider responsibility and powers of taxation for the dominion government. See *Intergovernmental committees.*

Drybones Case (The Queen v. Joseph Drybones [1969]). An appeal before the Supreme Court that resulted in the invalidation of a section of the Indian Act because it violated the federal Bill of Rights (1960). The judgment established that the Bill of Rights was not just an interpretation act setting out guidelines, but an act which could enlarge freedoms beyond existing legislation. However, the Supreme Court's ruling in 1975 on two cases concerning sex discrimination in the Indian Act has led to confusion about the Court's view of the Bill of Rights (see *Lavell and Bedard cases*).

In the particular case of the *Queen v. Drybones*, the Indian Act provided for a penalty for Indians being intoxicated in a public place in the Northwest Territories which was different for other citizens. Drybones had pleaded guilty and was convicted. Others took up the case in order to test the Bill of Rights, which outlawed discrimination "by reason of race, national origin, colour, religion, or sex." The decision in the Drybones Case, especially in view of other court rulings, has not diminished the pressure on the federal government from civil libertarians to entrench civil liberties or rights. See *Bill of Rights; Lavell-Bedard cases; Supreme Court.*

Duff Doctrine.   A judicial opinion that the preamble of the British North America Act, which asserts that Canada is to have a constitution similar in principle to that of the United Kingdom, precludes provincial legislatures from restricting "the right of free public discussion of public affairs, notwithstanding its incidental mischiefs ... " and other rights essential to the operation of parliamentary government. Thus, only Parliament "possesses authority to legislate for the protection of this right... " *(Reference re Alberta Statutes* [1938]). The so-called doctrine is associated with Chief Justice Duff, who wrote the decision in the Reference concerning the Alberta Accurate News and Information Act, which would have subjected newspapers to government censure and required "corrections" of stories. The doctrine was written as an *obiter dictum*, that is, as an opinion which did not bear on the elements of the case and therefore represented only a guide for subsequent judicial interpretations. Because Duff based federal competence in the "powers requisite for the protection of the constitution itself" (134), he felt that Parliament could only protect and not itself restrict the right of free public discussion of public affairs. Duff's view was reasserted in several decisions of the Supreme Court regarding provincial legislation. See *Alberta Press Bill Reference; Padlock Law; Saumur v. Quebec; Supreme Court.*

E

Economic Council of Canada.   A federal crown corporation established in 1963 to advise Parliament on measures to achieve high employment and efficient production, and a high and consistent rate of growth. In its annual report in 1979, for example, the Council recommended a conservative fiscal and monetary policy to deal with "deep-seated" structural difficulties in the economy which made for poor economic prospects in the early 1980's. The Council's membership is supposed to be representative of labour, agriculture, industry, and commerce. However, representatives of the Canadian Labour Congress withdrew from the ECC in 1976. The Council, which reports to Parliament annually through the prime minister, consists of a full-time chairman, vice-chairman, a director and twenty-five part-time members, the latter receiving no remuneration. For a brief period in 1978,

the Council housed the Centre for the Study of Inflation and Productiv-
ity, a short-lived anti-inflation monitoring group which succeeded the
Anti-Inflation Board following the wage and price control period.

Far from being a government agency for economic planning, the
Council's value is largely educative. On its own initiative or on direction by the government, the Economic Council investigates and reports
on specific problems related to its general mandate. In 1978, ECC
Chairman Sylvia Ostry argued for more discussion between the public
and the government prior to decision-making, but without resorting to
organizational structures. She also recommended that the ECC report
on the basis of a "substantial majority" rather than unanimity, and that
a parliamentary committee be formed to discuss economic matters regularly with members of the Council.

Economic nationalism.   A phrase associated with the opinion, especially widespread during the 1960's and 1970's, that the federal and
provincial governments should act to slow down the rate of increase,
and reduce the amount, of non-resident equity (ownership) capital in
the Canadian economy, and thereby reverse the "continentalist" policies of federal governments since 1945. The roots of economic nationalism may be found in the report of the (Gordon) Royal Commission on
Canada's Economic Prospects in the 1950's and Walter Gordon's later
career in the federal Liberal Governments of the 1960's. Important in
the latter were Gordon's abortive "foreign take-over" tax, when he was
minister of finance in 1963, and a commissioned study on foreign ownership by economist Mel Watkins (1968). A House committee (Wahn)
report in 1970 and a government review (Gray) the following year
added fuel to the fires of controversy. Kari Levitt's *Silent Surrender:
The Multinational Corporation in Canada* (Toronto: Macmillan Co. of
Canada Ltd., 1970) was an important academic work on the subject at
this time.

The greatest pressure from outside the Government came from the
left and was organized as a faction within the New Democratic party.
Its founders, Watkins and historian James Laxer among them, styled
the group "the Waffle" because they initially hesitated at its founding
in the late 1960's to argue for extensive public ownership as a solution
to foreign control. In 1969, the Waffle attempted unsuccessfully to
have the federal NDP adopt its manifesto. In 1971, Laxer unsuccessfully challenged veteran New Democrat David Lewis for the federal
party leadership. In 1972, the Ontario NDP denounced the Waffle as an
unacceptable "party within a party" and forced the group from the party.

The Committee for an Independent Canada, which was also established at this time, was composed mostly of Liberals and Conservatives. Walter Gordon and Conservative Eddie Goodman were prominent in the CIC's ranks at its founding. Publisher Mel Hurtig and economist Abraham Rotstein were also prominently associated with the organization. See Rotstein and Gary Lax (eds.), *Getting it Back: A Programme for Canadian Independence* (Toronto: Clarke Irwin and Co. Ltd., 1974), for essays and studies which the CIC sponsored.

The federal government and some provincial governments did respond to the issues raised by the economic nationalists. The most notable federal responses were the Canada Development Corporation, which is designed to develop Canadian-owned and -managed private corporations and investment opportunities for Canadians, and the Foreign Investment Review Agency, which assesses the benefit to Canada of proposed foreign purchases of established Canadian companies or new businesses. Since the mid-1970's, the issues raised by economic nationalists have been less prominent in public discussion. See *Canada Development Corporation; Continentalism; Foreign Investment Review Agency; Waffle, the.*

For a source book on the controversy at its peak, which was compiled by two economic nationalists, see David Godfrey and Mel Watkins (eds.), *Gordon to Watkins to You: A Documentary: The Battle for Control of Our Economy* (Toronto: New Press, 1970).

Eldorado Nuclear Limited.   Originally a privately owned exploration company, but a federal crown corporation since 1944; it is responsible for exploring and developing uranium deposits, and for refining and marketing nuclear fuel products domestically and internationally. The refining process takes place at Port Hope, Ontario, where Eldorado Nuclear also stockpiles uranium concentrates. Controversy arose in the late 1970's over stockpiling procedures, when ground leakage occurred in long-standing stockpiles. Eldorado Nuclear was one of several crown corporations which the Conservative Government in 1979 contemplated selling to private interests in its divestiture, or "privatization," programme. The board of Eldorado Nuclear reports to Parliament through the minister of energy, mines, and resources.

Election expenses (controls; subsidies).   Changes to provincial and federal election acts since the 1960's place limits on campaign contributions and campaign expenditures, provide for public disclosure of names of financial supporters, provide for controlled access to the mass media, and provide limited compensation for election expenses from the public treasury.

Under the federal Elections Act (1970, as amended), all parties must be registered by the Chief Electoral Officer, who has discretionary and mandatory powers to register and deregister parties. Recognized parties have protected names and guaranteed but limited broadcast time, with partial compensation during elections. They qualify for the tax credit scheme whereby contributors may deduct portions of their limited contributions from their income tax. Registered parties and their officially designated candidates also receive partial compensation for campaign expenses. The parties, however, assume legal responsibilities. The parties' and each candidate's official agents are responsible for all revenues and expenses incurred following the issuance of writs for the election. The Act also makes it illegal for anyone other than the candidate, his or her agent and the party's agent to incur expenses during a campaign for promoting or opposing a candidate or a party. This law attempts to preclude the creation of so-called non-partisan committees in support of a particular candidate or party for the purpose of evading the expense ceilings.

In the federal election campaign in 1979, the central party offices could spend 30 cents times the total number of voters in constituencies where they had candidates. Beyond this, individual candidates were limited to a formula based on the number of electors in their constituency. The value of goods and services had to be included in expenditures. Spending ceilings on broadcasts tended to limit the activities of the Liberal and Conservative parties but to increase advertising for the New Democratic party. Because the expenditure ceilings are in place only following the issuance of writs for the election, there was considerable activity before the date of the anticipated election in 1979 was announced. The Chief Electoral Officer, who is responsible for enforcing the provisions of the Act, has conceded that the publicly supported mailing and constituency office privileges of sitting members represent pre-writ advantages over their challengers.

It will take some time to ascertain the effect of public controls and subsidies on federal and provincial elections and the party system. Generally, the traditional supporters of Liberal and Conservative parties might be less disposed to contribute in view of the public disclosures, and those parties will attempt to broaden their base of financial support. The financial situation of the New Democratic parties should be improved because of the tax advantages for their mass membership. The Liberal and Conservative parties may depend less on advertising and more on constituency campaigning, while the New Democrats will increase their media activity, especially on radio and television. Of some importance to the federal nature of the party system, provincial and federal counterparts will become financially independent of each other, and presumably more politically independent; also, local constituency associations may become less dependent on the financial largesse of the central party and leadership. In short, the party system will probably become more fragmented.

For an analysis of federal law pertaining to parties and elections, see John C. Courtney, "Recognition of Canadian Political Parties in Parliament and in Law," *Canadian Journal of Political Science* 11 (1978), 33-60.

Electoral Boundaries Readjustment Act (redistribution) (1975). Provisions for the drawing of boundaries of constituencies based on population distribution according to the decennial census. The principle of the current federal Act (1975) pertaining to the House of Commons was established in 1964; it basically takes the task away from politicians and gives it to independent commissions. Otherwise, the business of drawing electoral boundaries would be left in the hands of the politicians in office, who would be tempted to establish constituency boundaries to maximize electoral support for their party (gerrymander) – a practice known relatively recently in some provinces.

Each of the federal boundary commissions, which are established after each census, contains four members. The chairmen are separately appointed by the chief justice of each province from judges of the court over which the chief justice presides. The Speaker of the House of Commons appoints two members from residents of the particular province. The final member of each commission is the federal representation commissioner, who sits on all commissions and is responsible for preparing maps showing the distribution of population in each province and for devising alternative proposals for the new boundaries.

Within one year of their appointment, each commission must report new boundaries to Parliament, through the representation commissioner and the Speaker. The House then has approximately 45 sitting days to object to the proposed changes. Naturally, MPs soon become familiar with changes proposed for their seats, applying the previous election results to the proposed constituencies. The commissions have the final authority to deal with MPs' objections before the representation commissioner sends their final reports to the Speaker.

In 1974, Parliament revised the formula for awarding a particular number of seats to each province and the territories. The figure having been established, the boundaries were then readjusted within each province on the basis of a total population of a constituency being neither more than 25 per cent above nor more than 25 per cent below an average constituency population for the province.

Malapportionment is generally tolerated for geographic reasons, particularly between densely and sparsely populated parts of a province, and with consideration for accessibility and rate of growth, but also for socio-political reasons, recognizing community or diversity of interests of the inhabitants of a particular region. In the 1960's, federal redistribution based on the 1961 census was completed by 1966, for the 1968 election. In the 1970's, redistribution based on the 1971 census was completed by 1977, for the 1979 election. Given the length of time between the census and redistribution and degree of urbanization in Canada, the tolerated malapportionment between urban and rural areas tends to be accentuated, with urban populations being considerably underrepresented. See *Gerrymander; Malapportionment.*

For an historic overview of the election process, see T.H. Qualter, *The Election Process in Canada* (Toronto: McGraw Hill Co. of Canada Ltd., 1970).

Electoral system.   The means by which votes cast for candidates are translated into legislative seats won. Elections to the provincial legislatures and to the House of Commons are based on the single-member constituency system with plurality win, or the first-past-the-post system. That is, the winner is the candidate who has received more votes than any other candidate irrespective of his percentage of the total number of votes cast. Thus a candidate may win with a plurality over his opponents, and without a majority of the votes cast. There are other types of electoral systems. For example, in federal elections in the United States, there are different electoral systems for election to the presidency, the Senate, and the House of Representatives. In the Federal Republic of Germany, one-half of the Bundestag's deputies are elected by the single-member constituency system with plurality win, while the other one-half are elected on a system of proportional representation using the party list system. The specific rules and procedures pertaining to elections concerning, for example, candidate selection, voter eligibility, and campaign procedures and financing, are usually referred to as election laws.

No electoral system is neutral. Each has inherent biases. The system used in Canada results, in effect, in two levels of electoral reality, only one of which counts. The important level of reality is the number of seats won by each party, and the other is the percentage of popular support for each party. Governments are appointed on the basis of seats held in the Commons or provincial legislatures, regardless of any discrepancy between the percentage of seats and the percentage of votes for that party.

On the consequences of electoral rules generally, see Douglas Rae, *The Political Consequences of Electoral Laws* (New Haven: Yale University Press, 1967). For an analysis of the biases of the electoral system as it has operated in federal elections in Canada in this century, and its impact on the party system, see Alan C. Cairns, "The Electoral System and the Party System in Canada, 1921-1965," *Canadian Journal of Political Science* 1 (1968), 55-80. Cairns argues in part that the electoral system has resulted in overrepresentation of the parties with the most and the least support, underrepresentation of the middle parties, overrepresentation of small parties with sectional support, and underrepresentation of small parties with nationally diffused support. See also J.A. Lovink, "On Analyzing the Impact of the Electoral System on the Party System in Canada," *Canadian Journal of Political Science* 3 (1971), 497-516; Cairns's "A Reply to J.A. Lovink," *Canadian Journal of Political Science* 3 (1971), 517-21; and Richard Johnston and Janet Ballantyne, "Geography and the Electoral System," *Canadian Journal of Political Science* 10 (1977) 857-66.

Elites.   Small groups of people who exercise considerable power in society. One may speak of economic, political, and bureaucratic elites, or collectively of a national elite or ruling class, as well as regional elites. In urbanized and industrialized societies generally, there tends to be a plurality of elites forming temporary coalitions of interests on different issues, rather than the well-defined, permanent ruling class which tends to appear in more traditional societies. Studies of community power have led to the "ruling elite" and "plural elite" models of community power. The methodology of the investigators may explain their different conclusions. If one follows a reputational method of study, one might arrive at the ruling class model; if one adopts a decisional approach, examining a variety of issues, the plural model might be confirmed. Nonetheless, in plural societies, some elites are better organized and financed than others and consequently have more impact on decision-making in that society. Also, elites tend to be drawn from the same strata of society.

In the manner of John Porter in *The Vertical Mosaic: An Analysis of*

Social Class and Power in Canada (Toronto: University of Toronto Press, 1965), many Canadian academics adopt an understanding of power as conflicts, not between those who are "in" and those who are "out," but rather among those who are "in": "The latter are those who have assumed the major decision-making roles in the various [hierarchically organized] institutional systems in a complex society in the modern world ... Elites ... compete to share in the making of decisions of major importance for the society, and they co-operate because together they keep the society working as a going concern" (27).

For Porter and for Robert Presthus (*Elite Accommodation in Canadian Politics* [Toronto: Macmillan of Canada Ltd., 1974]), the major forces dominating the political system are the political (elected) and bureaucratic (appointed public) elites, along with an elite based in the private sector of the economy, composed of representatives of large-scale business and financial interests. Moreover, these groups share a class background characterized by a high level of education that results in a secularism which values moderation, bargaining, and accommodation. This secularism may be contrasted with the particularism of the lower strata of each group, which may occasionally complicate the bargaining process.

A characteristic of such a horizontally accommodative elite system is the movement of personalities back and forth across groups, in addition to recruitment to the top vertically from within the groups. This is particularly evident in federal politics, where one political party (the Liberals) has been in power for most of the twentieth century. The federal Liberal party, then, is not so much a power structure in itself as a coalition for power including leaders drawn from across other elites.

The federal system in Canada enhances the elite structure of Canadian society. In 1977, Alan C. Cairns spoke of the two levels of government creating powerful support for their survival in their public employees and in the support of parties and interest groups in a complex network of mutually supportive relations ("The Government and Societies of Canadian Federalism," *Canadian Journal of Political Science* 10 [1977], 695-725). In the 1960's, Arend Lijphart devised the term "consociational democracy" to describe countries which had fragmented political cultures but were stable democracies. In such countries, he argued, the elite make a conscious decision to accommodate their differences while defending the particular values and interests of their constituency, or subgroup. Lijphart later classified Canada as a semi-consociational democracy, in which the cultural fragmentation was institutionalized by the elite in intergovernmental relations

(*Democracy in Plural Societies: A Comparative Exploration* [New Haven: Yale University Press, 1977]). See *Consociational democracy.*

Emergency powers. Virtually unlimited powers to be assumed by the federal Parliament in time of national peril, under the "Peace, Order and good Government" clause of Section 91 of the British North America Act. The occasion on which to invoke the powers and their duration are fundamentally political questions, determined by the cabinet with Parliament's approval. During World War One, Parliament passed the War Measures Act (revised in 1952), which gives authority to the governor-in-council to make orders and regulations which "it may deem necessary or advisable for the security, defense, peace, order and welfare of Canada . . . ." In 1945, when World War Two was concluded, Parliament passed the National Emergency Transitional Powers Act, which declared that the state of emergency under the War Measures Act, which had been invoked during the war, still existed. The powers were renewed under the Emergency Powers Act of 1951, which expired in 1954. Parliament exempted the War Measures Act from the Bill of Rights in 1960. In 1970, the War Measures Act was invoked, for the first time in peacetime, upon the Government's assertion of an "apprehended insurrection" when the so-called *Front de Libération du Québec* kidnapped a British trade official and a Quebec cabinet minister in separate incidents in Montreal (the cabinet minister was later murdered by his captors, and the trade official was released following negotiations).

Serious doubts were expressed during and after the events of 1945-1954 and 1970 about the emergency measures. For example, in 1979, the private Canadian Civil Liberties Association recommended in part that judicial review of a Government's reasons for invoking the Act be established, with the House of Commons able to overrule the court's approval of the government's decision only by a two-thirds vote. The Association also wanted the term "apprehended insurrection" replaced by a definition which included imminent violence sufficiently intense and widespread to overthrow the government. Currently, the House must approve the Government's action by majority vote. Sections 20 and 91:1 of the British North America Act require Parliament to sit at least once a year and assert that no House of Commons may continue for more than five years except "in time of real or apprehended war, invasion, or insurrection" and when "such continuation is not opposed by the votes of one-third of the members of such House." See *October Crisis; War Measures Act.*

Energy Supplies Emergency Act (Energy Supplies Allocation Board). Federal legislation enacted under the Liberal Government in 1979, by which an Energy Supplies Allocation Board may be established and given sweeping authority over the petroleum industry, petroleum, and other energy supplies. Such powers would constitute a major encroachment on provincial jurisdiction over natural resources. The legislation was introduced following a refusal by Imperial Oil of the Government's request that it purchase oil directly from the Venezuelan government to replace oil which its parent company, the Exxon Corporation, had diverted from the Canadian subsidiary to the United States.

The legislation was passed despite vocal Conservative opposition and under threat of closure. However, the Board was not established before the Government's electoral defeat. Later in 1979, Conservative Prime Minister Joe Clark promised to create the Board, in order to win crucial support from Social Credit MPs to defeat a Liberal motion of no confidence. Events overtook the Clark Government, however, and the Board was still not appointed before the the Government's electoral defeat in 1980. See *National oil policy; Natural resources.*

Entrenchment, constitutional. The removal of legislative competence from government by a constitutional act which may be altered only through a complex and difficult amendment of the constitution itself. Strictly speaking, no aspect of the Canadian constitution is entrenched, all of it being subject to change by provincial legislatures, Parliament, judicial interpretation, and the British Parliament.

The argument for entrenchment in the Canadian constitution usually focusses on language and education rights and on civil liberties, with judicial interpretation giving meaning to the entrenched rights. In 1969, Donald Smiley criticized the concept of entrenchment, noting the limitations of judicial interpretation and the "elemental wisdom" of the current constitution in that, within the restrictions of the federal distribution of legislative powers, legislatures can enact legislation as they desire with the one exception – they cannot bind successor legislatures ("The Case against the Canadian Charter of Human Rights," *Canadian Journal of Political Science* 2 [1969], 277-91).

Enumeration (of powers). The delineation of the legislative competence of Parliament and of the provincial legislatures in Canada, as outlined in the British North America Act and subsequently amended. The legislative competence is thus said to consist of powers listed under enumerated heads. See *Distribution (division) of powers.*

Enumeration (of voters).   The registration of people for the list of eligible voters prior to federal and provincial elections. At the federal level and in most provinces, the returning officer in each constituency prepares a list of enumerators when it appears that an election will be called. The returning officer tries to ensure that the urban enumerators, who will work in pairs, are members of different political parties. Thus, the returning officer approaches the first- and second-ranked parties in the previous election for names of people who would be willing to be paid enumerators. This is a source of minor patronage for local party organizations. The rural enumerators should be residents of the polling division in which they are collecting names for the list.

Because of the shortness of campaigns, especially at the provincial level, enumerators are sworn, trained, and set to work soon after the election date has been set. The paired urban enumerators must call at each urban dwelling, making return calls where necessary, and must agree to each name added to the list. However, some will divide their labour; and, especially in such violation of the rules, the voters list can be padded – that is, names added fraudulently. It is presumed that in the rural areas, where the population is more permanent and smaller, false enumeration cannot so easily take place.

Preliminary lists of voters are published and distributed to the political parties in each constituency and to each household in their respective polling divisions. This procedure is a check against fraud, but it also gives potential electors who were missed in the enumeration an opportunity to apply to the court of revision to be declared eligible to vote. There are also procedures to protect an eligible voter from having his name removed from the list at the courts of revision. The distribution of lists to voters may be discontinued in order to reduce the length of federal campaigns.

A permanent registration list is maintained in some countries, such as the United States. In this system, the onus is on the individual to ensure that he is on the list of voters in his constituency.

Equalization grants (unconditional transfer payments).   Unconditional financial payments made by the federal government to the provinces, based on their fiscal need, to achieve revenue equalization. From 1945 to 1956, the federal government's control over taxation was widened to achieve economic stabilization. During this period, in bilateral agreements with the provinces, the federal government "rented" provincial personal income and corporation taxes, as well as succession duties, and paid individually negotiated provincial subsidies

beyond a minimum level. In return, the federal government accepted responsibility for a range of welfare matters, including pensions and unemployment and health insurance. Only Quebec remained aloof from
these arrangements. In 1956, new federal-provincial arrangements led
to the determination of unconditional federal subsidies for provincial
revenue equalization based on objective criteria. The formula for determining the grants was designed, at that time, to bring the provincial per
capita yield of personal income and corporation tax and succession
duties to the per capita yield of the same taxes in the two wealthiest
provinces in each year.

Since then, the principle of equalization has been reaffirmed, but the
formula for calculating payments has been modified. In the 1970's,
provincial revenue which was to be "equalized" was established in 29
revenue sources, for each of which a revenue base was defined for the
calculation of equalization grants. Since 1977, revenue from provincial
crown corporations has been included in the calculation of provincial
revenue; the purpose is to prevent a provincial equalization grant from
being increased because of the nationalization of a profit-making business which no longer pays corporate income tax. This measure was introduced following Saskatchewan's nationalization of the potash industry. Also in the late 1970's, the federal government had to revise the
calculation to determine payments, because of the considerable rise in
revenue in Alberta which resulted from the international price increase in oil. For example, it announced a formula change for 1979-
1980 to avoid the anomaly of having Ontario, with almost the highest
provincial per capita income, about to qualify for equalization payments. In 1979, an increase in domestic oil and gas prices and increased revenues for the oil- and gas-producing provinces resulted in
an estimated $60 million increase in federal equalization grants to all
provinces except Alberta, British Columbia, and Ontario. In 1978, the
premier of Ontario had criticized equalization payments to the extent
that they hindered efficient economic development (presumably in
Ontario) by subsidizing inefficient industrial activity (presumably elsewhere). All premiers, however, reaffirmed support for equalization;
and some, such as the Nova Scotia premier, declared equalization payments "fundamental to ... Confederation." See *Federal-provincial tax-
sharing agreements.*

Established Programmes (Interim Arrangements) Act (1965). A
federal measure by which provinces objecting to federal conditional
grants in shared-cost programmes as unwarranted intrusions into their

spheres of authority could, by a specific date, opt or contract out of specific established programmes and receive financial compensation. The major programmes involved were: hospital insurance; assistance for elderly, blind, and disabled persons; unemployment insurance; vocational training; and health. The compensation then involved a reduction in personal income tax points, with transfer payments between the federal and provincial governments to match the difference between the tax yield and the amount that the province would have received in conditional grants. Specific reductions in tax points (percentages) were associated with each of the five programmes; and the revenue for the abated taxes was subject to equalization payment by, or recovery to, the federal government. Cash payments were involved in the contracting-out of several minor programmes. During specified transition periods, the provincial government had to agree to provide services comparable to those that would have been provided under the conditional grant programme.

Only Quebec, where concern about federal encroachment on provincial autonomy had been greatest at the time, took advantage of the Act. Thus, under the federal statute, the province managed to achieve a kind of special status in Canada. Federal-provincial programmes are otherwise financed until 1982 under the Fiscal Arrangements and Established Programmes Financing Act of 1977.

Estimates.   Funds which the cabinet wishes the legislature to appropriate to meet government spending needs. The following describes procedures for handling estimates at the federal level (procedures which the House of Commons could change). Departmental and agency estimates approved by the Treasury Board and cabinet, with a concern for the Government's priorities in spending as well as for economy, are usually tabled in the House of Commons in February as the main estimates (in the so-called "Blue Book"). The Government's main estimates take the form of a supply bill, or appropriation act, and are accompanied by detailed spending proposals of departments and agencies. The estimates for specific departments and agencies are then sent to the relevant standing committee of the House of Commons for intensive scrutiny. The committee members – at least the Opposition members – question the designated or responsible minister, who is accompanied by the senior civil servants to give advice. In some jurisdictions, the legislature sits as the committee of the whole, or a committee of supply, to question the minister. When the committees report back to the House of Commons, the estimates are voted on and passed through Parliament as one bill. Of course, the Opposition uses the committee meetings and supply periods in the House (25 days in three periods, also known as "Opposition days," or allotted days) to criticize not only government spending but policy priorities generally. Parliament may vote interim supply before the study of the main estimates is concluded.

Standing orders of the House of Commons require the main estimates to be referred to committees by March 1 in the expiring fiscal year. The committees must report back by May 31 in the new fiscal year. The three supply periods must end by December 10, March 26, and June 30. The first supplementary estimates for a fiscal year are usually dealt with in the December period, and the final supplementary estimates in the March period. Interim supply is voted in the March period also. Finally, in the June period, the House votes on full supply on main estimates.

All departments and agencies must spend appropriated funds as outlined in the detailed estimates examined by Parliament. A government body may deviate somewhat with the approval of the Treasury Board. However, Parliament requires the auditor general and the comptroller-general to investigate and report on government spending for purposes other than those for which funds were appropriated.

The Government introduces supplementary estimates and further supplementary estimates to meet financial needs purportedly unforeseen when the main estimates were drawn up and presented. These estimates are often introduced and acted on late in a parliamentary session, and they naturally receive less scrutiny than the main estimates. When Parliament is not in session and the government faces a serious appropriation shortfall, it can spend money through Governor General's Warrants. The governor-in-council issues warrants when the president of the Treasury Board reports that there is no appropriation for an expenditure which the relevant minister deems urgently required. These special warrants must be published in the *Canada Gazette* within 30 days of issue, be reported to Parliament within 15 days of the next session, and be approved as supplementary estimates. See *Budgetary process; Treasury Board; Treasury Board Secretariat.*

For a description of the federal, institutional machinery in the late 1970's, see H.V. Kroeker, *Accountability and Control: The Government Expenditure Process* (Montreal: C.D. Howe Research Institute, 1978).

Exchequer Court. A court of law, equity, and admiralty, a superior court with civil and criminal jurisdiction, established in the nineteenth century and replaced in 1970 by the Federal Court of Canada. Appointed by the governor-in-council and removable only by Parliament, the judges on the Exchequer Court had jurisdiction concurrent with the provincial courts in cases involving crown revenue (review of taxation) and exclusive jurisdiction over claims against the Crown in federal matters: for example, claims concerning expropriation of property by the Crown, and claims arising out of negligence by agents of the Crown. If a provincial legislature gave the necessary statutory authority, the Exchequer Court also had jurisdiction over federal-provincial and interprovincial disputes. In most cases, appeals were allowed to the Supreme Court on decisions by the Exchequer Court. See *Federal Court of Canada*.

Executive, the.   That part or branch of government which is responsible for the presentation of a programme to and for approval by the legislature, and for the implementation of laws by the administration. The executive also has certain legislative and quasi-judicial powers through delegated power under enabling legislation.

In Canada, an important distinction exists between the formal executive (that is, the Crown) and its representatives (the governor general and the provincial lieutenant-governors) and the political executive, that is, the cabinets, or Governments-of-the-day. The British North America Act invests the "Executive Government and Authority of and over Canada" in the Crown, its governor general, and the Privy Council for Canada (Sections 9-11), and the lieutenant-governors advised by their Executive Councils in each of the provinces (Sections 58-67). Although the political executives are the effective Governments, they have statutory existence only as the effective part of the Privy Council for Canada and the provincial Executive Councils. See *Cabinet; Crown; Crown prerogatives; Delegated power; Governor General; Letters Patent; Lieutenant-Governor; Public service (administration); Quasi-judicial decisions; Regulatory agencies (regulations)*.

Executive assistant, ministerial.   The chief of staff of a cabinet minister, a person who is hired and retained at the minister's "pleasure" and is not a public servant. Usually such personnel at the federal level, who are maintained on public salaries, are hired with the approval of senior members of the Prime Minister's Office and the Privy Council Office. The minister will determine how to allocate departmental, cabinet, and party responsibilities among his or her executive staff. From the minister's point of view, an executive assistant should bring to the minister's attention information and points of view from outside the cognizance of the departmental senior civil servants, and thereby improve political judgment on issues within the minister's responsibility. A possible post-ministerial staff career for executive assistants is in consultative work in the private sector with firms who do business with the public administration. Former executive assistants may also become elective politicians.

For an analysis of ministerial executive staffs, see Kenneth G. Tilley, "Ministerial Executive Staffs," in Paul Fox (ed.), *Politics: Canada* (4th ed.; Toronto: McGraw-Hill Ryerson Ltd., 1977), 409-14.

Executive Council.   The formal name for a provincial Government-of-the-day, cabinet, or ministry. Executive Councils are mentioned in the British North America Act only with respect to some provinces, and then only with respect to the lieutenant-governor. The principle of responsible government is observed in the provinces by convention; that is, while the lieutenant-governor may appoint the Executive Council, he or she is bound to appoint members who have, or may soon have, seats in the legislature and who have its support, or confidence. Subsequently, the lieutenant-governor will act virtually always on the Council's advice (formally, they through him or her as the lieutenant-governor-in-council), subject to the federal aspects of the lieutenant-governor's office (including appointment, tenure, and powers of disallowance and of reservation). See *Lieutenant-Governor; Lieutenant-Governor-in-Council; Disallowance; Reservation.*

Executive (administrative) federalism.   A term which describes a federal system such as Canada's, in which intergovernmental relations are characterized by a level of interdependence which puts great emphasis on multilateral and bilateral consultation, negotiation, and functional operations among the eleven governments of the two levels. This contrasts with a more classical federal system, in which intergovernmental relations are determined by a strict definition of jurisdictional competence between the two levels of government.

Donald Smiley defines and uses the phrase "executive federalism" in his analysis of Canadian federalism (*Canada in Question: Federalism in the Seventies* [2nd ed.; Toronto: McGraw-Hill Ryerson Ltd., 1976]).

Export Development Corporation (EDC).   A commercially self-sustaining federal crown corporation established in 1969 to develop and facilitate Canada's export trade by providing insurance, guarantees, and loans. EDC insures Canadian firms against non-payment by foreign buyers; provides surety insurance to protect exporters who must issue performance bonds and to the financial institutions supplying the guarantee; grants long-term loans to public and private foreign buyers of Canadian equipment and services; and provides guarantees to Canadian exporters against loss of investment abroad due to political action.

EDC, which succeeded the Export Credit Insurance Corporation (1944-1969), is directed by a 12-member board chaired by a full-time president. Five of the directors are from the private sector. The vice-chairman is the deputy minister of industry, trade, and commerce. The other government members of the Corporation's board are the governor of the Bank of Canada; the senior assistant deputy minister of international trade in the Department of Industry, Trade, and Commerce; the president of the Canadian International Development Agency; the under-secretary of state (deputy minister) for external affairs; and the deputy minister of finance. In 1977, EDC was decentralized, with regional offices in Montreal, Toronto, Vancouver, and Halifax. As the Corporation is self-sustaining (income is derived from premiums, interest, and guarantee fees), there is no allocation for EDC in government estimates. The Corporation is nonetheless audited by the auditor general.

In his annual report for 1977, the EDC president estimated that EDC programmes supported 40 per cent of Canada's shipment of capital goods and related services abroad, excluding the United States. In the process, EDC has earned a positive return on equity invested in the Corporation by taxpayers. As a crown corporation, EDC earnings are not subject to the Income Tax Act.

Extraterritoriality.   The extension and application of the laws of one country to another. The concept has relevance to Canada in the application of U.S. laws to American-owned businesses operating in Canada. The problem of the extraterritorial application of U.S. laws is particularly important in Canada because of the extensive ownership of Canadian companies by American firms. Thus, Canadian exports which involve components and technical data from the United States have been subjected to the U.S. Export Control Act of 1949. Also, the U.S. Foreign Asset Control Regulations and the Cuban Assets Control Regulations and the Trading With the Enemy Act apply to U.S.-owned operations abroad, even when no U.S. components are involved. Finally, American anti-trust (anti-combines) laws are also applied when

Canadian subsidiaries of U.S. firms are merged. There have been a few cases when Canadian-based but American-owned companies have lost export business because of the extraterritorial application of U.S. laws. However, the greatest impact of extraterritoriality is in the inhibition it places on Canadian managers of U.S.-owned firms when developing export markets.

F

Family Allowance.   A taxable federal benefit, known popularly as the "baby bonus," paid monthly on behalf of dependent children under 18 years of age. Although the mother usually receives the payment, it is taxable against the person who claims the child as a dependent. The government introduced the allowance, Canada's first universal welfare benefit, in 1944 and indexed it to the consumer price index in 1974. In 1976, the government suspended indexation as a measure of economic restraint.

Farm Credit Corporation (FCC).   A federal crown corporation established in 1959, successor to the Canadian Farm Loan Board, which makes long-term mortgage loans to farmers or syndicates of farmers. The FCC administers the Farm Credit Act and the Farm Syndicates Credit Act, and it is the agent of Agriculture Canada in administering the Land Transfer Plan of the small farm development programme. Most of the members of the FCC are civil servants who are responsible to the minister of agriculture. The minister appoints a committee, whose members include farmers, to advise the FCC on policy. In most provinces, there are also boards composed of farmers to deal with the appeals of dissatisfied applicants.

Federal Court.   Established in 1970, successor to the Exchequer Court, the Federal Court consists of a Trial Division (a court of original jurisdiction) and an Appeals Division, or Federal Court of Appeals. The Trial Division has: original jurisdiction in claims against or by the Crown and in federal-provincial and interprovincial disputes; concurrent jurisdiction in claims against or concerning officers or employees of the federal government; some jurisdiction with respect to relief sought against federal boards, commissions, and other tribunals; jurisdiction in certain property matters; admiralty jurisdiction; jurisdiction in appeals from income and estate tax assessments and citizenship court decisions; and residual jurisdiction where no other court has jurisdiction for relief under a law of Canada which, though not a statute of Parliament, falls "within the legislative competence" of Parliament. The Federal Court of Appeal hears appeals from cases in the Trial Division and appeals from some tribunals. Under freedom-of-information legislation which the Conservative Government introduced in Parliament in 1979 (and which died on the Order Paper), complainants would have been able to appeal to the Federal Court about the government's non-compliance with a recommendation of an information commissioner. Also, the legislation would have required changes in the Federal Court Act, which allows a minister to issue certificates denying access to information (see *Freedom-of-Information Act; Information Commissioner*).

The jurisdiction to hear and determine applications to review, and set aside orders of federal tribunals, is found in the Trial Division with two exceptions: first, in cases where the Federal Court of Appeal has statutory jurisdiction; second, where there is a statutory appeal elsewhere. For example, the Broadcasting Act, the Immigration Appeal Board Act, the National Energy Board Act, and the Railway Act explicitly allow for appeals to the Federal Court of Appeal. In the second case, appeals may be allowed by statute to the Supreme Court, the governor-in-council (that is, the cabinet), or the Treasury Board. Also, federal boards, commissions, and tribunals themselves may refer a question of law, jurisdiction, practice, and procedure to the Appeal Division for determination without delay.

The Court of Appeal consists of the chief justice of the court and five other justices. The Trial Division consists of the associate chief justice and nine other justices. The Federal Court has the authority to invite retired federally appointed judges to act as deputy judges of the Court. The Court may also invite federally appointed judges who are still on the bench, but only with the consent of the relevant chief justice or provincial attorney general. The administrator of the Court is the principal officer of the Registry in Ottawa. District administrators manage regional offices elsewhere.

Federal secretary (New Democratic party). The principal administrator of the federal New Democratic party, whose provincial counterparts are called provincial secretaries. The federal secretary, who is appointed by the party executive, is responsible for organizational matters both between and during elections. Because the NDP is a mass membership-based party, the role of the federal secretary's office has a

more separate and distinct identity apart from the parliamentary leadership than do the small bureaucracies and administrative officers and offices of the elite-based Liberal and Conservative parties. David Lewis, for
example, who became leader of the federal NDP in 1971, had been elected to the House of Commons only three years earlier. However, previ-
ously he had held party offices, including that of secretary.

Federal-provincial conferences.   Earlier styled dominion-provincial
and currently the Conference of First Ministers, federal-provincial conferences involve meetings of the prime minister and provincial premiers or their representatives; they have been held in 1963, 1964, 1966,
1968, 1971, 1973, 1974, 1977, 1978, and 1979. The term "federal-provincial conference" is also used to describe innumerable meetings involving ministers with particular portfolios and senior civil servants of
particular departments or with particular policy responsibilities.
While most of the conferences involving the heads of government have
been concerned with constitutional, fiscal, and economic matters,
other areas of joint concern, such as energy (1974, 1979), are also discussed. See *Intergovernmental committees.*

Federal-provincial relations.   See *Federalism; Intergovernmental
committees.*

*Federal-provincial Relations Office (Canada; secretary to the cabi-
net for . . .).*   A government department under the prime minister
which is headed by a senior civil servant designated secretary to the
cabinet for federal-provincial relations. Before Parliament established
the office in 1974, its responsibility had been in a division of the Privy
Council Office (PCO). The secretary and the Office assist the prime
minister in federal-provincial consultations and provide the cabinet
with advice on federal-provincial issues. The Office undertakes studies
and monitors provincial views on federal programmes and policies. It
participates in the work of interdepartmental committees of civil servants and co-ordinates federal involvement in the Conference of First
Ministers. The first secretary to the cabinet for federal-provincial relations was Gordon Robertson, a career public servant who had been
clerk of the Privy Council (that is, secretary to the cabinet) for many
years. Robertson resigned after the appointment of the Conservative
Government in 1979 so as not "to inhibit" Prime Minister Joe Clark's
"capacity to establish and carry out" new constitutional policies (Robertson to Clark, September 28, 1979). (Earlier, under Prime Minister

Pierre Trudeau, Robertson's responsibilities had also included the security and intelligence section of the PCO and the committee which advised the prime minister on senior appointments in the public service.)

The parliamentary debate on the establishment of the Federal-Provincial Relations Office and the role of the Privy Council Office casts some light on the operation of the senior executive, or central, agencies of the federal government; but it also illustrates the difficulty of parliamentary scrutiny of prime ministerial "departments of state." See J.R. Mallory, "The Two Clerks: Parliamentary Discussion on the Role of the Privy Council Office," *Canadian Journal of Political Science* 10 (1977), 3-19. On the Federal-Provincial Relations Office and other central agencies, see Colin Campbell and George J. Szablowski, *The Super-Bureaucrats: Structure and Behaviour in Central Agencies* (Toronto: Macmillan Co. of Canada Ltd., 1979).

Federal-provincial tax-sharing agreements (Fiscal Arrangements Act). Periodically renegotiated agreements whereby the provinces and the federal government share tax revenues and the federal government provides conditional grants in specific shared-cost programmes and unconditional equalization grants, in order to reduce regional disparities in the provision of government services. During the emergency conditions of World War Two, the provinces agreed not to levy personal income and corporation taxes. In return, the federal government made a tax rental payment to the provinces based either on the revenue yields in 1941, in the abandoned tax fields, or the cost of servicing the provincial debt; and it assumed the cost of certain social services. The federal government also entreated with the provinces not to increase succession duties by subtracting any increased yield in succession duties from the rental payments to those provinces opting for the payment for debt servicing. The Wartime Tax Agreement lasted until 1946; and since then, agreements have been negotiated for the periods 1947-1952, 1952-1957, 1957-1962, 1962-1967, 1967-1977, and 1977-1982. The current arrangements, which include important changes in federal funding of provincial programmes, are carried out under the Federal-Provincial Fiscal Arrangements and Established Programmes Financing Act of 1977.

The aim of the tax agreements is to reduce disparity in the provision of public services, notably in such costly areas as hospital and medical services, welfare, and post-secondary education. Since 1965, the trend has been to reduce the federal government's role and to make the calculation of unconditional equalization transfer payments more equitable. The following describes some characteristic developments since 1957.

The 1957-1962 arrangements continued the unconditional equalization payment to allow provinces to match the per capita yield in personal income tax, corporation taxes, and succession duties to the average per capita yield in the two wealthiest provinces. The agreement also provided for a stabilization grant in order to preclude large fluctuations in revenues from year to year. These arrangements were modified during the term. For example, unconditional special Atlantic Provinces Adjustment Grants were established in 1958; and additional aid was given to Newfoundland in 1959, in addition to the normal equalization payment.

Under the arrangements of 1962-1967, the tax rental system was abandoned. The federal government agreed to partial withdrawal from the three tax fields. The formula for calculating the equalization payment was also modified, in view of Alberta's increasing wealth through the resource tax field. In 1965, the federal Established Programmes (Interim Arrangements) Act allowed provinces to opt or contract out of particular shared-cost programmes without financial penalty, through abated tax points and cash transfers to make up any difference between the yield of the abated tax points and the amount of the conditional grant the province would have received. Only Quebec accepted this provision. In 1966, the federal government altered the funding of post-secondary education from conditional grants to tax abatements and cash transfers (that is, equalized tax points).

The agreement for 1967-1972 included a more complex formula for calculating the equalization payments. Instead of using the per capita yield of the three tax fields, the payment was calculated on the national average per capita provincial revenue in 16 fields. When a province's per capita yield in a given field was lower than the national average, the province was given a positive entitlement. When the opposite held, the province received a negative entitlement. If the total in the 16 fields indicated a positive figure, the province received that figure as a per capita equalization payment.

For the 1972-1977 period, there were further modifications to the financing of post-secondary education and medical care, and the tax fields used to calculate equalization payments were increased. In 1973, the federal government imposed a limit on support for post-secondary education; in 1976, a similar limit was placed on federal support for medicare.

The Federal-Provincial Fiscal Arrangements and Established Programmes Financing Act of 1977 represents a reversal of federal participation in shared-cost, conditional grant programmes. Until the 1970's, the federal government had subsidized one-half of the cost of certain provincial programmes which met federal standards. The most important and costly of these "fifty-cent dollar" programmes were medical and hospital insurance, the Canada Assistance Plan, and post-secondary education. Such conditional grant programmes allowed the federal government to establish minimum national standards in social services within provincial jurisdiction. The provincial governments, however, were increasingly opposed to federal "entanglement" in provincial matters, in effect establishing provincial policy and spending priorities; for its part, the federal government wanted to extricate itself from costly spending programmes over which it had no financial control. As noted above, Quebec had contracted out of some of these programmes under provisions of a 1965 act; and the federal government had later put ceilings on federal contributions to provincial medicare programmes and changed the nature of funding post-secondary education to abated tax points and cash transfer payments.

In the 1977 Act, the federal government abandoned the shared-cost approach to hospital and medical insurance, as well as post-secondary education. The federal government now uses tax abatement and cash transfers, the latter to make up any difference between the yields of the abated taxes or tax points and the amount that would have been received in federal conditional grants in these programmes (thus, equalized tax points). Specifically, the federal government provided an abatement of 13.5 personal income tax points and one corporation income tax point and cash payments in place of the matching "fifty-cent dollars."

The provinces now have control of their own spending priorities. They can individually spend their revenue from abated equalized tax points as they wish. The provinces alone are now responsible for deciding how to meet rising costs – by increasing revenue from provincial taxes, by moving funds from one programme to another, and by cutting back services.

In 1978, the federal government proposed (but later withdrew the proposal) that an unconditional block grant replace the conditional grants in social welfare. By 1979, there was public criticism of the federal-provincial arrangements, as several provinces were cutting back services in hospital and medical care and in post-secondary education. The decision of some provinces not to pay for rising doctors' fees, for example, was, according to the critics, threatening to make medicare less than universal.

The 1977 Act also redefined the formula for entitlement to equalization transfers because of the increasing wealth of some provincial governments due to oil prices. Ontario, a province with one of the highest per capita provincial incomes, was on the verge of qualifying for equalization transfers. The 1977 Act also included a provision that revenue from provincial crown corporations would be included as provincial revenue for the purposes of establishing entitlement. This provision would prevent a province's entitlement from rising as a result of nationalizing a profit-making business that no longer paid corporation tax. It was established specifically following the announcement in 1975 of the Saskatchewan Government's intention to nationalize the potash industry.

In an analysis of the 1977 agreement, Thomas J. Courchene, an economist, proposed a two-tier system of federal-provincial arrangements. The first tier would include all non-resource revenues, which the federal government would equalize among the provinces; the second tier would be a pool of resource revenue, which the provinces would transfer on the basis of need. Thus a province might be entitled to an equalization payment on one tier, but not on the other. See Courchene's *Refinancing the Canadian Federation: A Survey of the 1977 Fiscal Arrangements Act* (Montreal: C.D. Howe Research Institute, 1979). See also Marsha A. Chandler and William M. Chandler, *Public Policy and Provincial Politics* (Toronto: McGraw-Hill Ryerson Ltd., 1979), and Garth Stevenson, *Unfulfilled Union: Canadian Federalism and National Unity* (Toronto: Macmillan Co. of Canada Ltd., 1979).

Federalism.   A political system in which legislative power is distributed between a national (central), or federal, legislature and a level of state or provincial legislatures. In a theoretically pure, or classical, federal system, there is no superior-inferior relationship implied in the divided authority. The national legislature retains jurisdiction in matters crucial to the integrity of the nation, while the provincial legislatures have autonomy in matters of local concern. In practice, however, federal constitutions are usually biased in one direction; and the push-pull of political competition leads to inevitable conflict between the two levels of authority and the domination of one by the other in different areas of political activity. An indication of constitutional bias is the location of residual power: that is, which level of authority is given the powers not otherwise enumerated in the case of either level of government. The power of taxation is also an indication of real political power. In case of disputes, governments may resolve them either through negotiation or through judicial interpretation of the constitution.

In Canada, domination by the central, or federal, government characterized the early years of the federal system. In a short time, however, the provinces acquired a consciousness that led to the competitiveness that has been characteristic of federal-provincial relations. Since 1940, the underlying cause of tension in Canadian federalism has been the high level of jurisdictional responsibility on the part of the provinces in an era of positive government and the welfare state, but the considerably greater access of the federal government to tax revenue and a self-assumed responsibility to ensure national minimum standards in public services through its spending power. Attendant also with the enhanced role of the federal government is the tendency of contemporary policy questions to cut across the jurisdictional divide which was established in the nineteenth century. For approximately 20 years after World War Two, the federal government was pre-eminent in setting policy priorities and establishing conditions for shared-cost programmes and unconditional equalization payments. After 1960, the provinces – some more than others – began to assert themselves once again. Quebec's political elite, in particular, reflected a new aggressive nationalism in the province and made demands which were commensurate with its self-proclaimed role as defender of French civilization in America. This development led to the election in 1976 of a Government whose objective was to establish sovereignty for Quebec. Assertiveness by some other provinces, notably Alberta, was based on wealth accruing from natural resource developments and conflicts which arose as these resource commodities involved interprovincial and international marketing and pricing policies. See *National oil policy; Natural resources; Quiet Revolution; Sovereignty-association; Spending power.*

Until recently, the adjudication of federal-provincial differences was usually definitive. Since 1960, however, the Canadian federal system has experienced a trend toward behaviour that has been characterized as executive, or administrative, federalism. Conflict is not necessarily minimized, but judicial decisions can be part of the bargaining process among the eleven governments. Executive federalism has led to such a proliferation of intergovernmental organizations that some observers have become alarmed at the growth and power of politically non-responsible agencies whose decisions no provincial legislature or federal Parliament can effectively challenge, let alone reject.

In 1977, Alan C. Cairns spoke of the "ongoing capacity of the federal

system to manufacture the conditions necessary for its continuing survival," and of Canadian federalism as a function of the governments that
"work" the constitution. "The post-Confederation history of Canadian
federalism," he said, "is little more than the record of the efforts of governing elites to pyramid their resources and of the uses to which they
have put them. Possessed of tenacious instincts for their own preservation and growth, the governments of Canadian federalism have en-
dowed the cleavages between provinces, and between provinces and
nations which attended their birth, with an ever more comprehensive
political meaning" ("The Governments and Societies of Canadian Federalism," *Canadian Journal of Political Science* 10 [1977], 698, 699,
700).

For an analysis of the contemporary federal system, see also Edwin
R. Black, *Divided Loyalties: Canadian Concepts of Federalism*
(Montreal: McGill-Queen's University Press, 1975), Peter Meekison
(ed.), *Canadian Federalism: Myth or Reality* (3rd ed.; Toronto: Methuen Publications, 1977), Donald V. Smiley, *Canada in Question:
Federalism in the Seventies* (2nd ed.; Toronto: McGraw-Hill Ryerson
Ltd., 1976), and Garth Stevenson, *Unfulfilled Union: Canadian Federalism and National Unity* (Toronto: Macmillan Co. of Canada Ltd.,
1979).

Financial Administration Act.   A major federal statute, passed in
1951 and amended in 1967; it contains regulations pertaining to the expenditure, and accounting for the expenditure, of money, by the government of Canada. The Act defines and classifies departmental and
non-departmental organizations, such as crown corporations, and
gives authority for planning, programming, and administrative policy
operations in the government to the central body of administrative and
financial management, the Treasury Board Secretariat, which includes
the office of comptroller-general.

First Ministers' Conference.   See *Conference of First Ministers.*

First-past-the-post system.   A common term used to describe a particular electoral system, the single-member constituency system with
plurality win. This electoral system is used in all provincial and federal elections in Canada. Under this system, the winner is the candidate with more votes than any other candidate (plurality), but not necessarily more votes than all other candidates combined (majority). See
Electoral system.

Fiscal policy.   Government plans in the area of spending and taxation, which are outlined in an annual budget for the fiscal year. Fiscal policy includes several components such as: desired level of economic activity and concern over price levels, interest rates, and international currency exchange rates; desired relative productive activity of the public and private sectors of the economy; and the desired distribution of wealth in society. When government spending exceeds revenue, the fiscal policy is described as deficit financing and is designed to promote aggregate demand in a "sluggish" economy. When the Government wishes to curb demand, or "cool off" the economy, the appropriate fiscal policy involves increased government revenue and decreased government spending. See *Bank of Canada; Budgetary process; Federal-provincial tax-sharing agreements.*

Foreign Investment Review Agency (Act) (FIRA).   A federal agency established in 1973 to "advise" the Government on applications by non-Canadians to acquire control of Canadian businesses or to establish new businesses in Canada. FIRA bases its decisions on the likelihood of "significant benefit" to Canadians from foreign take-overs or initiatives. FIRA may consult other federal agencies and provincial governments on the applications, prepares ministerial rulings, and monitors the enforcement of the Act. The principal officers of the Agency are the commissioner and deputy commissioner.

The Agency resulted from concerns about foreign domination of the Canadian economy (see *Economic nationalism; Canada Development Corporation*). However, economic nationalists criticize FIRA because it does not have jurisdiction over the activities of non-Canadian businesses already in Canada, which dominate many fields of the economy. Nor does the Act contain provisions for "buying back" foreign-owned businesses. Indeed, FIRA has sought to allay the apprehension of potential foreign investors to the extent that it appears to some observers to be soliciting equity investment. In 1980, the Liberal Government promised to strengthen FIRA by introducing performance reviews of foreign firms in Canada.

Fragment parties.   Splinter political parties, whose leaders have usually abandoned a hitherto successful career in a governing party because of major policy differences with their leader. The fragment party receives notoriety because of the founder's prominence and the popularity of the grievance. However, lacking any real grassroots involvement and cut off from the traditional sources of financial support, fragment parties and their leaders' political careers are usually short-lived.

Henri Bourassa's Nationalist party in the early decades of the twentieth century, H.H. Stevens' Reconstruction party and W.D. Herridge's New Democracy in the 1930's are examples of fragment parties. Paul Hellyer's Action Canada in the 1960's was a fragment party which did not last to contest an election.

Franchise.   The right to vote in elections. From 1867 to 1884, the franchise in federal elections in Canada was based on provincial laws and included a property qualification. The distinct federal franchise, which was created in 1885, continued the property qualification and allowed for multiple voting for electors who held property in more than one constituency. At this time, only men qualified for the franchise. There was a return to the several provincial franchises for federal elections from 1898 to 1917, a combined franchise from 1917 to 1920, and finally a separate federal franchise from 1920 to the present.

Until it became universally held, the franchise was a topic of considerable political controversy. The most flagrant manipulation of the federal franchise occurred in 1917, during World War One. Then, the Union Government disfranchised Canadians of central European origin, extended the franchise to close female relatives of soldiers, and created a floating military vote (see *Wartime Elections Act* and *Military Voters' Act*). Since then, however, the history of the federal franchise is an account of its slow and controversial extension. Following the war, females were enfranchised on the same basis as men, and the franchise was extended periodically to lower age levels from the high twenties in the 1920's to the 'teens in the 1970's. Otherwise, exceptions in the federal franchise continued to exist for many years – for Hutterites, conscientious objectors, Indians and Innuit, and for Asians who were disqualified under provincial legislation (notably in British Columbia).

These discriminatory features were eliminated one by one after World War Two. In 1960, Indians were the last group to receive the federal franchise.

For a history of the franchise, see T.H. Qualter, *The Election Process in Canada* (Toronto: McGraw-Hill Co. of Canada Ltd., 1970).

(La) Francophonie.   A collective term used to designate countries which are wholly or partly French-speaking. The term also refers to a movement with economic, political, and cultural implications to provide a structured relationship among such countries. "La Francophonie" is also referred to as the Community of French-speaking nations. See *Community*.

Free vote. A division in a legislature when members, normally bound by party discipline, are free to vote as they wish. In a disciplined party system such as Canada's, divisions in the legislatures usually take place along party lines, with each party leadership using inducements or sanctions available to them to maintain discipline among the party members. Occasionally, however, a question will arise for which the leadership of even the most tightly disciplined party – the Government party – may wish to avoid explicit responsibility. In such a case, the Government will permit a free vote, suggesting that this move dignifies the legislature by making its debate and subsequent division a parliamentary, rather than a Government, question. If the question passes, the Government may take what amount of credit it can for having allowed the legislature to consider the question; if the question fails, the Government need not resign but may take credit for having allowed the legislature to express its will free of party discipline.

Freedom-of-Information Act. Legislation under which the government is obliged to make information public. In 1980, Canada's first freedom-of-information law came into effect in New Brunswick. In 1979, the short-lived federal Conservative Government introduced such legislation and several provincial governments were contemplating similar measures. The federal bill died on the Order Paper in 1979; but in 1980, the Liberal Government promised to introduce legislation similar in some ways to the Conservative measure which would have required the government to release requested non-exempted information, normally within 30 days of the request. If the information was refused, the government would have had to indicate the statutory basis of exemption.

The Conservative legislation included an appeals procedure with ultimate recourse to the courts. A complainant could have appealed to the Parliament-appointed commissioner of information on a refusal, the levying of costs, or the length of time taken to process a request. The commissioner could have refused unnecessary, impractical, trivial, frivolous, or vexatious investigations. In supporting a complainant, the commissioner would have reported his or her findings to the relevant government authority and might have recommended action. The commissioner would also have reported the findings to the complainant, but not the action recommended unless the government had failed to carry it out. If necessary, a complainant could have further appealed to the Federal Court, where the burden of proof not to release the information would have been on the government. In this respect, the proposed federal legislation was weaker than the United States legislation, which permits immediate access to the courts; but it was stronger than a proposal in the previous Liberal Government's Green Paper in 1977, which based the appeal procedure in the cabinet with no judicial review. In 1980, the Liberals promised an element of judicial review.

In addition to the appeal procedure, the categories of exemption are crucial to the effectiveness of such legislation. The federal legislation proposed in 1979 contained such categories as law enforcement and investigation, security of penal institutions, defence and international relations, federal-provincial relations, cabinet records, personal information, commercial and financial information, solicitor-client confidences, government testing and auditing procedures, and privacy provisions in other acts related to Statistics Canada and National Revenue. In most of these areas, the legislation gave ministers scope for broad definition of the categories of exemption and initial reaction to the legislation, though generally positive, focussed on the need to narrow the scope of ministerial and administrative discretion. To be effective, the legislation would necessitate amendments to the Official Secrets Act, which broadly prohibits people from distributing and possessing information, and the Federal Court Act which allows ministers to issue certificates denying access to information. See *Official Secrets Act; Secrecy.*

Fulton-Favreau Formula (1964).   A proposal in 1964 to effect constitutional changes, including a domestic amending procedure, named after the two successive federal ministers of justice who chaired federal-provincial discussions leading to the proposal (E. Davie Fulton and Guy Favreau). Two years later, the Quebec Government decided to "delay" the proposal, presumably because of the proposed principle of unanimous provincial consent. Thus, one province would have been able to veto amendments which Quebec wanted.

Under established statutory law and convention, the British North America Act is amended by the British Parliament responding to a petition from the Canadian Parliament. In a federally initiated amendment in 1949, the federal government made a distinction between matters subject to amendment by the Canadian Parliament alone and matters subject to amendment by the British Parliament involving, by convention, unanimous consent of the provinces.

The Fulton-Favreau amending procedure would have first clearly established that no future British statute would apply to Canada. Second, certain important constitutional components would have been amended only with the consent of Parliament and all provincial legislatures (for example, legislative powers allocated to the provinces, the use of English and French, denominational education rights, and the determination of representation by province in the House of Commons). Third, certain aspects of the constitution relating to the federal government would have been amended by Parliament only with the concurrence of at least two-thirds of the provincial legislatures which together represented at least one-half of the country's population (for example, the role of the monarchy and the governor general, Senate representation by provinces, and the five-year limit on the duration of a Parliament). Otherwise, Parliament would continue to have the right to amend the constitution with respect to the government of Canada. Finally, legislative power could have been delegated between the two levels of government by mutual consent of Parliament and at least four provincial legislatures. All provinces would have had to be consulted on such delegation, and Parliament would assert that the delegation was of concern to fewer than four provincial legislatures.

Federal-provincial conferences were held between 1968 and 1971 to discuss a new constitution and an amending formula. These discussions resulted in the so-called Victoria Charter of 1971, which was also rejected by the Government of Quebec. See *British North America Act; Victoria Charter.*

Fund for Rural Economic Development (FRED). A federal programme established in 1966 by which the minister of regional economic expansion (earlier the minister of agriculture) can enter into agreements with provincial governments to assist rural economic development. FRED represents one of several programmes established in the 1960's in the context of a federal concern for regional development, first established in the Agricultural Rehabilitation and Rural Development Act (ARDA) of 1961. This concern was expressed initially in policies to improve agricultural efficiency in depressed areas, but it later involved education for employment in non-primary industry. See *Agricultural Rehabilitation and Rural Development Act; Department of Regional Economic Expansion; Regional disparity.*

G

General Development Agreements (GDA). Separate agreements between the federal and provincial governments providing a framework for co-ordinated action on regional development in programmes in the Department of Regional Economic Expansion. Since 1974, the federal government has signed ten-year GDA's with all provinces except Prince Edward Island, which has a separate Comprehensive Development Plan. Subsidiary agreements, identifying specific joint actions in each provincial case, have also been signed. See *Department of Regional Economic Expansion.*

Geographic cleavage.   A social division delineating areal or spatial communities of interest. The cleavage is usually expressed in terms of the core, or metropolis, on one side and the periphery, or hinterland, on the other. The core/metropolis is that part of the political unit which is densely populated; it is where most of the manufacturing, industrial, research, and financial activity is carried out; and it contains major centres of advanced learning, the arts, the dominant communication media, and political decision-making. The remainder of the political unit is the periphery/hinterland.

In Canada, the national core has historically been the lower St. Lawrence Valley and the lower Great Lakes area, including Montreal, Toronto, and Ottawa. The two distinct peripheries have been the Maritimes and the West. Within the peripheries, one can distinguish an historic geographic cleavage between Halifax-Dartmouth and the remainder of the Maritimes, and between Winnipeg and the remainder of the West. In recent years, Winnipeg's dominance has been challenged by Edmonton and Calgary. One may speak of the "prairie West" to distinguish the prairie region from British Columbia, with its periphery dominated by the Vancouver-Victoria core. Neither of these latter developments within the western periphery has replaced the basic division between the central Canadian core of Montreal-Ottawa-Toronto and the rest of the country.

Canada's core and peripheries exhibit dependence on comparable spatial communities in the United States. Canada is an historically dependent country, and the models of behaviour for people in the core have historically been those of people in the British core and, currently, in the American core of New York-Washington. Likewise, behaviour in the Canadian West has been historically influenced by the agrarian populism of the northwestern states.

It is difficult to isolate issues that are purely spatial in meaning. Once apparent, however, the federal system promotes and perpetuates such issues through provincial representatives and institutions. Western disaffection toward the "East," or central Canada, is often ex-

pressed in terms which have bicultural or class meaning. This is so because the bulk of Canada's francophones and a high concentration of
wealth and economic decision-making are found in central Canada. Issues which highlight regional interests in Canada include transportation, agriculture, trade and resource, and regional development policies.

Historically, radical political behaviour of both the left and the right
was a manifestation of western disaffection with central Canada. The
prairie provinces were creations of the federal Parliament, and the
population was enticed there in the early decades of the twentieth century by the Canadian government's promise of a better life. Moreover,
the population was a northern European population which had already
experienced radical behaviour in trade unions, rural co-operatives, and
socialist and populist political parties. Thus, when expectations were
not met, the western population's rejection of the party system and the
two "eastern" parties was not surprising. The Maritimes, by contrast,
were a more settled region, where traditional elites who were better integrated in central Canadian political and economic institutions were
firmly established. It is instructive that the most solid regional support
at both federal and provincial levels for the parties of Confederation,
the Liberal and Conservative parties, is in Atlantic Canada.

The West, then, has been the origin and site for much radical political behaviour in Canada. Despite the federal New Democratic party's
attempts to make inroads in Ontario, the West remains an important
base of support for the NDP. The West was also the bastion of support
for the populist Social Credit party prior to the 1970's, and it contains
now the only jurisdiction which has a competitive Social Credit party.
Indeed, in provincial politics in British Columbia, the Social Credit
and New Democratic parties are the competitive parties, and the ideological polarization of politics there is a periphery counterpoint to the
traditional party loyalties in the eastern periphery. The general decline
of the Social Credit party and the rise of the provincial Conservative
parties in the prairie West is probably connected to the same populist
constituency. The popularity of the federal Conservatives in the West
in the 1970's was a popularity based in large part on the leadership of
the "eastern" party by westerner John Diefenbaker, from 1957 to 1967,
and on contemporary representatives such as Alberta's Premier Peter
Lougheed. While Diefenbaker's immediate predecessors as federal
Conservative leaders were central-Canadian personalities, his two immediate successors were from the periphery – Robert Stanfield from
Nova Scotia and Joe Clark from Alberta – though neither would be

styled a populist. No federal Liberal leader has come from the periphery though a successful leader such as William Lyon Mackenzie King had forceful periphery personalities in his cabinets. In the late 1970's, the Liberals were the "third" party in the provincial politics of Manitoba and Saskatchewan and virtually non-existent in the provincial politics of Alberta and British Columbia.

On the core-periphery cleavage, see Roger E. Kasperson and Julian V. Minhgi (eds.), The Structure of Political Geography (Chicago: Aldine, 1969), especially 69-186. On the geographic cleavage in Canada, see David J. Elkins and Richard Simeon, Small Worlds: Parties and Provinces in Canadian Political Life (Toronto: Methuen Publications, 1980); Mildred A. Schwartz, Politics and Territory: The Sociology of Regional Persistence in Canada (Montreal: McGill-Queen's University Press, 1974); and Simon McInnes, "Federal Systems and Centre-Periphery Analysis," a paper presented at the annual meeting of the Canadian Political Science Association, 1974. On voting behaviour and the geographic cleavage, see Schwartz, "Canadian Voting Behavior," in Richard Rose (ed.), Electoral Behavior: A Comparative Handbook (New York: Free Press, 1974). See also Douglas McCready and Conrad Winn, "Geographic Cleavage: Core vs. Periphery," in C. Winn and J. McMenemy, Political Parties in Canada (Toronto: McGraw-Hill Ryerson Ltd., 1976), 71-88. For an analysis of contemporary developments in the prairie West, see John Richards and Larry Pratt, Prairie Capitalism: Power and Influence in the New West (Toronto: McClelland and Stewart Ltd., 1979).

Gerrymander. A manipulation of constituency boundaries to minimize the effect of the opposition vote. A gerrymander is achieved by creating constituencies where the opposition vote is likely to be concentrated in a few constituencies and the vote for the party responsible for the gerrymander to be at least narrowly greater than the opposition vote in many constituencies. The word "gerrymander" comes from such a manipulation in Massachusetts in 1812 by the party of Governor Elbridge Gerry, which resulted in constituencies whose configurations resembled those of a salamander. Gerrymandering can take place effectively only when one party has control over the drawing of constituency boundaries. Thus, the possibilities for gerrymandering have diminished considerably in Canada since the 1960's, as federal and provincial legislatures have delegated the responsibility for redesigning constituency boundaries to independent boundary commissions. See Electoral Boundaries Readjustment Act.

Government bills.   Public bills, or legislation, introduced by a minister or a parliamentary secretary, which the Government therefore sponsors and to whose passage the Government is committed. Consideration of such bills dominates legislative sessions. The Government may be embarrassed if it is forced by the Opposition's criticism and public opinion to withdraw a bill. In Canada, Government bills are questions of confidence on which, if defeated, the Government is obliged by convention to seek dissolution of Parliament for an election or offer to resign. See *Legislation.*

Governor General.   The officer who exercises the functions of the Crown in Canada under Letters Patent made effective by the sovereign. The appointment of the governor general is formally a function of the sovereign, but informally the action of the federal cabinet. The appointment is usually for five years although this term may be modified by the "advice" of the cabinet. The British North America Act describes a role for the governor general, but Letters Patent from the sovereign also delineate this role. Since 1947, the governor general may exercise the crown perogative in Canada at his or her discretion with the advice of the sovereign's Canadian Privy Council, effectively the federal cabinet. Important powers granted by the Letters Patent of 1947 include appointment of federal ministers of the Crown, notably the prime minister, provincial lieutenant-governors, judges, and commissioners; they also include the power to dismiss federal ministers of the Crown and the power to summon, prorogue, and dissolve Parliament. The BNA Act grants the governor general exclusive power to recommend legislation which involves expenditures from the public purse or revenue from taxation. Under the BNA Act, the governor general may also appoint senators, refuse royal assent to federal legislation, and disallow provincial legislation.

In all the matters listed above and others, the governor general usually acts on the advice of the Canadian Privy Council, the effective part of which is the federal cabinet, or Government-of-the-day. Nonetheless, there remains a residue of discretionary authority, or crown prerogatives, pertaining to the dissolution of Parliament and the appointment and dismissal of prime ministers. In this respect, the governor general's primary constitutional duty is to ensure that there is a Government in office which has the confidence of the House of Commons. In cases of independent action, however, the governor general would have to be responding to a violation of the constitution and acting beyond a reasonable doubt as to his or her personal judgment. See *Crown; Crown prerogatives; Governor-in-council.*

Since 1947, the office of governor general has been continually "nationalized." In 1952, Vincent Massey was the first Canadian appointed governor general. Since then, practice suggests not only that Canadians hold that office but that there be appointed alternately an anglophone and a francophone (Georges Vanier, Roland Michener, Jules Leger, Edward Schreyer). Moreover, since the 1970's the federal Government has "advised" the governor general to engage in activity which suggests more the role of head of state than a representative of a non-resident head of state. Domestically, the presence of the governor general in the Arctic, for example, has been understood as an exercise of national sovereignty over the archipelago; internationally, the governor general has made official visits to the Caribbean area and Europe.

For examinations of the office and role of governor general, see R. MacGregor Dawson, *The Government of Canada* (5th ed., rev. by Norman Ward; Toronto: University of Toronto Press, 1970), 143-66; and J.R. Mallory, *The Structure of Canadian Government* (Toronto: Macmillan Co. of Canada Ltd., 1971), 41-62.

Governor General's warrants. Authorization issued through an order-in-council for unforseen emergency expenditure of public money not approved by Parliament. According to provisions of the federal Financial Administration Act, the governor-in-council issues warrants when the Treasury Board reports, on the advice of the relevant minister, that such authorization is necessary. Warrants can be issued only when Parliament is not in session or has adjourned and will not meet for at least two weeks. The Government must report the issuance of warrants in the *Canada Gazette* within 30 days. Within 15 days of Parliament's return or opening, the Government must also inform Parliament of the amount of the warrant issued and include the expenditures as part of the next estimates.

Only the Government has the authority to put before Parliament bills involving public expenditure; but Parliament must sanction such expenditures. Normally, this precedes the actual disbursement of the funds. Thus, the use of governor general's warrants to finance government operations can suggest poor government management. See *Budgetary process.*

Governor-in-council. A formal, constitutional body through which the federal cabinet exercises executive power. Under the British North America Act and Letters Patent (1947), the governor general, advised by the Canadian Privy Council, is the executive power. The cabinet, or the Government-of-the-day which the governor general appoints, has no statutory status. Nonetheless, the cabinet is the effective part of the council, whose advice the governor general almost always accepts. Thus, the governor-in-council is the governor general acting on the advice of cabinet; and the executive instrument of the governor-in-council is the order-in-council, or minute of the council. The governor general does not attend cabinet meetings but signs the orders or minutes which are sent from cabinet.

In the provinces, a similar relationship exists between the lieutenant-governors and their executive councils – effectively the provincial cabinets, or Governments-of-the-day. The federal nature of the lieutenant-governors' office, however, modifies this relationship. That is, the federal cabinet "recommends" appointments of governors general, and the governor-in-council also appoints the provincial lieutenant-governors. The lieutenant-governors may also receive instructions effectively from the federal cabinet with respect to reservation. See *Reservation*.

Green Book (1946). A federal document which, along with a white paper on employment and income, declared the federal Government's commitment to the welfare state and was published a few months prior to the Dominion-Provincial Conference on Reconstruction. The proposals contained in the Green Book and white paper provided a federal initiative for national economic development and reconstruction following World War Two.

In the documents, the federal government accepted Keynesian objectives of maintaining a high and stable level of income and employment. However, to accomplish this through revenue and expenditure policies, the federal government sought exclusive access to personal and corporate income tax fields and to succession duties. With provincial agreement and through shared-cost programmes, the federal Government proposed to establish a health insurance programme and a universal unemployment insurance plan, and to assume all administrative and financial responsibilities for universal old age pensions for people over 70 years of age.

Particularly because of objections from Ontario and Quebec, the Dominion-Provincial Conference adjourned without agreement. Ultimately, however, the welfare state was established incrementally. See *Federal-provincial tax-sharing agreements; Wartime Tax Rental Agreement*.

Green paper. A Government document which contains legislative proposals for discussion. Governments are not committed to the proposals in green papers and can use the publication to test public opinion. When a green paper is received by the legislature, it is usually sent to a committee of the legislature which will hold hearings and report to the legislature on the proposals.

In 1977, for example, the federal Government published a green paper on procedures for dealing with the release of government documents or information (see *Freedom-of-Information Act*). In this case, the paper included a discussion of several alternatives and suggested the Government's preference for one of them. The paper was referred to the joint Commons-Senate committee on regulations and other statutory instruments, which held hearings and reported its own view on the matter to Parliament.

Grit (Clear Grit). A popular term to refer to Liberals and the Liberal party in Canada. The phrase "Clear Grit" was popularized by editor and political reformer George Brown in Canada West in 1849-1850. It indicates the quality of character which Brown thought necessary for members of his wing of the Reform party in the Province of Canada. The term was applied in the post-Confederation period to the Liberal party, which represented the same rural Protestant interests in Ontario and included Brown himself as a prominent member. See *Liberal party*.

Gross national expenditure (GNE); Gross national product (GNP). Two of several statistical statements which the federal government publishes concerning economic activity; they are based on the Canadian System of National Accounts. This system is closely related to an international standard of national accounts. By totalling all costs incurred in production, the GNP measures the market value of all final goods and services produced in a specific period by Canadian factors of production. The GNE measures the same production aggregate by tracing the disposition of production through final sales to resident and non-resident (exports) individuals and to public and private institutions on capital account. Statistics Canada compiles the data and publishes the statements under provisions of the Federal Statistics Act (1971).

H

Hansard. The popular designation for the daily verbatim record of debates in the House of Commons. Edited, translated, printed in English and in French, it is distributed to MPs the following day and made available to the public. A revised and bound edition is later published, with a separate index. Hansard is named after Luke Hansard, who began printing the debates of the British House in the eighteenth century. The official title in Canada is *Debates of the House of Commons.* The daily record, with minor editorial amendments to correct grammar and achieve clarity, is compiled from shorthand notes of House of Commons reporters, who sit on the floor of the House during the debate.

The term Hansard is sometimes used with reference to the record of debate in the Senate and in the provincial legislatures. As late as 1972, the legislature of British Columbia was the only provincial legislature which did not have an official record of daily debate.

Have (have-not) provinces. A popular term which designates provinces which do or do not receive unconditional equalization payments or other adjustment grants from the federal government under federal-provincial tax agreements. "Have-not" provinces receive the payments. Various formulae have been in effect since the 1950's to calculate payments to make equitable the tax revenue of each province. See *Equalization grants; Federal-provincial tax-sharing agreements.*

Head of state. The person who holds the political office which represents the authority and power of the state – in Canada, the monarch, in whose name the governor general acts. Statute, custom and usage, and convention limit the powers of the Canadian head of state. See *Crown; Crown prerogatives; Governor General.*

High Commissioner (Commission). The representatives of Canada in Commonwealth countries and of Commonwealth countries in Canada. The terms are used instead of "ambassador" and "embassy" to distinguish member-states of the Commonwealth from other countries. The terms are of nineteenth-century origin, when Canadian agents had no international status except as associates of British diplomats. Canada's representative in London was designated a high commissioner rather than an ambassador and had consular rather than diplomatic rank. This model was followed in the cases of Australia, New Zealand, and South Africa when they gained self-governing status in their internal affairs.

In time, Canada and the other dominions acquired status in external relations in their own right. Since the transformation of the British Empire to the large Commonwealth of Nations following World War Two, the terms "high commissioner" and "high commission" have continued to distinguish the relationship of the former colonies with Britain and, indirectly, to each other.

Horizontal agencies. An informal term which denotes administrative bodies in government which are not integrated hierarchically in a single structure. Such agencies may be a department, a portfolio, or a staff agency to assist a minister. At the federal level, many responsibilities of the minister of transport lie outside the departmental structure – in such autonomous agencies as Air Canada, Canadian National Railways, and the Canadian Transport Commission. The president of the Treasury Board has authority over cabinet colleagues and across the government in consolidating and co-ordinating procedures and policy; and some ministries of state – such as those for Economic Development and for Trade since 1979–1980 – are also designed to achieve policy co-ordination across other cabinet portfolios.

House leaders. MPs designated from each party as managers of party conduct in the House of Commons. Recognizing that the Government and Opposition parties have different objectives in parliamentary debate and tactics, each party nonetheless designates a House leader to confer with his or her counterparts from other parties in order to expedite business. The Government's House leader, a member of the cabinet holding the honorific position of president of the Privy Council, is responsible for obtaining agreement among the parties on the Commons' timetable. Each chosen by their party leader, the House leaders have the authority to negotiate a timetable and list of speakers, and have considerable influence to hold their respective parties to the negotiated agreement.

House of Assembly. The official name for the elected legislatures of Ontario, Nova Scotia, and Newfoundland. The legislature in Quebec is styled the "national assembly" and those of the other provinces the "legislative assembly."

House of Commons.   The elected lower house of the Parliament of Canada, some of whose members are the Government, others the Opposition parties' leaders (shadow, or alternate, government); the remainder are usually backbench supporters of one of the parties. Few MPs are formally Independent.

The 282 members of the House (known as members of Parliament, or MPs) are elected in single-member constituency contests among candidates, most of whom are representing established political parties. The contests take place on the same day, in a general election; but some MPs are elected in by-elections to fill vacancies. The successful candidates sit with other MPs elected from their party. The House is divided by an aisle; the Government MPs sit on one side, and the Opposition MPs sit on the other side, the two factions facing each other. MPs' behaviour is almost invariably dictated by the Government or Opposition status of their party.

The principle of responsible government requires that Government ministers have seats in the House (or, though less politically desirable, in the appointed Senate) and retain the confidence of the House. The governor general must appoint as prime minister someone who is likely to have the confidence of the House. Subsequently, the House responds to the guidance of the Government – Government MPs willingly, and Opposition MPs unwillingly. A Parliament may last five years. Usually, however, the governor general dissolves it on the advice of the prime minister and issues writs for another election for a new House sometime within the five-year term.

The House of Commons is the site for two contradictory and conflicting roles. The Government, on the one hand, must have parliamentary endorsement of its legislative proposals and expenditures; the Opposition's role is to criticize those proposals and try to bring about the Government's defeat in the next election, if not in the House itself (see *Legislation*).

In majority Government situations, the Opposition will not likely bring down the Government, but it may influence the Government's policy through various tactics. Normally, the Government controls the legislative timetable. However, the oral question period, so-called "Opposition days," as well as motions to adjourn the House to debate urgent matters, are opportunities available to the Opposition to throw the Government off balance. Subject to closure, the Opposition can also prolong debate on a Government measure (see *Closure*). In these various manoeuvres, the role of the mass media in transmitting the parliamentary debate to the public and generating public opinion is crucial.

Since 1977, debates of the House of Commons have been available for broadcast by radio and television.

During the question period, the principle of responsible government is manifested in the exchanges between ministers and Opposition critics. Some questions may be written down and placed on the Order Paper to receive a printed reply later. The oral question period, however, permits direct questioning of ministers. Any private member may ask a question of a minister; but usually the leading Opposition speakers and selected backbenchers on the Opposition side of the House dominate question period. Ministers may be asked questions about activities in currently held portfolios only; in 1979, shortly before its defeat, the federal Conservative Government proposed that cabinet ministers (but not former ministers still in the House as backbenchers) be required to answer questions about activities that occurred within the jurisdiction of earlier portfolios. Dissatisfied questioners may give notice that they intend to raise a matter on adjournment later in the day. In the so-called "late show," the minister's parliamentary secretary usually defends the Government against the Opposition attack (see *Question period*).

Up to 25 days are allotted to the Opposition in three supply periods to determine the subject of debate. Supply periods are those occasions in which the Government is seeking passage of various appropriation bills in a session (see *Budgetary process; Supply period*). The object here is to force the Government to defend measures which the Opposition feels are weak points in the Government's armour.

The Opposition may also move adjournment of the House to discuss an important matter of great urgency that has risen unexpectedly and is not likely to be considered in normal business that day. If the Speaker, a neutralized MP usually from the Government's side, determines the matter is appropriate, he or she will hold over the motion to adjourn until the evening sitting, at which time debate will take place on the subject. When satisfied that the debate has been concluded, the Speaker will declare the motion to adjourn carried and adjourn the House until the next day. Even if the Speaker does not accept the motion to adjourn, the Opposition will have raised the issue to the Government's potential embarrassment (see *Urgent debate*).

The debate on the Speech from the Throne – formally a debate on a Government motion commending the governor general for his address opening the session – and the debate on the budget brought down by the minister of finance are occasions for general debate. In those cases, the opportunity for backbenchers to participate in House debate is

greater than in the situations discussed above, which tend to be dominated on both sides by frontbenchers. There has been, however, a tendency in recent years to devote less time to the general debates.

The role of the private member (that is, an MP who is not a cabinet
minister) is severely restricted by party discipline. Within this stric-
ture, however, MPs participate in in-camera sessions of the party caucus and caucus committees; they may have an impact on party positions in House debate, may participate actively in committees of the
House, may introduce private member's legislation, and may act as a
constituency ombudsman, redressing grievances of constituents (see
*Caucus; House of Commons committees; Standing [select, special]
committees; Member of Parliament; Private member's legislation).*

The chief officer of the House of Commons is the Speaker. The
Speaker's election is the prime order of business when the House first
assembles after an election, and his or her duties are outlined in standing orders of the House. Once elected by the House, the Speaker is responsible to it, and not to the Government, although the Speaker is
usually a Government party MP. In 1979, the House accepted Conservative Prime Minister Joe Clark's nomination – a customary act of prime
ministers – of the previous Speaker, a Liberal MP, to the position. The
Speaker's main function is to preside over proceedings impartially,
and also to maintain the rights and privileges of MPs (see
Parliamentary privilege). The Speaker also manages the administration of the House and its permanent employees, who staff the House
and the committees (see *Speaker).*

Other officers of the House are: the House-elected deputy speaker (or
chairman of committees of the whole House), deputy chairman, assistant deputy chairman; and such appointed officers as the Clerk of the
House, the clerk assistants, the sergeant-at-arms, the law clerk, and
parliamentary counsel. The deputy speaker, who is usually proficient
in the official language that is not the Speaker's first language, occupies
the Speaker's chair when the Speaker is absent and otherwise chairs
the committee of the whole House. Like the Speaker, the deputy chairman and assistant deputy chairman are MPs chosen at the beginning of
a Parliament and usually for its duration. The Clerk, who holds the
rank of deputy minister, is the recording officer and is responsible for
the safekeeping of House documents. The clerk assistants act as reading clerks when documents must be read in the House, and as clerks
when the House is in committee. They are also responsible for ensuring that relevant documents are available to MPs. The sergeant-at-arms
attends the Speaker with the Mace (the symbol of the authority of the

House vested in the Speaker) and is responsible for House fittings; in addition, the sergeant-at-arms engages messengers, pages, and temporary constables and labourers when necessary. The law clerk assists MPs in drafting bills, motions, and resolutions. The counsel prepares memoranda and opinions on legal and constitutional matters and advises MPs on proposed amendments.

Finally, there is an administrative organization of the House – involving personnel, building services, and legislative services – that is responsible to the Clerk of the House; and there is a financial administration in the commissioners of internal economy, consisting of the Speaker and four ministers. Changes in the administration of the Commons are likely, following criticism by the auditor general in 1979.

On the House of Commons, see John B. Stewart, *The Canadian House of Commons: Procedure and Reform* (Montreal: McGill-Queen's University Press, 1977); and Norman Ward, *The Canadian House of Commons: Representation* (2nd ed.; Toronto: University of Toronto Press, 1963). On the legislative system generally, see Robert Jackson and Michael Atkinson, *The Canadian Legislative System* (Toronto: Macmillan Co. of Canada Ltd., 1974), and W.A.W. Neilson and J.C. MacPherson (eds.), *The Legislative Process in Canada* (Montreal: Institute for Research on Public Policy, 1978). Finally, see the special issue devoted to the House of Commons and some provincial assemblies, "Responsible Government Reconsidered / *Le parlementarisme: bilan et prospective*," *Journal of Canadian Studies* 14 (1979) Summer, *passim*.

House of Commons committees.   Meetings of all or some members of Parliament in form other than as the House of Commons. In addition to committees of the whole House, which are chaired by the deputy or assistant deputy speakers who are chosen shortly after the opening of the first session of a Parliament, there are standing and special committees of the House as well as joint committees with the Senate. House rules allow for the striking, or appointment, of 19 standing committees to consider bills and estimates from government departments and agencies and to perform other duties as instructed by the House. There is also provision for three standing joint committees. Finally, special committees and special joint committees may be appointed as required. The chairmen of standing committees are selected at the beginning of each session and (except in the case of the committee on public accounts) are usually Government members. Party representation on committees approximates the proportion of party representation in the House, and membership is determined by party leaders. During its brief life, the Conservative Government of 1979-1980 proposed in a white paper that standing committees be reduced in size to a maximum of eleven members, and that committee inquiries be authorized by motions of the House supported by at least 50 MPs, ten or more from each of two parties. The Government would have to respond to the committee reports within 21 days. However, only five such investigations could be conducted concurrently and research budgets would have to be approved by the House of Commons' commissioners of internal economy, that is, the Speaker and four ministers. A list of committee members is published in each Wednesday edition of *Hansard*. See *Committee of the whole; Standing (select, special) committees.*

I

Ideological parties.   Organized groups seeking political power whose members subscribe to an ideology – that is, a set of values which help determine attitudes towards political events and objects such as elections and public policy. The particular ideology may be congruent or incongruent with the dominant values of society, and may be expressed explicitly or implicitly. In Canada, the Social Credit and *Ralliement des créditistes* are ideological parties whose values, at their origin, were relatively implicit and congruent. Their populist leadership explains their success better than their ideology, and they came to constitute a conservative political force (see *Social Credit party; Ralliement des créditistes*). The Co-operative Commonwealth Federation was an ideological party whose values were explicit and incongruent; its successor, the New Democratic party, is based on a more implicit and congruent value system (see *Co-operative Commonwealth Federation; New Democratic party*). The relatively unimportant Communist party of Canada and its various offshoots constitute ideological parties whose values are explicit and incongruent with society (see *Communist party of Canada*). See *Movement parties; Populism; Socialism.*

For a contrary style of political party, see *Brokerage politics; Parliamentary parties.*

Immigration Appeal Board.   A court of record established by Parliament in 1967, with broad discretionary powers to permit immigration (provisions of the Immigration Act notwithstanding) and to hear appeals from individuals against deportation, detention, and refusal of admission of sponsored relatives so ordered under the Immigration Act. The decisions of the Board may be appealed to the Federal Court and to the Supreme Court of Canada.

The Board's headquarters are in Ottawa, but it also has court facilities and members in Montreal, Toronto, and Vancouver. The minister responsible is the minister of employment and immigration. The Board, however, is independent from the ministry. The ministry's Canadian immigration division, its recruitment and selection and facilitation branch, and its enforcement and control branch are responsible for the decisions which are appealed to the Board.

Imperial conferences. Forums of prime ministers and colleagues from the self-governing colonies and dominions of the British Empire, held occasionally between 1887 and 1930 in London. The conference was neither an executive nor a legislative body, though it would express opinions in resolutions. Topics of the early conferences included imperial federation, defence, and tariffs; but in later years, topics included foreign policy and national autonomy.

When World War One began in 1914, the British assumed the dominions to be at war when Britain declared war without consulting them. The dominions did join the war; but they each signed the peace treaties and joined the League of Nations following the war. The imperial conference of 1926 issued a declaration of equality between Britain and the dominions in imperial and international affairs. This declaration was a turning point from subordination in the Empire to association in a Commonwealth of nations. The declaration read in part: "They [the dominions] are autonomous Communities within the British Empire, equal in status, in no way subordinate one to another in any aspect of their domestic or external affairs, though united by a common allegiance to the Crown, and freely associated as members of the British Commonwealth of Nations. ... " The imperial conference of 1930 (the last so styled) requested that the British Parliament pass certain resolutions of the conferences of 1926 and 1930, clarifying the new association. Thus, the British Statute of Westminster (1931) became a constitutional statute, removing most statutory impediments to national autonomy of the dominions. See *Statute of Westminster.*

Independence-of-Parliament Bill. Conflict-of-interest legislation to govern the private financial affairs of legislators. The federal Liberal Government introduced such legislation in 1978, but it died on the Order Paper in 1979. Because all parties support conflict-of-interest legislation in principle, a similar bill will likely be introduced in Parliament.

Under the Liberal bill of 1978, parliamentarians would not have been allowed to be officers or directors, legal counsel, financial auditors, or consultants with corporations that received contracts, licenses, permits, or other authorizations from the government. The legislation would also have prohibited parliamentarians from having large shareholdings in such companies. However, involvement would have been permitted through assets that were in trusts that met the requirements of acceptance to be established by the governor-in-council. Parliamentarians would have been prohibited from accepting fees for activities that could be construed as lobbying. They would also have been compelled to declare any personal financial interests when speaking or voting in Parliament or communicating with the administration or other parliamentarians.

Parliamentarians would also have had to declare publicly their sources of income over $1000, trusts, unsecured debts of themselves and their spouses of more than $5000 (including names of creditors), land and buildings owned by themselves and their spouses, shares and bonds worth more than $1000, travel outside the country (especially sponsored trips), honorariums, employment, directorships, partnerships, leave of absence, grants or loans from the government, and gifts received by them or their spouses worth more than $100. Parliamentarians, however, would have been given the option of avoiding this publicity by placing their financial holdings in a blind or frozen trust. See *Conflict of interest*.

Indirect taxation.   Any tax which will likely be passed on by the actual payer to another source. The federal government has access to both direct and indirect taxation, and the provinces to direct taxation only. Section 125 of the British North America Act exempts public land or property belonging to "Canada or any Province" from taxation. See *Direct (indirect) taxation*.

Information commissioner.   An officer of Parliament proposed in freedom-of-information legislation introduced by the Conservative Government in 1979, but which died on·the Order Paper. The proposed office constituted an intermediate step between a complainant and the courts in the appeal procedure to have the government disclose information. On its refusal, the government would have had to cite the statutory basis for the exemption and remind the applicant that he or she could appeal to the information commissioner. Complaints could also be lodged if the government were taking too long or if it charged too much for the information. Under the 1979 proposal, the commissioner could also have refused to investigate unnecessary, impractical, trivial, frivolous, or vexatious complaints. On finding for a complainant, the commissioner would have informed the relevant government office and could have recommended action. The commissioner would also have informed the complainant of the results of the investigation, but not the action requested unless the government failed to comply. In the case of non-compliance, the complainant could then have appealed to the Federal Court. See *Freedom-of-Information Act.*

Inner cabinet. A select group of cabinet ministers, whose meetings are chaired by the prime minister and who may assume decision-making power on behalf of the whole cabinet. In 1979, Prime Minister Joe Clark created Canada's first publicly designated inner cabinet, a 12-member body from the approximately 30-member cabinet. Until then, Prime Minister Pierre Trudeau's smaller cabinet committee on priorities and planning, which he chaired but which reported to the full cabinet, constituted an inner circle of key ministers.

Canada's first inner cabinet did not contain all senior ministers. Also, the body's membership appeared to have been subjected to the federal pressures of Canadian politics. For example, the minister who headed the large, expensive, and politically sensitive Department of National Health and Welfare was not in the inner cabinet. That minister was from Ontario, a province which had five ministers in the inner cabinet. Meanwhile, the holder of the relatively minor portfolio, Postmaster General, was belatedly appointed to the inner cabinet; presumably this was because he was from British Columbia, a province which had no representation in the original inner cabinet. See *Cabinet; Cabinet organization.*

Interdelegation Reference (Nova Scotia, 1951). A reference in which the Supreme Court of Canada declared the direct delegation of powers between Parliament and the provincial legislatures to be incompatible with the federal constitution (*Attorney-General for Nova Scotia v. Attorney-General for Canada* [1951]). From time to time, the federal and provincial governments have encountered areas where the jurisdiction of one level was inadequate to cope with a problem – for example, the marketing of farm products across provincial boundaries. The Rowell-Sirois Royal Commission on Dominion-Provincial Relations (1940) had recommended a constitutional amendment to permit such legislative co-operation. In the Interdelegation Reference, the Court declared unconstitutional a Nova Scotia statute which delegated provincial authority to the federal government and anticipated delegation of federal power to the province. Thus, the Supreme Court upheld the "watertight compartment" approach to Sections 91 and 92 of the British North America Act; and indirect means were tried in order to effect the same outcome as direct delegation of jurisdictional competence. One year after the Interdelegation Reference, the Supreme Court validated the indirect device of parliamentary delegation of powers to a board established by a provincial legislature, rather than to the legislature itself *(PEI Potato Marketing Board v. H.B. Willis Inc.,* 1952). See *Judicial Committee of the Privy Council; Supreme Court.*

Interdepartmental committees. An important bureaucratic device to achieve co-ordination of government priorities and planning. Many government departments have responsibility for programmes which bear on particular areas of public policy. Thus, governments often create committees of high-level civil servants to advise individual ministers or a cabinet committee on new policy or improvements in established programmes. Not surprisingly, these committees are also the site for the protection of departmental jurisdictions and bureaucratic fiefdoms. Such committees may therefore become an obstacle rather than a route to problem-oriented consideration of public policy.

The federal Interdepartmental Committee on External Relations is an example of a highly structured interdepartmental committee. Established by the cabinet in 1970, the Committee is responsible for integrating Canadian government efforts in foreign policy and operations. The Committee has a secretariat from the departments involved and a stipulated membership from the deputy minister ranks of the departments of external affairs, industry, trade and commerce, employment and immigration, and public works. The committee also includes the president of the Canadian International Development Agency, the secretary of the Treasury Board, and the clerk of the Privy Council (secretary to the cabinet). The Committee's secretariat develops methods for integrating policies and programmes of departments and agencies with activities abroad. The Committee has a personnel management subcommittee to advise on staffing abroad and on common policies related to foreign career development. In 1971, another subcommittee was established to advise the government on foreign information policy. In 1973, a third subcommittee was established at the assistant deputy minister level to deal with *ad hoc* problems.

Interest groups. Organizations which make demands on political authorities for specific policy outputs, and are therefore often termed "pressure groups." Interests which are aggregated in groups are more likely to be given consideration by government than are unaggregated interests. Whether group politics is inimical or not to democratic politics, it is certainly a clear and irreversible feature of the collectivist age. There are few citizens who are not at least passive members and supporters of an organization whose leadership seeks some protection or enhancement from the government on their behalf. There are many types of interest groups – such as the non-economic and economic, the permanent and *ad hoc*, the self-interested and public-oriented, the elite- or mass membership-based, the regional, national, or international, and the constantly active or politically latent groups.

The political behaviour of an interest group often depends on its type and, in Canada, upon the federal and parliamentary nature of the political system. Some groups – such as the Canadian Bar Association, the Canadian Federation of Agriculture, the Canadian Legion, and the Consumers' Association of Canada – have easy access to the public decision-makers who are responsible for formulating policies directly in the areas of these groups' concerns. Indeed, some groups have had at times an occupational affinity with specific political roles. Usually, the federal minister of justice and the provincial attorneys-general are lawyers, with membership in the bar association. Until recently in Ontario, a doctor MPP was usually the minister of health. In the latter case, since the introduction of public medicare, the relationship between provincial medical associations and the provincial public bureaucracies may have become more formal and less friendly; but the relationships are still necessarily close. On the other hand, *ad hoc* groups, especially those which are created in opposition to a proposed government action, have a more clear-cut adversary relationship with the political authorities.

The federal system in Canada makes it necessary for an interest group to select its target and allocate its resources very carefully. Some groups will have to operate at both levels, and possibly in all provinces; others may be able to concentrate on one level and in only some provinces. For example, the Canadian labour movement's central body, the Canadian Labour Congress, is a weak federation of provincial groups. This reflects the particular need for effective lobbying for labour's interests at the provincial level, where much of the labour law is drawn up and administered in Canada. The Canadian Bankers Association, on the other hand, operates in large part at the federal level, as

Parliament has jurisdiction over banking. When the insurance industry opposed the introduction of government medicare in the 1960's, it had to operate at both levels of government – at the federal level, where legislation would allow the federal government to enter shared-cost agreements with the provinces, and at the provincial level, where the programmes would be implemented. Lobbying by the insurance industry against public automobile insurance, on the other hand, has been conducted only at the provincial level, particularly in those provinces where governments were clearly moving toward the introduction of such programmes. The federal government has no jurisdiction or interest in the matter.

Because parliamentary government in Canada concentrates power in the political and administrative executive, the cabinet and the civil service are the chief targets for interest group activity. If, for example, the group is working against a declared government objective, then legislators, the mass media, and the public become the more obvious targets in a campaign which does not appear likely to be successful. Ongoing activity by interest groups may include directing attention to legislators, party caucuses, and the mass media; but this is more to affect the environment for future discussions than to achieve a specific current campaign objective.

There are several signs of an interest group's influence on public decision-making. Reference has already been made to group representation on advisory boards in a public bureaucracy. Formal appearances before cabinet (for example, the annual public presentation of briefs by the Canadian Labour Congress and the Canadian Chamber of Commerce) are occasions for the Government to convince the group and the public of its concerns for the economy – and for the group to convince its own members and public opinion of its competence and influence on the Government. Some banks, insurance companies, manufacturing and resource companies, and other businesses make a practice of appointing former cabinet ministers, former senior civil servants, and current senators to their boards of directors; this represents an attempt to forge a positive, symbiotic relationship between themselves and the public decision-makers.

There has been an historic affinity between certain private interests and political parties in Canada. While much of the bargaining between interest groups and governments is secular and accommodative, these historic and current affinities do have some effect on the attitudes of the interest groups toward particular governments. Banks and manufacturing concerns, for example, have long been important financial contributors to the Liberal and Conservative parties; and the cabinets and Opposition front benches of these parties have generally been peopled with MPs who are integrated in the business and social environment of these interests. The Co-operative Commonwealth Federation, precursor of the New Democratic party, was a federation of many groups, including farm and labour organizations. The transformation of the CCF to the NDP in the 1956-1961 period was designed to achieve, in part, a larger and more effective affiliation of the Canadian labour movement to the social democratic party. Not a few NDP candidates and officials have held positions with some trade unions and farm organizations.

For an analysis of interest groups in Canada, see John Porter, *The Vertical Mosaic: An Analysis of Social Class and Power in Canada* (Toronto: University of Toronto Press, 1965); Robert Presthus, *Elite Accommodation in Canadian Politics* (Toronto: Macmillan Co. of Canada Ltd., 1973); and A. Paul Pross, *Pressure Group Behaviour in Canadian Politics* (Toronto: McGraw-Hill Ryerson Ltd., 1975).

Intergovernmental committees. Federal-provincial and interprovincial forums in which bargaining takes place in the context of contemporary executive, or administrative, federalism in Canada. Executive federalism has involved a constant interaction between the two levels of government since the 1960's and, in a later development, interaction among the provincial governments, especially those in the Maritimes and the prairie West. The bureaucratic process of accommodation has become so important in Canada that some observers have, perhaps prematurely, likened the intergovernmental committee system to a fourth branch of government, one that operates largely in private and for which there is no effective legislative oversight.

Federal-provincial committees have become numerous since the 1960's. They have involved more policy areas and lower levels of the public administration; and they have developed a variety of organizational structures. Such intergovernmental consultation has widened over many policy areas, but it usually has meant federal involvement in discussions on matters of provincial jurisdiction. The federal government's greater access to tax revenues has given it the power to offer money to provinces for programmes in provincial jurisdiction, as long as federal legislation (which the courts could declare unconstitutional) was not involved (see *Spending power*). Thus, there is no intergovernmental committee on foreign policy, national defense, or banking – all matters of federal jurisdiction; but there is intergovernmental consultation on urban affairs, highways, and education – matters of provincial jurisdiction. Of course, the provinces resent the centralist bias of executive federalism. In 1978, for example, the provincial attorneys-general refused to grant observor status to interested federal ministers at their annual conference, where federal incursion in the provincial realm of law enforcement was being discussed.

The highest level of intergovernmental committees is at the heads-of-government conferences – for example, the Conference of First Ministers, the Conference of Premiers, the Western Premiers' Conference, and the Maritime Premiers' Conference. Various ministerial conferences comprise second-rank intergovernmental committees, and they are closely associated with committees of senior officials (that is, deputy and assistant deputy ministers). Finally, there is a level involving technical officials charged with making operational the agreements of the higher officials. For example, in the area of finance and economy, the ministers of finance and provincial treasurers meet at least once a year and are supported administratively by the continuing committee on fiscal and economic matters (a committee of deputy ministers and deputy provincial treasurers). As one moves down the ranks of officials involved in intergovernmental committees, there are more multi- and bilateral, rather than universal, committees. The administration, for example, of the separate federal-provincial General Development Agreements negotiated by the federal government's Department of Regional and Economic Expansion, and the various programmes developed in the 1970's through the now-defunct federal Ministry of State for Urban Affairs, involved bilateral consultation.

Most of the governments have separate departments of intergovernmental affairs, with a cabinet minister holding that portfolio. Some provincial premiers were reluctant to establish such an organization outside their own office, perhaps much as Canadian prime ministers were reluctant to let foreign affairs out of their hands a generation earlier. In 1975, Parliament established a second cabinet secretary specifically for federal-provincial relations; this secretary is responsible to the prime minister. A section of the Privy Council Office, or cabinet secretariat – the Federal-Provincial Relations Office – was established to deal with policy and programmes in federal-provincial relations and to carry out studies and research dealing with the constitutional and administrative aspects of federalism.

The lack of a truly intergovernmental secretariat or permanent support staff for intergovernmental committees suggests that the institution of intergovernmental committees does not yet qualify for "fourth-branch" status in government. However, since 1973 there has been a Canadian Intergovernmental Conference Secretariat, whose secretary reports to the prime minister on administrative matters and to all heads of government on operational questions. The Conference of First Ministers established the secretariat as successor to a secretariat specifically dealing with constitutional review which had been created in 1968. The revised secretariat now provides support services for all federal-provincial conferences once the ministers have met and determined an agenda. The secretariat, however, has no independent policy functions. It is based in Ottawa and has departmental status through a federal order-in-council.

The attenuation of federal power in the 1960's that gave rise to executive federalism has thus also given rise to a more bureaucratic political system in Canada. The fragmentation of the Canadian party system, the lack of interaction among legislators across the eleven Canadian legislatures, and the lack of national mass media of communication lead to reasonable concern about the growth of the intergovernmental committee system as an apparently impervious and non-responsible political force in Canada's future. Especially as the elected ministers may shift portfolios or leave office more regularly than the senior officials, the senior officials' committees would seem to be a particular focus of effective, but non-responsible, power in the Canadian federal system. See *Federalism.*

For an account of federal-provincial relations in this bureaucratic environment, see Richard Simeon, *Federal-Provincial Diplomacy: The Making of Recent Policy in Canada* (Toronto: University of Toronto Press, 1972). For an early article on the subject co-authored by Edgar Gallant, then a deputy secretary to the cabinet in the Privy Council Office, see Edgar Gallant and R.M. Burns, "The Machinery of Federal-Provincial Relations: I and II," *Canadian Public Administration* 8 (1965), 514-34. See also Donald V. Smiley, *Canada in Question: Federalism in the Seventies* (2nd ed.; Toronto: McGraw-Hill Ryerson Ltd., 1976); and Garth Stevenson, *Unfulfilled Union: Canadian Federalism and National Unity* (Toronto: Macmillan Co. of Canada Ltd., 1979).

Interim supply, vote of.   A vote by which a legislature authorizes government expenditures prior to the passage of the main estimates. In recent practice, the vote on interim supply occurs in the House of Commons in the supply period which ends March 26. The House votes full supply on the main estimates in the next supply period, which ends June 30. A vote of interim supply assumes that the full supply will be voted in the subsequent period, and it is not unusual for some departments to have large parts of their estimates voted on interim supply by the time the vote on the main estimates takes place. See *Budgetary process.*

International Development Research Centre. A corporation created by federal statute in 1970 to conduct research into the problems of developing countries and methods of applying technical and scientific knowledge to their benefit. The Centre is managed by a board of governors composed of a chairman, a president, and nineteen other members appointed by the governor-in-council for renewable terms. Though most of the Centre's income is derived from the government of Canada, the board includes foreign nationals and the Centre may accept grants or bequests from elsewhere. The president of the Centre sits on the board of the Canadian International Development Agency, whose president is also on the board of the Centre. See *Canadian International Development Agency.*

International Joint Commission (IJC). A commission established under the Boundary Waters Treaty of 1909, with Canadian and United States sections. These must approve any use, obstruction, or diversion of boundary waters affecting the natural level or flow of boundary waters in the other country; and they examine and make recommendations on the matters referred to the Commission by the two national governments. The IJC has no independent, international status; but each of the national sections, for a total of two chairmen and four commissioners, is appointed by the relevant government, and the Commission is responsible to the national governments.

   Occasionally, the IJC has been the site for national political controversy and high-priority policy implementation. In 1963, the Canadian chairman, General A.G.L. McNaughton, resigned in order to publicize his disagreement with the Canadian Government over the Columbia River Treaty. In 1972, Canada and the U.S. gave the IJC responsibility to co-ordinate and monitor programmes to implement the Canada-U.S. agreement on Great Lakes water quality.

Intra (ultra) vires. A phrase which describes the statutes of federal or provincial legislatures as being within (or beyond) their legislative competence, as determined through judicial review by the Judicial Committee of the Privy Council until 1949, and by the Supreme Court.

J

Judicial Committee of the Privy Council (London).   Until 1949, the final appeal court for all cases except criminal cases in Canada. As a constitutional court, the Judicial Committee was particularly important in the development of Canadian federalism and is still of contemporary interest, as its decisions could be cited as precedent. The Judicial Committee was composed of British privy councillors who had held high positions on the bench. There were also judges on the Judicial Committee from Empire and Commonwealth countries, such as the chief justice of the Canadian Supreme Court. The Judicial Committee, as an imperial appeal court, did not give split judgments; rather, it offered unanimous advice to the sovereign (in the manner of the Privy Council itself). In 1949, the Supreme Court of Canada became the final court of appeal for Canadian cases.

Unlike the Supreme Court of the United States, which has a broad scope for judicial review and whose judges were clearly interpreting a constitution, the British judges on the Judicial Committee saw their role as interpreting a statute – which the British North America act literally was. This exercise was particularly narrow in the case of the Canadian constitution, perhaps because the judges were so removed physically and intellectually from the country whose constitutional statute they interpreted for 82 years. The problem of legalism was enhanced by the probable lack of understanding of federalism, a political system which does not allow (as does a unitary state) for easy modification of the constitution by a subsequent act of a single legislature. The narrowness was further reinforced by the unanimity of the Court, which did not allow subsequent "distinction" on a case based on a variety of expressed opinions.

Some important constitutional judgments by the Judicial Committee of the Privy Council have been the following: *Russell* v. *The Queen*, 1882, in which the Judicial Committee ruled, in a case involving a federal statute permitting local areas to prohibit the sale of liquor, that the federal government was dealing with "public order and safety" under the "Peace, Order and good Government" clause (Section 91), an action which took precedence over the provincial jurisdiction of property and civil rights (92:13); *Hodge* v. *The Queen*, 1883, in which the Judicial Committee began to retreat from the approval of the exercise of federal power under the "Peace, Order and good Government" clause, declaring that in one aspect an Ontario statute providing for licensing and control of the sale of liquor locally by provincial authority was constitutional (92:8, :9, :15) and that each level of legislature was sovereign and not subordinate to the other (see *Aspect Doctrine*); *Maritime Bank v. Receiver-General of New Brunswick*, 1892, in which the principle of equality was declared among legislatures – in Lord Watson's words, the object of the BNA Act was neither "to weld the provinces into one, nor to subordinate provincial government to a central authority"; *Attorney-General for Ontario v. Attorney-General for Canada*, 1896, also known as the Local Prohibition Case, in which Parliament's power to encroach on provincial jurisdiction enumerated in Section 92, using the "Peace, Order and good Government" clause, was further denied. The "Peace, Order and good Government" clause, which earlier had been declared effective when the legislation was of nation-wide importance, was now declared to be only a supplementary statement to the enumerated powers of Parliament which could not take primacy over the enumerated powers of the provincial legislatures. In a reference (*Re Board of Commerce Act and Combines and Fair Prices Act* [1919] in 1922, and *Toronto Electric Commissioners v. Snider*, 1925), the Judicial Committee, under Viscount Haldane, came to look upon Parliament's general power in the preamble to Section 91 as an emergency power only. Attempting to reconcile the Judicial Committee's view in 1925 with its view in *Russell v. The Queen* in 1882, Haldane suggested that their lordships then must have considered drunkenness a threat to the nation. In the reference in 1937 concerning the federal Employment and Social Insurance Act, which involved one measure in Prime Minister R.B. Bennett's New Deal, the Judicial Committee declared the measure unconstitutional and the economic depression insufficient to invoke emergency powers. In effect, "Property and Civil Rights" had become the residual power clause of the constitution, favouring the provinces.

The Judicial Committee eventually denied not only the "Peace, Order and good Government" clause as a source of comprehensive legislative competence but also "The Regulation of Trade and Commerce" power (91:2). Important cases here include *Citizens Insurance Co. v. Parsons and Queen Insurance Co. v. Parsons*, 1881, and a reference in 1937 on the Natural Products Marketing Act, another part of Bennett's New Deal.

The decisions of the Judicial Committee of the Privy Council were important in delineating jurisdictional responsibilities in a collectivist age. The Judicial Committee, for example, declared the federal role in establishing laws relating to collective bargaining to be restricted to areas in which Parliament had jurisdiction (Snider Case, 1925). Nor did the treaty-making powers of the federal government give it the power to legislate nationally on such labour-related issues as hours of work, holidays, and minimum wages (*Attorney-General for Canada* v. *Attorney-General for Ontario* [Labour Conventions Case, 1937]) – also part of the abortive New Deal. In the "new" fields of aeronautics and radio, however, Parliament acquired jurisdiction (Aeronautics Reference, 1932; Radio Reference, 1932). By now, the "watertight compartments" view, so called by Lord Atkin in the Labour Conventions Case, was dominant. Matters enumerated under Section 91 were the responsibility of Parliament; matters enumerated under Section 92 were the responsibilities of the provincial legislatures; and this clear-cut distinction would be maintained except for the sole emergency of war.

In cases in 1945 and in 1946, the Judicial Committee wove an unsteady pattern in the matter of emergency powers. In 1946 (*Attorney-General of Ontario* v. *Canadian Temperance Federation*), Lord Simon asserted the Aspect Doctrine in *Hodge* v. *The Queen* — that the nation-wide importance of the issue (and not an emergency situation) was the litmus test of jurisdictional competence. In 1947 (*Co-operative Committee on Japanese Canadians* v. *Attorney-General for Canada*), however, the Judicial Committee reasserted the narrow emergency doctrine.

Since 1949, the Supreme Court of Canada has been the final court of appeal. The question of constitutional development has become, however, a matter of accommodative bargaining among the various federal and provincial political elites; and the court's declarations are often viewed as a factor in political bargaining, rather than as decisive statements (see *Federalism*). See *Supreme Court*.

For an analysis of constitutional development, see R.I. Cheffins and R.N. Tucker, *The Constitutional Process in Canada* (2nd ed.; Toronto: McGraw-Hill Ryerson Ltd., 1969). See also Alan C. Cairns, "The Judicial Committee and Its Critics," *Canadian Journal of Political Science* 4 (1971), 301-45; J. Noel Lyon and Ronald G. Atkey (eds.), *Canadian Constitutional Law in a Modern Perspective* (Toronto: University of Toronto Press, 1970); Peter H. Russell (ed.), *Leading Constitutional Decisions: Cases on the British North America Act* (rev.; Toronto: McClelland and Stewart Ltd., Carleton Library, No. 23, 1973); and Edward McWhinney, *Judicial Review in the English-Speaking World* (4th ed.; Toronto: University of Toronto Press, 1969).

Judicial (commission of) inquiry.   Investigation by a panel composed
of judges and lawyers or a single judge, established and accountable to
the legislature. Such commissions of inquiry may be designated as
"royal commissions" and have statutory powers usually associated
with courts of law, in order to inquire into and report on specific questions which may give rise to criminal charges. Thus, the commissions
may have legal staff and power of subpeona with respect to individuals
and documents. Witnesses may be represented by lawyers, and interested parties may also seek the right to be represented in order to comment on procedure and to cross-examine witnesses.

The statutes establishing inquiries and the procedures of the commission are themselves subject to judicial review. In 1978, the Supreme Court of Canada declared that the powers of a commission of inquiry investigating the administration of justice within a province
were constitutionally limited. It supported the federal government's
opposition to the broad inquiry of a Quebec commission investigating
the affairs of the RCMP, a federal police force. Declaring one section of
the mandate to be unconstitutional, the Court observed: "Inasmuch as
these are the regulations and practices of an agency of the federal government, it is clearly not within the proper scope of the authority of
provincial government" (Mr. Justice Louis-Philippe Pigeon). Ruling
that the provincial inquiry could not force a federal cabinet minister to
appear as a witness, the Supreme Court said that in common law a
commission of inquiry has no power to compel the attendance of witnesses and to require the production of documents. Any jurisdiction
for such purposes depends on statutory authority, the Court declared;
"and it seems that provincial legislation cannot be effective by itself to
confer such jurisdiction as against the Crown in right of Canada."
Thus, a commission's orders are not like those of a superior court,
which must be obeyed without question, as they may be challenged on
constitutional grounds.

Also in 1978-1979, a federally appointed royal commission of inquiry into certain RCMP activities sparred with the federal government
over access to cabinet documents. The government may invoke Crown
privilege and the Official Secrets Act to deny documents to the federal
commission or, indeed, alter the commission's mandate. Two days before Prime Minister Pierre Trudeau's Government resigned in 1979, an
order-in-council was signed which allowed the commission access to
cabinet material in Trudeau's ministry only with Trudeau's approval.
A subsequent order-in-council could again alter the procedure. See
Royal commission.

Judicial Review.   Judicial judgment on the constitutionality of statutes. In Canada, legislatures are supreme in their areas of competence
as specified in the British North America Act. It is therefore a matter
for the Court (Judicial Committee of the Privy Council prior to 1949,
and the Supreme Court of Canada) to determine the constitutionality of
federal and provincial statutes when brought to the Court, or to supply
an opinion (reference) when the constitutionality of a proposed statute
is referred to it. Judicial review also exists indirectly in the power that
courts have in interpreting legislation. A legislature can, of course,
later amend the disputed legislation to clarify its original intent.
Whether direct or indirect, judicial review gives the courts an important political role. See *Judicial Committee of the Privy Council; Supreme Court.*

For an examination of this question, see Edward McWhinney,
Judicial Review in the English-Speaking World (Toronto: University of
Toronto Press, 1969).

Judicial system (judiciary).   The administering of justice in courts of
law. In Canada, the judicial system involves integrated provincial and
federal court jurisdictions. Under provisions of the British North
America Act (Sections 96-101), the federal government appoints and
pays superior, county, and district court judges in the provinces, as
well as federal court judges. The provinces appoint only low-level provincial court judges; but under Section 92:14 they may enact laws pertaining to the administration of justice in the provinces. Though appointed by government, judges are paid salaries which are fixed and
provided formally by Parliament. Judicial independence from government is further safeguarded by provisions which allow for removal before the age of retirement only with the approval of the legislature.

The law which the courts apply is based on legislative statute and on
earlier judicial decisions, or precedents. The rule of precedence, or
stare decisis, is that judges must take account of decisions that have
been made in similar cases. The lower courts are bound by the precedents of upper courts, and individual courts may be guided by their own
earlier decisions. The legal system in Canada is based on the common
law tradition of England and the codified civil law. Private law in Quebec is rooted in the Roman-French civil code, and private law in the
other provinces in the English common law tradition. Criminal law,
which is within the legislative competence of Parliament (91:27), is applied across Canada (see *Judicial review*).

The lowest level of courts involves provincial courts, surrogate courts, and division courts with civil and criminal jurisdiction. The mid-level includes the supreme courts of the provinces, which include courts of original jurisdiction and courts of appeal. The highest level includes the Supreme Court of Canada and the Federal Court of Canada. There is also a territorial judiciary in the Yukon and in the Northwest Territories. Until 1949, the Judicial Committee of the Privy Council was Canada's final court of appeal in non-criminal matters and effectively a constitutional court (see *Judicial Committee of the Privy Council*).

The Supreme Court of Canada, which was established in 1875, is composed of nine judges; they sit in Ottawa and exercise appellate jurisdiction in both civil and criminal cases. The Supreme Court is also required to consider references by the governor-in-council and advise Parliament on private bills. In 1978, for example, the federal Government asked the Supreme Court for an opinion on the constitutionality of its intention under Section 91:1 of the British North America Act to have Parliament amend the Act on representation in, and the role of, the Senate. In 1979, the Court ruled that such fundamental changes proposed could not be made unilaterally; in effect, such changes could be made only by the British Parliament on joint address by the two houses of the Canadian Parliament with, by convention, the consent of the provinces (see *Supreme Court*). The Federal Court of Canada, which was established in 1970, consists of a trial division and an appeals division and has up to ten judges. The Federal Court hears claims against and by the Crown and claims against or concerning officers and servants of the Crown, by individuals seeking relief from decisions of federal boards, commissions, and other tribunals. The Court also has certain jurisdiction in disputes between provinces or between Canada and a province (see *Federal Court of Canada*).

The appointment of the judiciary in general, and of the Supreme Court in particular, has occasionally been a controversial subject. Apart from the question of appointments as manifestations of party patronage, a federal-provincial debate centres on the monopoly of appointment power held by the federal government and the potential centralist bias that may pervade the courts – especially the Supreme Court, which is the final constitutional court of appeal in Canada. In its short-lived constitutional amendment bill in 1978, the federal Liberal Government proposed that the number of Supreme Court judges be increased to eleven, and that appointments involve regional distribution and agreement between the federal government and the relevant provincial governments.

K

King-Byng Dispute. A constitutional dispute concerning the role of
the governor general in Canada and crown prerogatives. Following the
federal general election of 1925, the governing Liberals remained in
office – though the party had fewer seats than the Conservatives, and a
third party (the Progressives) held the balance of power. Less than one
year later, in order to avoid a vote of censure concerning a scandal in
the customs department, Prime Minister William Lyon Mackenzie
King asked Governor General Lord Byng for a dissolution of Parliament. When Byng refused the request, King resigned and left the governor general without a Government. Arthur Meighen, the Conservative
leader, accepted Byng's request to form a Government. Meighen's Government, however, lasted only three sitting days before it was defeated
in the House. Byng accepted Meighen's request for dissolution, and in
the election of 1926 the Liberals were returned with a majority. King
managed to turn an election campaign which might have centred on a
scandal under his Government into one which focussed on the alleged
attempt to relegate Canada to colonial status by a non-responsible official exercising an imperial function of his office.

Indeed, the governor general had, and continues to have, the right to
grant or refuse the prime minister's request for dissolution. However,
King was wrong to portray the action as an imperial function rather
than the constitutional prerogative of the governor general as the sovereign's representative in Canada; Byng also exaggerated the scope of his
prerogative power. The governor general can exercise discretionary
judgment to counter a clear violation of the intent of the constitution,
but only when there is no reasonable doubt about the judgment and the
justice of such an independent action. While King's attempt to evade
the vote of censure in the House may have been an abuse of power to
be checked by the governor general, the latter overestimated Meighen's
ability to carry on in a House in which the Progressives held the balance of power.

For an examination of this question, see Eugene A. Forsey, *The
Royal Power of Dissolution of Parliament in the British
Commonwealth* (Toronto: University of Toronto Press, 1943); and R.
MacGregor Dawson, *Constitutional Issues in Canada, 1900-1931* (To-
ronto: University of Toronto Press, 1933). See also J.E. Esberey, "Per-
sonality and Politics: A New Look at the King-Byng Dispute,"
Canadian Journal of Political Science 6 (1973), 37-55.

L

Labour Conventions Reference (Attorney-General for Canada v. Attorney-General for Ontario, 1937). A constitutional judgment by the Judicial Committee of the Privy Council that Parliament could not acquire, through international obligation, legislative powers which it did not possess under the British North America Act. Though the judgment was a reference to "treaty power," it was also important in the development of provincial authority on class-related matters of public policy.

In the particular reference, the Judicial Committee declared unconstitutional three federal statutes which were part of Prime Minister R.B. Bennett's "New Deal." These dealt with limiting working hours, minimum wages, and holidays from industrial work. The federal government had argued that the legislation was constitutional under Section 132, in which Canada was carrying out obligations incurred when Canada became a member of the International Labour Organization. The Judicial Committee's decision in the reference on radio communication (Radio Case) had encouraged the Conservative Government to proceed with the labour legislation. According to Lord Atkin, however, the regulation of a new subject such as radio might fall under the federal residual power of the "Peace, Order and good Government" clause of Section 91; but power to implement a treaty depends on subject matter and the division of power under the BNA Act. The Judicial Committee declared that the legislation was the provincial governments' jurisdiction under Section 92:13 ("Property and Civil Rights"). Because the federal government cannot use "treaty power" as an excuse to enlarge its sphere of activity, it must be careful not to sign treaties which it does not have the power to implement under the distribution of power in Sections 91 and 92 of the BNA Act. See *Treaty power.*

Language ombudsman. An informal name for the federal Commissioner of Official Languages, who is responsible for ensuring the recognition of equal status for French and English in the operations of the government of Canada according to the Official Languages Act of 1969. See *Commissioner of Official Languages.*

Lavell-Bedard cases (Attorney-General of Canada v. Lavell, 1974). A decision by the Supreme Court of Canada which upheld sex discrimination in the Indian Act despite the "equality before the law" provision of the Canadian Bill of Rights (1960). Under the Indian Act, an Indian woman who marries a non-Indian is not entitled to be registered as an Indian, but an Indian man who marries a non-Indian retains his Indian status. The decision came several years after the decision in the Drybones case, which appeared to strengthen the Bill of Rights as a measure widening civil rights and against which the validity of established Acts could be tested. The majority decision and the several dissenting views in the Lavell-Bedard cases have led to some confusion about the Court's view of the Bill of Rights.

In the Drybones case, Mr. Justice Ritchie had declared the Indian Act a violation of the Bill of Right's "equality before the law" provision. However, in the majority decision in the Lavell-Bedard cases, he ruled that the discrimination in the Act was constitutional, as it applied only within Indian reserves while the Drybones case involved all Indians in Canada. The British North America Act granted the regulation of Indian status to Parliament, and patriarchy had been legally sanctioned for a century. Mr. Justice Ritchie now argued that equality in the application of the law was the determining factor more than equality before the law.

Mr. Justice Laskin, who later became chief justice, dissented strongly. He wrote that sex discrimination among Indians compounded racial inequality beyond the point that the Drybones case found unacceptable. When the opinions of other justices in this case are matched with their opinions in the Drybones case, the confusion is heightened. See *Bill of Rights.*

See the analysis by Peter H. Russell in "The Supreme Court since 1960," in Paul W. Fox (ed.), *Politics: Canada* (4th ed.; Toronto: McGraw-Hill Ryerson Ltd., 1977), 536-46. Fox also includes extracts from the Lavell-Bedard decision (581-94).

Law Reform Commission of Canada.   A body created in 1970 to report to Parliament through the minister of justice on the improvement, modernization, and reform of Canadian law. The four-member Commission, with two part-time members, maintains a continuous review process to complement the normal legislative and judicial review processes. The Commission is particularly charged to make recommendations on removing anachronisms and anomalies in the law and obsolete laws, the reconciliation of differences and discrepancies in the application of law arising from the differences in the common law and civil law systems, and the development of new approaches and concepts of the law.

The Commission's research is usually carried out on a contract basis and has involved projects in these areas: family law (property rights, resolution of family conflicts, and divorce laws); criminal procedure (police powers, pre-trial procedures, appeals, and non-prosecutorial disposition of cases); criminal law (sexual misconduct, obscenity, contempt of court, conspiracy and dishonest acquisition of property, and mental disorder and the law); sentencing (compensation and restitution, diversion, imprisonment and release, and hospitalization as a therapeutic alternative to imprisonment); administrative law pertaining to public sector agencies, which perform a range of functions from regulating individual and corporate behaviour to providing money and other benefits (expropriation laws and procedures and public information programmes in the regulatory process); and evidence (elimination of expense and delay involved in the rules of evidence).

The Law Reform Commission does not hold public hearings. However, it publishes background papers, study papers, and working papers to encourage public and professional discussion and comment before making final reports. For example, in 1979, the Commission published a critical review of the Official Secrets Act which gave direction to the Commission's consideration of reform of administrative law and procedures.

Leadership conventions (selection).   Meetings of party members to select a parliamentary leader. Leadership conventions are an American practice imported to Canada and adapted firmly, if awkwardly, to the parliamentary system which was imported from Britain. In the American presidential-congressional system, with fixed terms of office for elected officials, party conventions to select presidential and vice-presidential candidates are regular quadrennial events. In the parliamentary system, however – where there is no nation-wide contest to fill the "prime ministership," and no fixed term for a Government except for the constitutional five-year limit on Parliaments – leaders were traditionally selected by the parliamentary caucus. In Canada, the leaders of all parties are now selected by conventions. For Liberals and Conservatives the selection is without fixed term; for New Democrats the selection is, formally at least, for a fixed term. In the Canadian practice of selecting leaders in convention, the candidates are usually drawn from the parliamentary caucus, the successful candidates are usually elite-supported. In all parties, the delegates cast a secret ballot. If no candidate has a majority of the votes cast, further balloting takes place, with the least popular candidate in the previous tally disqualified.

The federal Liberal party held the first leadership convention in 1919. The Opposition Liberals had held a convention in 1893 to boost morale; and the leader, Wilfrid Laurier, again in Opposition in 1918, announced a convention for similar reasons to be held the following year. However, Laurier died in February 1919, and the parliamentary caucus which would have normally selected a leader decided to hold the convention to "First ... draft, discuss, and adopt the platform ... ; Second ... deal with ... party organization; Third ... select a leader ... " (the official call quoted in John C. Courtney, *The Selection of National Party Leaders in Canada* [Toronto: Macmillan Co. of Canada Ltd., 1973], 64). However, after the selection of William Lyon Mackenzie King in 1919, no Liberal convention was held for any reason until 1949, after King announced his retirement and a successor had to be chosen. King had been prime minister for 22 of those 30 years; and, on the occasion of his retirement while in office, a party convention for the first time selected not only a new leader but effectively the next prime minister. When King submitted his Government's resignation, the governor general asked the party-selected leader, Louis St. Laurent, to form the next Government.

The federal Conservatives adopted the convention model in 1927, and the socialist Co-operative Commonwealth Federation not surprisingly adopted it at the party's inception in 1933. The Ontario Conservatives had selected their provincial leader in convention in 1920. Therefore, by the time Arthur Meighen resigned as federal leader in 1926, the convention model was trumpeted as preferable to selection by a parliamentary cabal. The convention model by contrast seemed democratic and representative of the party, and the Conservatives could not afford to appear otherwise.

As the CCF and its successor, the New Democratic party, originated as a grassroots political movement, there was no question as to how the party would select its leader. Its leaders are chosen by convention and and for a fixed term. In 1971, when the party met to choose T.C. Douglas' successor, veteran CCF-New Democrat David Lewis had to endure four ballots before defeating his remaining opponent, James Laxer, a relative newcomer to party activism. Likewise, MP Ed Broadbent succeeded the retiring David Lewis in 1975 only after defeating his final opponent, a provincial MPP, on the fourth ballot.

The leadership convention gives the impression of openness, liveliness, and ultimately unity behind the new leader; but the element of control is very strong, especially in the Conservative and Liberal parties. The party executives, over whom the parliamentary leader usually has considerable influence, are responsible for naming delegates to conventions. Leadership-appointed delegates-at-large have usually accounted for one-third to one-half of the delegates at federal Conservative and Liberal conventions (although the tendency in recent years has been for the proportion of constituency-elected delegates to increase). The comparable brake on counter-elite activism in NDP leadership conventions is usually located among trade union representation.

The lack of fixed terms for Liberal and Conservative leaders, the concern of some party activists over leadership-dominated conventions, and possibly the bitter struggle within the federal Conservative party during the final years of John Diefenbaker's leadership in the mid-1960's led to the development in the 1970's in those parties of instruments of accountability. While the precise nature of the instrument varies, the intent is to have the leader submit to a periodic vote of confidence at conventions held, for example, within a certain period following a general election. If the leader does not obtain a certain level of confidence, the party executive may then be obliged to call a leadership convention within a specific period. Such a device, then, allows a party whose leader does not have a fixed term to debate the leader's future, which may be appropriate following electoral defeat.

For an analysis of leadership conventions in Canada up to 1968, see John C. Courtney, *The Selection of National Party Leaders in Canada* (Toronto: Macmillan Co. of Canada Ltd., 1973).

League for Social Reconstruction (LSR). A group of largely university-based intellectuals which existed from 1932 until World War Two; it was the "brains trust" of the socialist Co-operative Commonwealth Federation. Modelled on the British Fabian Society, the LSR published pamphlets and articles to educate the public on socialist approaches to the social and economic order. In 1932, members of the LSR met with Labour and some Progressive MPs in Ottawa to pass resolutions leading to the founding of the CCF a few months later.

The CCF's Regina Manifesto, which was published in 1933, was the work of such LSR members as Frank Underhill (historian), F.R. Scott (constitutional lawyer, professor, and poet), and Eugene Forsey (labour and economic historian). In 1935, the LSR published *Social Planning for Canada*, its most influential critique of Canadian society and the economic order. See *Co-operative Commonwealth Federation; Regina Manifesto.*

On the LSR, see Michiel Horn, "The League for Social Reconstruction and the Development of Canadian Socialism," *Journal of Canadian Studies* 7 (1972), 3-17.

***Legislation (public, financial or money, enabling, private, passage
of).*** Bills introduced in a legislature. Once introduced, legislation
may be removed or withdrawn from consideration, may be defeated,
may "die on the Order Paper" when the legislature recesses, may be
amended, and may pass the legislature. When passed, bills become
statutes upon receiving royal assent.

Public bills are of a public or general nature and may be introduced
by any member of the legislature. Such legislation, which is sponsored
by private members (that is, MPs who are not in the Government), may
not involve the expenditure of money; they are often introduced for
reasons of public education, as they do not often pass (see *Private
member's legislation*). Public bills, which are introduced by a member
of the cabinet, constitute Government legislation and take up the bulk
of the legislature's time. Government legislation is either financial or
non-financial. Financial legislation deals with the spending of money
(supply bills) or with the raising of money (tax measures and ways and
means legislation). Only the Government, then, may introduce financial legislation, or money bills (see *Budgetary process; Estimates*). The
power of the Senate to amend federal money bills is debatable – such
bills must first be introduced in the House, and the Senate cannot increase the sums. Non-financial Government legislation may involve
new programmes and the creation of administrative agencies to carry
out the objectives of the legislation (enabling legislation), or it may involve amendments to statutes.

Private bills are non-Government legislation designed to alter the
law relating to some particular interest, or to confer rights on or relieve
the obligations of some person or group of people. For example, bills to
incorporate private companies are private bills. In practice, such bills
at the federal level are usually introduced in the Senate and dealt with
perfunctorily by the House of Commons.

Legislation must receive three readings in the legislature. In the Canadian Parliament, the public bills and private bills receive different
treatment. Because Government legislation is more important and because consideration in the House is more extensive and effective than
in the Senate, the following describes procedure for the passage of
most Government legislation in the House of Commons (otherwise, see
Private bills; Private member's legislation).

The minister sponsoring the legislation first gives notice to the
House of the Government's intention to introduce the bill. At least two
days later, the minister moves for leave to introduce the bill and moves
that the bill receive first reading. The House usually approves first

reading automatically, sometimes following a brief explanation of the bill. The bill is then printed and distributed.

Subject to the negotiation of the schedule of the House by the party House leaders, the minister later moves that the bill be given second reading and referred to a committee of the House. The vote on second reading represents approval in principle and is preceded by extensive debate.

At the committee stage, the committee may call witnesses to testify in public for or against the legislation. This stage may take weeks and involve considerable debate among the parties, who are represented roughly in proportion to their representation in the legislature. Following hearings on the measure, the committee holds private sessions to prepare its final report, including suggested amendments to the legislation. The House then decides whether to accept the report, including amendments proposed by the committee. At this stage, any MP may move an amendment on one day's notice. This is the occasion for Opposition MPs whose amendments have been rejected in committee to put their argument and the amendment to a public vote in the House. After all such amendments are voted on, a motion that the bill (as amended) be "concurred in" is voted.

After the report stage, the minister moves third reading. Debate at this stage is limited, and amendments of a general nature only are permitted. If the measure receives approval on third reading, it goes to the Senate for consideration and passage. If the Senate alters the legislation, the House must concur in the changes or the legislation may not proceed to the governor general for royal assent. See *House of Commons; Standing (select, special) committees.*

Legislative assembly.   The official name for the elected legislatures of all Canadian provinces except Ontario, Nova Scotia, Newfoundland, and Quebec. The legislatures of the first three are called the house of assembly, and the legislature of Quebec is called the national assembly.

Legislative process.   A series of actions involving consideration of bills by a legislature which may result in their passage to become law. On the passage of legislation, see *House of Commons; Legislature.* However, on pre-legislative activities to encourage or discourage certain legislation, see *Budgetary process; Interest groups; Lobby.* On post-legislative activities which in turn may lead to pressure for legislative change, see *Judicial review; Policy (analysis; -making; public); Regulatory agencies (regulations).*

Legislature. That part or branch of government which has the power to make or amend laws. A legislature may be elected (as in the cases of all provincial legislatures in Canada, and in the House of Commons) or appointed, as in the case of the Canadian Senate. In other countries, some legislatures are filled by heredity or by a combination of heredity, appointment, and election. In a less formal but still effective sense, some administrative bodies perform legislative functions through making regulations under enabling legislation passed by a legislature (subordinate legislation). See *Delegated powers; House of Commons; Legislation.*

Letters Patent (1947). The prerogative instruments defining the office of governor general, which the sovereign makes applicable to each governor general through the commission of appointment. Aside from provincial governments, there is a distinction between prerogative powers exercised by the governor general as the Crown's representative in Canada and those exercised by the sovereign on Canadian advice. That is, not all of the sovereign's prerogative powers with regard to Canada were historically transferred by the Letters Patent to the governors general. However, by the Letters Patent of 1947, the sovereign delegated all powers to the governor general to be exercised "on the advice of his Canadian ministers" as they affect Canada.

Liberal party. The federal Liberal party of Canada originated in the reform politics of mid-nineteenth-century Canada. In response to the dominant Tory element, the Reformers in Upper Canada (now Ontario) and the Maritimes joined with the anti-clerical *Rouges* of Lower Canada (now Quebec) in an uneasy alliance. The alignment was notably unsuccessful until the late nineteenth century. The Liberal party lacked French-Canadian support because of its extreme anti-clerical element in Quebec and its rural anti-Catholic and pro-Protestant element elsewhere. The party came to office in 1873, in the wake of a scandal in the Conservative party. It left office five years later, in the wake of an economic depression and under a wave of popular support for the Conservative's National Policy of railway construction, immigration, and tariff increases.

Since 1896, however, the Liberal party has been pre-eminent in federal politics. Considerable credit for the change in party fortunes is usually given to Wilfrid Laurier, leader from 1887 to 1919. In the 60 years since then, the Liberals have had only four leaders, two of whom came into the position of prime minister when they became leader and all of whom were eventually prime ministers. In contrast to the dour quality of Liberal leadership before him, Laurier's style was one of moderation and "sunny ways."

Laurier's success, and that subsequently of his party, may be understood in terms of Liberal failure and Conservative success earlier on a bicultural and class strategy. The Liberals under Laurier developed a French leadership that was, and continues to be, integrated in Quebec society, and an English leadership that was at least sympathetic to French-Canadian survival. In federal elections since 1891, the Liberals have led the Conservatives in popular vote in Quebec in all but the 1958 election. Two of the four leaders since Laurier have been French Canadians, while no French Canadian has led the Conservative party.

In addition to a *"Québec solide,"* the Liberals have generally followed the earlier Conservative model of maintaining the good will of the economic elite as well as a progressive image. The sole instance of clear alienation from the business community involved Laurier's support for reciprocity in 1911, and the Liberals suffered electorally for that temporary lapse. Since the rise of the industrial trade union movement in the 1920's, with its formal if occasionally tenuous link with the socialist Co-operative Commonwealth Federation (and later the New Democratic party), the Liberals have seemed more right-wing than left-wing in leadership and economic and social policy. Nonetheless, Liberal Governments have introduced redistributive programmes. They seem, however, to prefer to maintain a progressive image with such non-redistributive social policies as law reform, internationalist foreign policy, cultural nationalism, and minority rights.

As did the Conservatives in the nineteenth century, so the Liberals in this century have constantly sought to project an image of their party as the sole political vehicle of Canadian nationalism. However, especially since the 1940's, the Liberals have seemed to identify national interest with the predominant views of the central-Canadian economic elite. This patriotic image held as long as elite opinion in central Canada was effectively that of the national economic elite, as long as French Canada's strategy for survival was largely internalized in Quebec, and as long as the population of central Canada elected the bulk of members of Parliament. A long-term problem for federal Liberals in the 1980's may be that two of these conditions no longer hold, and the third condition is becoming problematic. The Canadian West has developed strong, indigenous economic interests at odds with those of central Canada and better reflected in provincial government policy. French-Canadian nationalism is more aggressive than in the past. The western population is growing, while the central-Canadian population is in a steady state. By the late 1970's, the federal Conservatives appeared to have benefitted more than the Liberals from these changes, although the flexibility of Liberal leadership in the past has stood that party well in adapting to new conditions.

On the federal Liberal party, see Joseph Wearing, *The Liberal Party of Canada, 1958-1979* (Toronto: McGraw-Hill Ryerson Ltd., 1980); and Reginald Whitaker, *The Government Party: Organizing and Financing the Liberal Party of Canada, 1930-1958* (Toronto: University of Toronto Press, 1977). See also J.M.S. Careless, *Brown of the Globe* (2 vols.; Toronto: Macmillan Co. of Canada Ltd., 1959, 1963); Dale Thomson, *Alexander Mackenzie: Clear Grit* (Toronto: Macmillan Co. of Canada Ltd., 1960); Joseph Schull, *Edward Blake* (2 vols.; Toronto: Macmillan Co. of Canada Ltd., 1975, 1976); Joseph Schull, *Laurier: The First Canadian* (Toronto: Macmillan Co. of Canada Ltd., 1965); R. MacGregor Dawson, *William Lyon MacKenzie King, I, 1874-1923* and Blair Neatby, *William Lyon MacKenzie King, II, 1924-1932* (Toronto: University of Toronto Press, 1958-1963); J.W. Pickersgill, *The Mackenzie King Record, 1939-1944, 1944-1954, 1945-1946, 1947-1948* (4 vols.; Toronto: University of Toronto Press, 1960 –); and Dale C. Thomson, *Louis St. Laurent: Canadian* (Toronto: Macmillan Co. of Canada Ltd., 1967). See also Lester B. Pearson's memoirs, *Mike: The Memoirs of the Right Honourable Lester B. Pearson, 1897-1948, 1948-1957, 1957-1968* (3 vols.; Toronto: University of Toronto Press, 1973 –). For a journalist's account of the Pearson Governments, see Peter C. Newman, *The Distemper of Our Times: Canadian Politics in Transition* (Toronto: McClelland and Stewart Ltd., 1968). For a critical examination of Liberal government policy since World War Two, but focussing on contemporary policy under Pierre Trudeau's leadership, see James Laxer and Robert Laxer, *The Liberal Idea of Canada: Pierre Trudeau and the Question of Canada's Survival* (Toronto: Lorimer, 1977). See also Walter Stewart, *Shrug: Trudeau in Power* (Toronto: New Press, 1971); and George Radwanski, *Trudeau* (Toronto: Macmillan Co. of Canada Ltd., 1978). For an examination of a provincial Liberal party which was important at one time for the federal party, see David E. Smith, *Prairie Liberalism: The Liberal Party in Saskatchewan, 1905-1971* (Toronto: University of Toronto Press, 1975).

Liberalism. Political beliefs associated with the idea of progress achieved through the free play of each person's will to self-aggrandizement. Liberalism developed in the eighteenth and nineteenth centuries, in the context of political struggles against arbitrary government, and usually found support among European nationalists or the rising bourgeoisie of industrial capitalism. A liberal views the state as the instrument to maintain "equality of opportunity." In the nineteenth century, a liberal held the state's role to be minimal. In the twentieth century, however, liberals are more inclined to rely upon the social policy and the regulatory power of the state, rather than the "free market forces," to achieve this equality. Contemporary liberalism is also basically anti-nationalist, except when imperial bonds are being challenged as a prior condition to the creation of individual freedom.

As a broad set of beliefs, liberal ideas are prevalent in all Canadian parties — in the *laissez-faire* individualism of western Conservatism or in the mild reformism of the socialist New Democratic party, as well as in the Liberal party. As the national political elite since 1935, the federal Liberal party has been criticized on the one hand for its excessive involvement of the state in the economic life of the country and, on the other hand, for its unwillingness to control economic development to achieve nationalist as opposed to continentalist American goals. The "achievement" of the Liberal elite in the twentieth century, one might argue, has been to remove Canada from the faltering British empire and to place it in the sphere of influence of the rising American empire.

For an analysis of Canadian liberalism, see Frank Underhill, *In Search of Canadian Liberalism* (Toronto: Macmillan Co. of Canada Ltd., 1960); and James Laxer and Robert Laxer, *The Liberal Idea of Canada: Pierre Trudeau and the Question of Canada's Survival* (Toronto: Lorimer, 1977). The British philosopher L.T. Hobhouse is often acclaimed for his contribution to development of the "New Liberalism," that is, the rejection of the *laissez-faire* approach for the new approach through state social policy and regulatory power. See John W. Seaman's assessment in "L.T. Hobhouse and the Theory of Social Liberalism," *Canadian Journal of Political Science* 11 (1978), 777-801. For a trenchant criticism of both liberalism and the federal Liberal party, see George P. Grant, *Lament for a Nation: The Defeat of Canadian Nationalism* (Toronto: McClelland and Stewart Ltd., 1965).

Lieutenant-governor. The representative of the Crown in each of the Canadian provinces. The lieutenant-governors act virtually always on the advice of their provincial ministers, the Executive Council (provincial cabinet). See *Crown prerogatives*. However, the lieutenant-governor's office is a federal one. The governor general-in-council appoints a lieutenant-governor for five-year terms, removable only for cause communicated to the governor general and to Parliament in writing. The Canadian Parliament also pays the lieutenant-governors' salaries (British North America Act, Sections 58-60). The BNA Act prohibits provincial legislatures from legislating with respect to the office of lieutenant-governor (92:1). Under Sections 56 and 90, lieutenant-governors have the right to refuse royal assent to provincial legislation and to "reserve" the legislation for consideration by the governor-in-council. While there are no legal restraints upon the powers of reservation, these powers have not been serious limitations on provincial authorities recently. The last case occurred in Saskatchewan in 1961, and the lieutenant-governor did not fare well in that episode. Since 1970, the federal government has indicated that a revised constitution would not include the powers of reservation. See *Governor General; Reservation (of provincial legislation).*

See J.R. Mallory, "The Lieutenant-Governors' Discretionary Powers," *Canadian Journal of Economics and Political Science* 27 (1961), 518-21. On the office generally, see John T. Saywell, *The Office of Lieutenant-Governor* (Toronto: University of Toronto Press, 1957).

Lieutenant-governor-in-council. The formal constitutional body through which a provincial cabinet (formally the Executive Council) exercises executive power. The lieutenant-governor appoints the council, or the Government-of-the-day. Thus, the lieutenant-governor-in-council is the lieutenant-governor acting on the advice of the cabinet; and the executive instrument of the lieutenant-governor-in-council is the order-in-council, or a minute of the council. The lieutenant-governor does not attend cabinet meetings, but signs the orders or minutes which are sent to him or her from cabinet.

Lobby. While "the lobby" is an area adjacent to a legislative chamber, where legislators and guests may meet, "a lobby" usually refers to people who individually or collectively seek to influence legislators or other decision-makers in the executive and the administration of government (lobbying). A lobbyist is a person whose business is to advance the interest of clients in representations to parliamentarians and government officials. In the United States, the weak party system, separation of powers, and the large and diffuse administration make lobbying a crucial and pervasive part of the political system. By contrast, Canada's disciplined party and parliamentary systems, along with the compactness and cohesiveness of the administration, result in less initiative and control by lobbyists.

In Canada, parliamentarians and former parliamentarians, former ministerial executive aides, and former civil servants have been known to act as lobbyists or "management consultants" in Ottawa. If a single industry is important in an MP's constituency, the MP may – party discipline and possible conflict-of-interest legislation (see *Independence-of-Parliament Bill*) notwithstanding – represent the interests of that industry. Senators, who are not electorally accountable and who hold office until 75 years of age, have also been known to represent interests before government officials. Such lobbying may be carried out in the context of lawyer-client relationships (see Colin Campbell, *The Canadian Senate: A Lobby from Within* [Toronto: Macmillan Co. of Canada Ltd., 1978]; and John McMenemy, "Influence and Party Activity in the Senate: A Matter of Conflict of Interest?" in Paul W. Fox [ed.], *Politics: Canada* [4th ed.; Toronto: McGraw-Hill Ryerson Ltd., 1976] 454-61). See *Interest groups.*

Lord Durham's Report. A report on the affairs of British North America following the rebellions in Upper and Lower Canada in 1837. It is described by R. MacGregor Dawson as "the greatest constitutional document in British colonial history" (*The Government of Canada* [5th ed., rev. by Norman Ward; Toronto: University of Toronto Press, 1970], 12). The *Report* recommended the reunion of the two Canadas and the granting of responsible government. The imperial government acted expeditiously on the first recommendation. However, the second recommendation, which was greeted favourably by the Reformers, was not acted upon.

The most famous passage from the *Report* bears on the first recommendation: "I expected to find a contest between a government and a people," wrote Durham. "I found two nations warring in the bosom of a single state; I found a struggle, not of principles but of races; and I perceived that it would be idle to attempt any amelioration of laws or institutions until we could first succeed in terminating the deadly animosity that now separates the inhabitants of Lower Canada into the hostile divisions of French and English" (*Report on the Affairs of British North America*, Sir C.P. Lucas [ed.], [Oxford: Clarendon Press, 1912], II, 16. By permission of Oxford University Press.) Clearly, Durham's expectation was that the reunion of the two Canadas would result in the absorption of the French society by the British. "I have little doubt," Durham said, "that the French, when once placed . . . in a minority would abandon their vain hopes of nationality" (*ibid.*, 307).

On responsible government, Durham wrote: "it was a vain delusion to imagine that . . . a body [legislature], strong in the consciousness of wielding the public opinion of the majority . . . could look on as a passive or indifferent spectator, while [its] laws were carried into effect or evaded, and the whole business of the country was conducted by men [executive], in whose intentions or capacity it had not the slightest confidence" (76-77).

The imperial government united Upper and Lower Canada by the Act of Union of 1840. Responsible government, however, did not come to the province of Canada until 1848, and then by custom and usage. See *Bicultural cleavage; Responsible government.*

Lower Canada.   A political entity which existed in British North America from 1791 to 1840, and in which the French-speaking population outnumbered the British. Under the Quebec Act of 1774: the colony extended west to include land between the Ohio and Mississippi Rivers; and the political system included provisions for freedom of worship and the right of Roman Catholics to hold public office, and for the use of civil law on non-criminal matters unless changed by the colony. In 1791, the Constitutional Act divided Quebec into Upper and Lower Canada and continued the protection for French law and society in Lower Canada. The possibility for French survival was enhanced, because the population of Lower Canada (unlike that of Upper Canada) was predominantly French. In 1840, the Act of Union reunited the two Canadas once again, partly in a vain attempt to absorb the French into the English-speaking community. See *Lord Durham's Report.*

Lower House.   In a bicameral legislature, the electorally accountable and more representative chamber. In Canada's bicameral Parliament, the lower house is the House of Commons, to which 282 MPs are elected, each to represent one constituency. See *House of Commons.*

M

MHA/MLA/MNA/MPP.   Initials designating elected members of provincial legislatures: member of the house of assembly, MHA; member of the legislative assembly, MLA; member of the national assembly, MNA; member of the provincial parliament, MPP.

MP.   Initials designating the elected members of the House of Commons: member of Parliament, MP. See *Member of Parliament.*

"Maîtres Chez Nous".   "Masters in our own House," a slogan of the Liberal Government in Quebec in the 1960's, expressing the assertive statism associated with French nationalism and the Quiet Revolution. See *Quiet Revolution.*

Majority government.   A government formed by a party which holds the majority of seats in the legislature. Of course, majority governments are less likely to be found in competitive multi-party than in two-party systems. From 1921 – when a multi-party system developed in Canada – to 1980, eleven of Canada's 20 Governments were majority governments. However, half of these 20 Governments have occurred since 1957, and only four of them have been majority governments. In other words, the dominant Liberal party constituted a "national" party in a multi-party system from 1935 to 1957; but since then, no party has achieved support from across the country sufficiently strong to form comparable long-lasting majority administrations.

Malapportionment.   A situation in which the population of constituencies is significantly unequal; this usually results in a particular bias favourable to one party. Malapportionment is usually tolerated on an urban-rural basis because rural constituencies tend to contain far fewer people than urban constituencies. Thus, using the representation by population criterion, the rural population is overrepresented. Malapportionment favours political parties with a rural base of support, and unfairness has been more prevalent at the provincial than at the federal level. The boundaries of constituencies are redrawn every decade in an attempt to deal in part with malapportionment caused by patterns of population growth and mobility. See *Electoral boundaries readjustment.*

Mandarin(ate).   An informal and somewhat pejorative reference to senior civil servants, implying cohesiveness, power, and privilege allegedly reminiscent of the traditional class of imperial Chinese officialdom.

Manitoba Schools Question.   The controversy which followed the abolition of Catholic and French-language education in Manitoba in 1890. Because the schools existed before Confederation, they were to be guaranteed by the British North America Act. When the provincial government refused the federal Conservative Government's request to redress minority rights, Prime Minister Sir MacKenzie Bowell introduced remedial legislation in Parliament in 1896. The Liberals, led by Wilfrid Laurier, a Quebec-based French Canadian, prevented passage of the legislation, arguing that it infringed on provincial rights. When in power, Laurier struck a compromise with the provincial government which protected the minority only temporarily. Earlier, in 1879, the lieutenant-governor of Manitoba had reserved a measure to abolish the printing of public documents in French. In 1889, the government passed an order-in-council ending the publication of the *Manitoba Gazette* in French. The Official Language Act of 1890 abolished French as a language of the courts and of the legislature (that is, the provincial government).

In 1959, Frank Scott, a constitutional lawyer, had observed that the Manitoba action and the failure of Parliament to enact remedial legislation weakened the position of the English language in Quebec (*Civil Liberties and Canadian Federalism* [Toronto: University of Toronto Press, 1959], 32). In 1978, Quebec abolished English as an official language in the province. Later that year, the Quebec Court of Appeals overturned the abolition of English as a language of the courts and the legislature. In 1979, the Manitoba Court of Appeals declared the abolition of French in the courts and the legislature to be a violation of the constitutional federal statute, the Manitoba Act of 1870. Later in 1979 the Supreme Court of Canada sustained the decisions of both courts. The Court's action, however, did not pertain to the language of instruction in the schools. See *Bicultural cleavage; Bill 101 (Charter of the French Language)*.

Maritime union.   A long-standing idea to amalgamate the provinces of New Brunswick, Nova Scotia, and Prince Edward Island. As a practical matter, union has not been high on the public agenda since the 1860's, when a conference was held in Charlottetown to discuss the matter. An unofficial delegation from Canada caused the subject of Maritime union to be replaced by a discussion of the wider union including Canada. Later sessions in Charlottetown resulted in a decision to hold a conference in Quebec on the larger union and postpone discussion of Maritime union. Ultimately, the larger union took place. While Maritime union is not now a foreseeable event, some functional interdependence has been achieved as a result of negotiations since the 1960's. For example, the Council of Maritime Premiers was established by statute in 1971, partly as a result of a recommendation of the (Deutsch) Report on Maritime Union in 1965, which recommended amalgamation of the three provinces. See *Council of Maritime Premiers*.

Marketing boards. A reference usually to the co-operative and compulsory marketing of agricultural products in the country. However, regulatory agencies, such as the federal National Energy Board and the Canadian Transport Commission, are in part marketing boards although not producer-managed. The regulation of the marketing of products within a province is a provincial matter (British North America Act, 92:13, "Property and Civil Rights," 92:16, "Generally all Matters of a merely local or private Nature . . . ," and other sections with particular regard to natural resources), but it comes under federal jurisdiction when the marketing becomes interprovincial or international (Section 91:2, "Regulation of Trade and Commerce"). Important contemporary cases decided by the Supreme Court include a reference on Ontario's Farm Products Marketing Act, 1957, and the so-called Chicken and Egg Reference (*Attorney-General for Manitoba* v. *Manitoba Egg and Poultry Association,* 1971). Attempts to delegate powers in marketing from Parliament to a provincial legislature, or vice versa, have been declared unconstitutional by the courts. The courts, however, later accepted as constitutional the delegation of federal power to a provincial administrative agency (Nova Scotia Interdelegation Case, 1951; *P.E.I. Potato Marketing Board* v. *H.B. Willis Inc.,* 1952). The problem of delegated jurisdiction is one matter dealt with in federal-provincial constitutional proposals in the 1960's and 1970's. See *"Trade and Commerce" power.*

Mass media of communication. A reference to television, radio, newspapers and magazines, and film as intermediaries between the public and politicians. Social scientists usually assume that the media are not neutral, and scholarly inquiries pursue the question of bias on the part of both the transmitters and the receivers of information. The concern is to discover systematic and hence predictable (as opposed to accidental) patterns of bias or distortion. Observing that most of the mass media in Canada are in the private sector, some people identify a right-wing, ideological bias to the media, while others attribute a conservative economic bias. Also, because there are no national newspapers in Canada and because Canadians tend to read either the English- or French-language daily press, and listen to or watch either English- or French-language news programming, the communication system reinforces the geographic and cultural cleavages in Canada. See *Alberta Press Bill Reference; Canadian Broadcasting Corporation (Radio-Canada); Canadian Radio-Television and Telecommunications Commission.*

On the mass media, see Wallace Clement, *The Canadian Corporate Elite: An Analysis of Economic Power* (Toronto: McClelland and Stewart Ltd., Carleton Library, No. 89, 1975); and Conrad Winn, "Mass Communications," in C. Winn and J. McMenemy, *Political Parties in Canada* (Toronto: McGraw-Hill, Ryerson Ltd., 1976), 129-50. See also Carol Charlebois, "The Structure of Federal-Provincial News," a paper presented to the annual meeting of the Canadian Political Science Association, 1977; Arthur Siegel, "French and English Broadcasting in Canada: A Political Evaluation," *Canadian Journal of Communication* 5 (1979), 1–17; and Walter C. Soderlund, Ronald H. Wagenberg, E. Donald Briggs, and Ralph C. Nelson, "Regional and Linguistic Agenda-setting in Canada: A Study of Newspaper Coverage of Issues Affecting Political Integration in 1976," *Canadian Journal of Political Science* 13 (1980), 347–56.

Means test.   Any regulatory device which distinguishes those who are eligible for a social benefit which is not "universal." Tests which require proof of eligibility before one can receive the benefit are generally considered anathema, because they have often required people to declare their poverty and they involve high administrative costs. User fees in such public programmes as medicare are effectively a means test, as level of income will determine usage. Far more popular a means test is to make the benefit universally available but taxable (and hence, given a progressive income tax system, recapturable from those with high incomes).

Medicare.   A popular term for the universal, comprehensive, public medical insurance plans operated on a shared-cost basis between the federal and provincial governments. In 1962, when medicare was introduced by the CCF Government in Saskatchewan, most doctors in the province withdrew their services from the public. In 1968, a federal Medical Care Act set standards by which the provinces would qualify for federal shared-cost funding. By 1972, all provinces had medicare plans which met the criteria. Because of rising provincial costs, the federal government imposed a ceiling in 1976 on the growth of federal payments for medicare. Under the Fiscal Arrangements and Established Programmes Financing Act of 1977, the federal government abolished many costly shared-cost programmes and now contributes to provincial medicare schemes through equalized tax point abatements. By 1980, some provinces had allowed underfinancing of their medicare plan, leading effectively to the proliferation of user fees and a potentially less than universal programme. See *Federal-provincial tax-sharing agreements*.

For an analysis of decisions which Malcolm G. Taylor considers crucial to the development of universal public health insurance in Canada, see his *Health Insurance and Canadian Public Policy: The Seven Decisions That Created the Canadian Health Insurance System* (Montreal: McGill-Queen's University Press, 1978).

Member of Parliament. The members of the House of Commons elected in single-member constituencies. Paradoxically, while MPs are probably the most widely recognized link between the public and the federal government, their actual role in determining public policy is at best minimal. Members of Parliament do not represent a cross-section of the population in terms of ethnicity, education, and occupation. British Canadians and French Canadians, Protestants, and high-status Canadians tend to be "overrepresented." MPs as a group have high levels of formal education and many are lawyers. Because MPs are elected in constituencies whose boundaries are objectively related to population distribution, most MPs come from the densely populated parts of the country. Also, MPs are nearly all male and predominantly middle-aged.

Most MPs are elected on a party "label." In recent years, Liberal MPs have tended to be French, Catholic, central Canadian, and very high status; Conservative MPs, of British origin, Protestant, periphery-based, and high status; New Democratic party MPs, of British origin, from west of Quebec, and less high status than the former; and Social Credit MPs from 1962 to 1980, French, Catholic, from rural areas of Quebec, and the least high status of all party MPs.

In recent years, very few MPs have had prior political experience in public office, although they have had local office-holding experience in their party. While some MPs have held parliamentary office for lengthy periods, the career of an MP is usually short-lived. Electoral defeat is the most common reason for an MP to leave the House. Government MPs may be offered a post-parliamentary career in the public service; Opposition MPs and less fortunate Government MPs usually return quietly to their private careers – often law, as noted above.

MPs do not as a group have a large impact on policy-making. The parliamentary system and the disciplined party system necessarily relegate MPs to a predictable and theatrical "reactive" role to Government policies, which are determined in private by the cabinet and the senior civil service. Government MPs will support the Government;

Opposition MPs will criticize it. Some MPs, especially on the Government side, therefore claim that their impact on policy debate and determination occurs in the private meetings of the parliamentary party caucus. Otherwise, the MPs' representative role is more often that of redressing constituents' grievances with some administrative body. See *Caucus; House of Commons; Parliamentary indemnity; Parliamentary privilege (immunities)*.

On members of Parliament, see David Hoffman and Norman Ward, *Bilingualism and Biculturalism in the Canadian House of Commons* (Royal Commission on Bilingualism and Biculturalism, Study No.3 [Ottawa, 1970]); Norman Ward, *The Canadian House of Commons: Representation* (2nd ed.; Toronto: University of Toronto Press, 1963); Allan Kornberg, *Canadian Legislative Behavior: A Study of the 25th Parliament* (New York: Holt, Rinehart and Winston, 1967); Robert Presthus, *Elite Accommodation in Canadian Politics* (Toronto: Macmillan Co. of Canada Ltd., 1974); and John Porter, *The Vertical Mosaic: An Analysis of Social Class and Power in Canada* (Toronto: University of Toronto Press, 1965).

Merit system (in the public service).   The principle of recruiting and promoting career civil servants on the basis of objective and public standards. Prior to 1918, the federal civil service was based on patronage appointments by the party in power. Since then, the Public Service Commission has been responsible in the main for promotion, recruitment, and discipline in the federal administration (except at the most senior levels and in certain crown corporations and agencies). The only recent intrusion of note by the government into the realm of appointment and promotion with respect to the merit system and the Commission has been related to the provisions of the Official Languages Act of 1969. The "free" operations of the merit system tended in this century to create a unilingual, predominantly anglophone federal administration. During the 1970's, there was an effort to attract French Canadians to the federal public service by creating unilingual French-speaking units and rewarding bilingualism among civil servants and would-be appointees. See *Bilingualism and biculturalism; Official Languages Act (1969)*.

Ministerial responsibility.   The principle that cabinet ministers are individually responsible to the legislature for actions and policies within their portfolios. Ministers are also responsible to each other and collectively to the legislature. This constitutional requirement is central to responsible government, that is, the legislature's control of the executive.

If a cabinet minister has been derelict in his or her duties, that minister may, if not supported by the prime minister, be censured by the legislature. The convention that a minister cannot be questioned on departmental responsibilities which he or she no longer holds somewhat insulates ministers and the cabinet from Opposition criticism. In a white paper on the reform of Parliament in 1979, the federal Conservative Government proposed that ministers answer questions in the House on activities involving former portfolios. This proposed responsibility, however, did not extent to former ministers sitting as backbench MPs. In the event of an effective Opposition charge against a minister, a "voluntary" resignation from the cabinet is a likely outcome. Depending on the circumstances, the withdrawal from the cabinet may be only short-lived. As long as a majority of MPs ignore an evasion of, or delinquency in, ministerial responsibility, there is no way to enforce it, at least until the next election.

In 1977, there were numerous Opposition charges in the House of Commons of lack of ministerial responsibility in supervising the activities of the security service division of the Royal Canadian Mounted Police. It was the difficulty encountered by the Conservatives, when in opposition, in asking of the Liberal solicitor general about his predecessors' activities (one of whom was still in the cabinet) with respect to the RCMP that led to the proposal in the white paper.

See T.M. Denton, "Ministerial Responsibility: A Contemporary Perspective," in Richard Schultz, Orest M. Kruhlak, and John C. Terry (eds.), *The Canadian Political Process* (3rd ed.; Toronto: Holt, Rhinehart and Winston, 1979), 344–62. See *Cabinet; Responsible government.*

Ministers (of the Crown).   Members of a cabinet whom the governor general (or a provincial lieutenant-governor) appoints on the advice of the prime minister (or provincial premier). By convention, cabinet ministers must hold seats in the legislature (in the bicameral Parliament, usually the House of Commons). Some ministerial appointments represent moves by a prime minister or premier to give cabinet representation to a particular group that may be important in electoral calculations. For example, prime ministers usually like to have a cabinet minister from each province and several from particular cities or subprovincial regions. While French Canadians have tended to be prominent in Canadian cabinets, either as prime ministers or as close confidants of anglophone prime ministers, they did not hold important economic or financial portfolios until the 1970's.

Theoretically, the legislature itself and the political party are training grounds for future ministers. However, especially since World War Two, a frequent route to the federal cabinet of Liberal Governments was from the leadership of groups outside the legislature and the party system in business, university, and public administration. Three of the five prime ministers since 1949 had little parliamentary experience before becoming cabinet ministers – and little experience, if any, as cabinet ministers before becoming party leader or prime minister. Appointment to an administrative office, the Senate, the judiciary, or a business career commonly follows a minister's exit from the cabinet. It has been rare since World War Two for federal cabinet ministers to tolerate post-cabinet careers in the backbenches of the Government or the Opposition.

Most ministers are heads of particular departments of the government and are responsible for the exercise of duties within the particular department or designated government agencies. Other ministers may be ministers with special parliamentary responsibilities, ministers of state responsible for "designated purposes" or, as an "undesignated" minister, appointed to aid a departmental minister. The prime minister or premier may also appoint ministers without portfolio to satisfy some representative or other political requirement.

Ministers are not only accountable to the House for policy and administrative performance in their areas of designated responsibility, but are collectively responsible for government policy and administrative behaviour. Ministers are bound for life by their oath of secrecy not to discuss cabinet matters publicly and may publicly dissociate themselves from a Government policy only by resigning from the cabinet and thereby ceasing to be a minister. See *Cabinet; Cabinet organization; Collective ministerial responsibility; Executive assistants; Inner cabinet; Ministerial responsibility.*

Ministry.   A loosely used term which can refer to a particular government department, the cabinet excluding parliamentary secretaries, or (generally) the Government-of-the-day, including all executive office-holders. See *Cabinet.*

Ministry (minister) of state.   Areas of special ministerial responsibility at the federal level, each established (and disbanded) by order-in-council. Ministers of state may be appointed responsible either for "designated purposes" or, as an "undesignated" minister, to aid a departmental minister. The federal ministry-of-state system was a device established in 1970 to achieve co-ordinated policy development and implementation across departments. In 1980, for example, the ministries of state in the Liberal cabinet were for social development, economic development, science and technology, the Canadian Wheat Board, sports, multiculturalism, finance, small business, trade, and mines. In the short-lived Conservative cabinet of 1979-1980, there had been ministries of state for federal-provincial relations, science and technology, transport, international trade, Treasury Board, fitness and amateur sport and multiculturalism, and small business.

Minority government.   A government formed by a party which holds only a minority of seats in the legislature. Thus, the Government's existence depends on the support of another party or some members of another party who then hold the "balance of power." From 1900 to 1957, there were only three federal minority governments. From 1957 to 1980, however, six of the ten federal Governments were minorities. An important difference between a minority and a majority government is the relationship of the cabinet to the legislature. In the federal minority Government of 1957-1958, the electoral momentum was with the governing Conservatives. Thus, the Government "toyed" with the House of Commons until it felt it propitious to dissolve Parliament in the reasonable expectation of winning a majority. From 1962 to 1968, from 1972 to 1974, and in 1979-1980, the ruling parties possessed no comparable momentum, and the House of Commons became an effective forum for debate and potential Government defeat. The Conservative Government from 1962 to 1963 possessed the reverse qualities of the 1957-1958 Government and seemed fated to be defeated. From 1963 to 1968, the Liberal Governments could survive with the easily achieved support of a few outside MPs, while from 1972 to 1974 and in 1979-1980, the Liberal and Conservative Governments respectively had to rely on support from, or absence of votes by, Opposition MPs.

   In 1968, a parliamentary precedent was established to deal with "accidental" defeat, a high risk for minority governments. The federal Liberal Government was defeated on the third reading of a financial bill. Instead of resigning at once, Prime Minister Lester Pearson announced his intention to introduce a motion of confidence in the Government at the next sitting of the House. When the House met, the Government won the vote of confidence and thereby remained in office. In 1979, the federal Conservative Government lost a vote on the New Democratic party's sub-amendment to a Liberal amendment to a Government motion approving the budget. Prime Minister Joe Clark immediately accepted the vote as want of confidence in the Government. The following day, he advised the governor general to dissolve Parliament and issue writs for an election (which he lost).

Monetary policy. The policy of a national government or central bank in varying the amount of money in circulation and the availability of credit. One major device to achieve desired policy is the central bank's regulation of interest rates charged by banks and other financial institutions; another involves such market operations as the purchasing or selling of government securities, either to restrict or expand the amount of money in circulation. For example, to combat high rates of inflation, the central bank would act to curb the availability of credit and the flow of money. See *Bank of Canada*.

Money bills. Financial legislation which deals with the spending of money (supply) or with the raising of money (tax measures, ways and means). In Canada, only cabinet ministers can introduce money bills; and in the bicameral Parliament, money bills must be introduced first in the elected House of Commons. While the power of the appointed Senate to amend money bills is debatable, the Senate may not increase the sums. This treatment of money bills reflects the historic relationship of Parliament to the Crown, which can raise and spend revenue only with the legislature's approval. The legislative voting of supply (or its denial) is the important foundation of responsible government. See *Budgetary process; Estimates; Legislation; Responsible government.*

Movement parties. Political parties which are created in society outside the parliamentary environment in times of social stress and crisis. In the first half of the twentieth century, such parties were a response to the failure of the established parliamentary parties to deal effectively with serious social tensions associated with immigration and with western settlement, and economic dislocation. Such parties usually combine educational and electoral activities, stressing mass involvement in party affairs and a desire to alter radically some aspects of the economic and political order. Some movement parties (such as the Social Credit party) may be classified as populist and leader-oriented; others, for whom their redistributive ideology is more important (such as the Co-operative Commonwealth Federation, now the New Democratic party) are socialist.

The disciplined party, parliamentary, and federal systems in Canada have encouraged and sustained movement parties. The disciplined party system, which requires members of Parliament to vote along party lines, encourages disaffection among sectional representatives who may be in a permanent minority. The rise of the so-called "third parties" in the Canadian West was caused in part by the central Canadian dominance of the federal Conservative and Liberal parties. The focus of elections in a parliamentary system is the numerous constituency elections. The election of only a handful of members legitimizes a party by giving it a parliamentary forum in which to criticize the Government and represents a base of operation for further electoral gains. The federal system also legitimizes sectional elites in the provincial political systems. The early and sustained success of both the Social Credit and the CCF-NDP as well as their precursors in various farmer movements was in provincial political arenas in the Canadian West and in Ontario. See *Co-operative Commonwealth Federation; Social Credit party; Ralliement des Créditistes; Third parties.*

Multiculturalism.   Policy associated with the federal Liberal Government in the 1970's, which supports the expression of the cultural heritage of ethnic groups, notably other than British and French-Canadian. The policy of promoting multiculturalism was formally a recognition and encouragement of the cultural mosaic of Canadian society. However, the programme was designed in political terms to sustain traditional electoral support of these ethnic communities for the Liberal party, especially in view of widespread disaffection among these groups with the special attention given francophones under the policy of "bilingualism and biculturalism." While most federal support is channeled through the secretary of state, a ministry of state for multiculturalism has existed during the 1970's.

N

National assembly (Quebec).   The unicameral provincial legislature of Quebec. From 1867 to 1968, the legislature had been styled the legislative assembly. The change of name illustrates the assertive nationalism associated with the Quiet Revolution of the 1960's.

National director (Liberal and Conservative parties).   The leading official in each of the federal Liberal and Conservative parties. Their counterpart in the New Democratic party is the federal secretary. Formally, the national director of each party is appointed by the party executive; but informally the confidence of the parliamentary leader is required for this position. These senior officials deal largely with organizational matters, but they may have influence on policy and election campaign decisions in particular circumstances. Because the Liberals and Conservatives have been traditionally less dependent on mass organization than the New Democratic party, their national directors may generally be less influential in the party elite than the New Democrats' federal secretary.

National Energy Board (NEB).   A federal board established in 1959 to regulate the oil, gas, and electrical industries and to advise the cabinet on the development and use of energy resources. The Board regulates the construction and operation of oil and gas pipelines that are under the jurisdiction of Parliament – that is, those which relate to interprovincial and international trade. The Board regulates charges for transmission and the export of crude oil and some refined products, as well as natural gas, in interprovincial and international trade. In allowing exports, the NEB must be satisfied that the quantities of energy to be exported do not exceed surplus, given foreseeable Canadian requirements. In the late 1970's, the Board recommended that exports of crude oil and petroleum products to the United States be progressively reduced, with minimum injury to those areas dependent on Canadian oil. The NEB is a court of record; its nine members are appointed by the governor-in-council for seven-year terms, and it reports to Parliament through the minister of energy, mines, and resources.

National Film Board (NFB).   A federal agency established in 1939 to produce and distribute films in the national interest, especially films "designed to interpret Canada to Canadians and to other nations." As well as producing films for government departments for specific informational purposes, the NFB is widely known for the production of documentaries and short and long features; it also encourages filmmakers to experiment in styles and techniques. The NFB also has a still-photography division. The NFB's headquarters is technically in Ottawa; however, its production studios, laboratories, administration offices, and distribution headquarters are in Montreal. Production offices exist in several other cities to encourage regional production. The NFB's board of governors consists of nine members: the Government Film Commissioner, who serves as chairman and is appointed by the governor-in-council; three members appointed from within the public service; and five members appointed from the Canadian public. The NFB reports to Parliament through the secretary of state.

National Housing Act (NHA).   Originally the Dominion Housing Act (1935), the often-amended legislation under which the federal government provides funds for housing production. Its major areas of responsibility are in: the middle- and low-price ranges and co-operative, non-profit, and public housing; residential rehabilitation and neighbourhood improvement; the elimination and prevention of water and soil pollution; land assembly for new communities; site clearance for areas outside the neighbourhood improvement areas; and mortgage assistance. The National Housing Act is designed to complement the private housing industry, rather than to assume political responsibilities in urban affairs that are under provincial jurisdiction or to take on economic responsibilities that traditionally have been part of the private sector. Many programmes under the National Housing Act require provincial agreement in order to be effective. The Canada Mortgage and Housing Corporation (CMHC) is the federal crown corporation (created in 1945) which chiefly administers the provisions of the National Housing Act. See *Canada Mortgage and Housing Corporation.*

National oil policy.   Federal policy on oil supply and pricing, which is periodically negotiated with the provinces, especially the major oil-producing province of Alberta. The policy was first established by the Conservative Government in 1961, when there was an oversupply of cheap oil. Then, the federal government assured sale of domestic oil in Canada west of the Ottawa River and in the United States, with the remainder of Canada supplied by cheaper foreign oil. In addition, federal and provincial tax concessions to the private, predominantly multinational petroleum industry bolstered the economies of the oil-producing provinces.

This policy was significantly changed when world oil prices rose dramatically in 1973 and a temporary embargo on oil shipments was established by the Arab oil-producing states. The federal Liberal Government imposed a temporary price freeze in Canada and imposed an export tax on Canadian oil equal to the difference between the domestic and world prices; this prevented "windfall" revenue either to the private oil companies or to the oil-producing provinces. Later, the federal government proposed sharing the additional revenue with those provinces. The federal government also committed itself to the completion of an oil pipeline to Montreal and a guaranteed outlet for domestic oil east of the Ottawa River. A federal-provincial conference in 1974 established the policy of a single price for oil throughout Canada, to be modified by transportation costs and the taxing policies of individual provinces. Canadian oil would be made available at a price below world levels, and the federal government would subsidize the costs of foreign oil in part through revenue from the export tax on Canadian oil.

In 1975, the federal government created Petro-Canada (Petro-Can), a crown corporation designed to participate actively in the petroleum industry. Also, Parliament passed the Petroleum Administration Act, which allows the federal cabinet to fix the price of domestic oil and gas in interprovincial trade in the absence of a negotiated agreement with the producing provinces, following Parliament's approval.

Since 1973, oil policy and other energy and resource questions have been the subject of bitter federal-provincial and interprovincial disputes. Alberta, for example, has consistently opposed the export tax on oil and the subsidized domestic price. Nonetheless, the revenue accruing to the oil-producing provinces has been so considerable that the federal government has periodically revised the formula by which equalization grants to provinces are calculated. In 1978, Ontario, which has one of the highest per capita income levels in Canada, was on the verge of qualifying as a "have-not" province. In 1979, a one-dollar-a-barrel increase in the price of domestic oil was estimated to cost the federal treasury an additional $60 million in equalization payments to all provinces except Alberta, British Columbia, and Ontario. Other post-1973 disputes include a federal proposal to end the exemption of royalties paid to provincial governments from corporate income taxable by the federal government. The government of Alberta was not sympathetic to the federal Petroleum Administration Act or to the activities of Petro-Canada.

In 1979, the federal Conservative Government (which was defeated in 1980) intended to reverse the direction of the previous Liberal Government's policy, notably its centralism. The Government was under pressure from Alberta to raise the price of domestic oil to the world level. In 1979, the Economic Council of Canada recommended that the domestic price be raised to match the world price in the 1980's. The Conservative Government also debated the future of Petro-Canada. In 1980, the federal Liberal Government proposed a strengthening of Petro-Canada, increased Canadian ownership in the private sector of the petroleum industry, and an agency to audit prices and profits in the industry. See *Natural resources; Petro-Canada; Resource rents and royalties*.

On the background of the national oil policy, see J.G. Debanne, "Oil and Canadian Policy," in Edward W. Erickson and Leonard Waverman (eds.), *The Energy Question: An International Failure of Policy*, Volume 2, *North America* (Toronto: University of Toronto Press, 1974), especially 125-36. On the changed circumstances in 1973, see Glyn R. Berry, "The Oil Lobby and the Energy Crisis," *Canadian Public Administration* 17 (1974), 600-35. See also the sixteenth annual report of the Economic Council of Canada. On the implications of oil policy for Canada's federal and provincial governments, see D.V. Smiley, *Canada in Question: Federalism in the Seventies* (2nd ed.; Toronto: McGraw-Hill Ryerson Ltd., 1976), 143–51.

National Policy (NP).   A policy for national development which Sir John A. Macdonald and the Conservative party advocated in the 1870's and 1880's; it involved railway construction, large-scale immigration and Western settlement, and an increase in the protective tariff. The NP is generally credited for the business and popular support which returned the Conservatives to power in the general election of 1878 and re-elected them in 1882.

The "nationalistes".   A political movement in the first two decades of the twentieth century; its most prominent spokesman was Henri Bourassa. The movement expressed the anxieties of French Canadians at a time when industrialization was threatening traditional French-Canadian society. The movement spoke to social and economic matters, as well as to cultural matters such as French-language rights in education and imperial foreign and military policy. Once a successful Liberal member of Parliament and a likely successor to the leader Sir Wilfrid Laurier, Bourassa and his movement eventually constituted an electoral threat to the Liberal party. The *nationalistes* and anglophone Conservatives in Quebec struck a curious anti-Liberal alliance in 1911. In the election that year, the pro-Conservative sentiment in English Canada which the reciprocity issue generated and the split vote in Quebec resulted in a majority Conservative Government. The *nationalistes* thus helped to defeat the Liberals, but they did not hold a balance of power in the House of Commons. In the following decade, French nationalist sentiment was fostered by further attacks on French-language rights in education, particularly in Ontario. However, in the polarized politics of the wartime election of 1917, French Quebeckers returned to the Liberal party. After 1917, Bourassa's influence in French-Canadian politics was restricted to journalism in the pages of *Le Devoir*, the *nationaliste* organ which Bourassa established in 1911. *Le Devoir*, the influential Montreal daily, continues to espouse nationalist sentiments in the context of a federal constitution.

On the *nationaliste* movement, see H. Blair Neatby, *Laurier and a Liberal Quebec: A Study in Political Management* (Toronto: McClelland and Stewart Ltd., 1973); Joseph Levitt, *Henri Bourassa and the Golden Calf: The Social Programme of the* Nationalistes *of Quebec, 1900-1914* (Ottawa: les Editions de l'Université d'Ottawa, 1968); and Robert Craig Brown and Ramsay Cook, *Canada: 1896-1921: A Nation Transformed* (Toronto: McClelland and Stewart Ltd., 1974), 127-43. On the 1911 election, see J. Murray Beck, *Pendulum of Power: Canada's Federal Election* (Scarborough: Prentice-Hall of Canada Ltd., 1968), 120-35.

Natural resources.   Commodities involving "Lands, Mines, Minerals, and Royalties," which, within the provinces, are under provincial jurisdiction (British North America Act, Section 109). Provincial jurisdiction is also assured under Sections: 92:5 ("The Management and Sale of the Public Lands belonging to the Province ... "); 92:13 ("Property and Civil Rights"); and 92:16 ("Generally all Matters of a merely local or private Nature . . . "). Of contemporary importance are resources such as oil, gas, and water, which are related to energy. Provincial jurisdiction means provincial power to determine the manner in which the resources are developed and to determine the prices that will be charged for the resources in the province. Under the "Trade and Commerce" clause (Section 91:2) and "Works and Undertakings ... extending beyond the Limits of the Province" (Section 92:10[a]), the federal government can regulate the conditions under which the resource commodities (once they are made available) move beyond a province in interprovincial and international trade. Thus, the volume, price, and means of transportation of oil and natural gas, for example, are subject to federal control when they are moving across provincial and international borders. On the one hand, the federal government is prohibited from taxing public land and property owned by the provinces (Section 125); but, on the other hand, it could use its declaratory power (Section 92:10[c]) or emergency powers under the "Peace, Order and good Government" clause (preamble, Section 91) to nationalize a resource industry. The federal government has exclusive jurisdiction over natural resources in the territories. In 1967, the Supreme Court declared off-shore mineral rights on the west coast to be under federal jurisdiction. Although the question of jurisdiction on the east coast was not determined, the brief federal Conservative Government in 1979 was prepared to relinquish claims to rights off the shores of Newfoundland.

Since the steep rise in world oil prices in the 1970's, the debate over natural resources and energy policy has become a major concern in Canada, because the Canadian economy and society have been used to an abundant supply of cheap energy. Apart from the question of jurisdiction, the debate has touched on the distribution of wealth, regional disparities and equalization agreements, foreign ownership in the Canadian economy, the appropriate role of the state in economic enterprises, the rights of native peoples, conservation of energy, and preservation of the environment. See *National oil policy*.

On the question of jurisdiction over natural resources, see A.R. Thompson and H.R. Eddy, "Jurisdictional Problems in Natural Resource Management in Canada," in W.D. Bennett et al., *Essays on Aspects of Resource Policy* (Ottawa: Science Council of Canada, 1973).

New Deal (R.B. Bennett's).   Social welfare and marketing legislation which Prime Minister R.B. Bennett's Conservative Government proposed in 1935 to "ensure a greater degree of equality in the distribution of the capitalistic system" (Speech from the Throne). The New Deal legislation was announced in the final year of Bennett's Government. It is usually interpreted as a last-minute gambit to save the Government from electoral defeat. Some have interpreted it in part as an example of Red Tory politics in Canada. Bennett announced the programme in radio speeches written by close aides and without the knowledge of most of the cabinet.

Following the election of 1935, Liberal Prime Minister William Lyon Mackenzie King referred eight of the New Deal measures to the courts to test their constitutionality. In 1937, the Judicial Committee of the Privy Council invalidated five of the statutes; they related to hours of work, holidays, minimum wages (*Attorney-General for Canada* v. *Attorney-General for Ontario* [Labour Conventions Case]), and unemployment insurance (*Attorney-General for British Columbia* v. *Attorney-General for Canada*).

The judicial decisions involved narrow interpretations of: federal power to implement treaties (British North America Act, Section 132); federal emergency powers under the "Peace, Order and good Government" clause (Section 91); and federal power in "Trade and Commerce" (Section 91:2). Concomitantly, the judicial decisions strengthened provincial legislative competence under "Property and Civil Rights" (Section 92:13). See *Judicial Committee of the Privy Council.*

New Democracy.   A political party founded in 1939 by W.D. Herridge, the brother-in-law and confidant of former Conservative Prime Minister R.B. Bennett. This left-wing fragment of the Conservative party fielded only a few candidates in Ontario and the West in the general election of 1940. The party was linked with the Social Credit party in Alberta and received only token support outside that province. Herridge lost his own constituency contest in Saskatchewan. See *Fragment party.*

On the New Democracy, see Mary Hallett, "The Social Credit Party and the New Democracy Movement: 1939-1940," *Canadian Historical Review* 47 (1966), 301-25.

New Democratic party (NDP).   Founded in 1961, the social democratic successor to the socialist Co-operative Commonwealth Federation (CCF). The New Democratic party's programme is based on the Winnipeg Declaration of 1956, which professes a mild reformism dedicated to improving the quality of life through government regulation of the economy. The organization of the NDP was also designed to facilitate greater involvement in the party by trade unions; it was hoped that this would gain electoral support among the younger, self-perceived upwardly mobile population of urban Canada.

The party has been more successful than the CCF. Its gains, however, have been in provincial rather than in federal politics. The party has formed Governments in British Columbia, Saskatchewan, and Manitoba, and it has been the official Opposition in Ontario. In federal elections, the party has fared better in popular vote percentages than the CCF; however, NDP has never gained more than 20 per cent of the vote. From 1972 to 1974, it held the balance of power during a minority Liberal Government.

Traditional federal voting habits and the weak perception of the party (compared to that of the Liberal and Conservative parties) on the powerful bicultural cleavage partly explain the NDP's weak federal performance. Also, since the 1960's, the Conservative party has tended to share the support of "aggrieved" westerners on the geographic cleavage, a source of political tension from which the NDP (and the CCF before it) has traditionally benefitted. The strongest perception of the NDP is that of a left-wing party on the class cleavage. Class-based issues and support for the NDP, however, tend to be more prevalent in provincial politics – where matters such as resource development, housing, medicare and hospital insurance, and labour law assist the New Democratic party in particular provinces. In the 1970's, the federal NDP hoped to benefit from disaffection with federal wage and price controls policy, resource development, and the domination of foreign ownership in the economy. In the federal election campaigns of 1979 and 1980, the Canadian Labour Congress encouraged close involvement with the NDP campaign. Analysis of election survey data may determine the effect of this support. See *Co-operative Commonwealth Federation; Movement parties; Waffle, the.*

On the New Democratic party, see Desmond Morton, *NDP: Social Democracy in Canada* (2nd ed.; Sarasota: S. Stevens, 1977). The first edition was titled *NDP: The Dream of Power* (Toronto: Hakkert, 1974). See also Ivan Avakumovic, *Socialism in Canada: A Study of the CCF-NDP in Federal and Provincial Politics* (Toronto: McClelland and Stewart Ltd., 1978). For a series of party-sponsored essays published when the NDP was founded, see Michael Oliver (ed.), *Social Purpose for Canada* (Toronto: University of Toronto Press, 1961).

North American Air Defence Command (NORAD). An integrated United States-Canada continental air-defence system involving military surveillance and warning systems, anti-submarine defences, and protection of the retaliatory nuclear force of the United States. The NORAD agreement (which was designed for protection against the Soviet Union) was negotiated by the Liberal Government in the 1950's and signed by the Conservative Government in 1957. The Liberal Government reaffirmed the agreement in 1975 for a further five years without a parliamentary debate. The agreement calls for a joint command headed by an American, with a Canadian deputy commander. It represents a culmination of military collaboration with the United States which began in 1940.

North Atlantic Treaty Organization (NATO). A military alliance involving Canada, the United States, and 13 European countries; it was designed for mutual defence against the Soviet Union and its European allies. In the early years following NATO's creation in 1949, Canada attempted unsuccessfully to promote non-military functions within the alliance (Article 2). Some critics have opposed Canada's involvement in NATO as contributing to the cold-war environment, while critics on the other side of the issue have described as insufficient Canada's commitment of forces in Europe and national defence generally. Earlier federal governments defended Canada's involvement in NATO with reference to maintaining good relations with the United States and opposing the expansion of communism in Europe. In recent years, the government has rationalized support for NATO by arguing that some military involvement in Europe is necessary in order to benefit from economic, scientific, and technological relations with Europe.

Northwest (Riel) Rebellion.   Armed revolts by Métis and Indians in the Saskatchewan area of the Northwest Territories in the 1880's. In 1869-1870, the Red River uprising led by Louis Riel resulted in the declaration of a provisional government of Manitoba, the taking of prisoners, and the execution of an officer from Ontario. As an expeditionary force approached Fort Garry (Winnipeg), the insurrection collapsed and Riel fled. Parliament established the province of Manitoba in 1870. Riel was elected to the House of Commons in 1874, but was prevented by other MPs from taking his seat. In 1875, he was granted amnesty and exiled for five years. He returned to lead another rebellion in the 1880's in an area of present-day Saskatchewan. The Métis wanted the Canadian government to give them recognition and representation as a province, and to acknowledge their right to the land. Several engagements took place between the rebels and government troops. Riel surrendered, was tried, found guilty, and sentenced to death for treason.

Riel's fate created a political storm in Ontario and Quebec. Anti-Catholic Ontario Protestants demanded his execution. French Catholics saw Riel as a hero, defending French Catholic communities from English encroachment. Under extreme pressure from Ontario supporters, Conservative Prime Minister Sir John A. Macdonald, assuming that Quebec's support for his Government would hold, refused to stay Riel's execution. Riel himself refused to plead insanity in order to avoid the death penalty. The prime minister could not overcome the bitterness engendered in Quebec by Riel's death in 1885. Nor did Riel's death diminish the extreme anti-Catholic, anti-French sentiment among Macdonald's supporters in Ontario. In the federal election of 1887, Conservative representation from Quebec was drastically reduced. In the same year, Wilfrid Laurier, who had publicly sympathized with the rebels, became leader of the Liberal party. These events and others preceded the historic switch of support among French Canadians from the federal Conservative party to the federal Liberal party in the 1890's. In recent years, some westerners have sought to portray Riel and the other rebels as early heroes in an ongoing struggle on the prairie West against central Canadian domination.

On Riel, see Thomas Flanagan, *Louis "David" Riel: "Prophet of the New World"* (Toronto: University of Toronto Press, 1979).

O

Occupational representation. Electoral representation in legislatures by occupational groups, rather than by conventional political parties. This non-party theory of representation was popular among western farmers in the early twentieth century. Supporters of occupational representation then saw the conventional disciplined party system as representative only of those business interests which financed the established parties, and not of the electors who elected the members to the legislature. See *Delegate theory of representation.*

October Crisis (1970). The kidnapping for ransom under the threat of death of a British trade commissioner and of a provincial cabinet minister in Montreal by two cells of the *Front de libération du Québec* (FLQ) – an action which led to the declaration of an "apprehended insurrection" by the federal Government and the invocation of the War Measures Act. Shortly after the Act was invoked, the Quebec minister was killed by his captors. The police found the location of the British official shortly afterwards and negotiated his release in return for the safe passage overseas of his kidnappers. Judicial proceedings took place against members of both cells, most recently upon the return of some exiles in 1979. While the "Crisis" generated no support for the terrorists, the federal Government itself was subsequently criticized for invoking the War Measures Act in peacetime. The Government provided no evidence to indicate that the eventual location and apprehension of the kidnappers and murderers depended on using the extraordinary powers of the Act. The cabinet's subsequent attempts to replace the Act with a less overwhelming and volatile public order bill failed. See *War Measures Act.*

On the October Crisis, see Ron Haggart and Aubrey Golden, *Rumours of War* (Toronto: New Press, 1971); Gérard Pelletier (trans. by Joyce Marshall), *The October Crisis* (Toronto: McClelland and Stewart Ltd., 1971); Abraham Rotstein (ed.), *Power Corrupted: The October Crisis and the Repression of Quebec* (Toronto: New Press, 1971); and Dennis Smith, *Bleeding Hearts – Bleeding Country: Canada and the Quebec Crisis* (Edmonton: Hurtig, 1971).

Official agent (party; candidate). Under election finance legislation, the person designated responsible for maintaining proper accounts of candidate and party finances. Federal legislation, for example, allows for limited tax credit for financial contributions to registered parties and their candidates. It also defines and limits election expenses, requires the filing of returns accounting for election contributions and expenses, and allows for the reimbursement of candidates. The agent is legally responsible for adherence to the law. See *Election expenses (controls; subsidies)*.

Official Languages Act (1969).   The federal statute which declares French and English to be official languages of Canada and under which the use of both languages in the federal public service is specified. The Act requires the establishment of a Bilingual District Advisory Board following each census. This board determines the boundaries of districts in which the services of the Canadian government will be provided in both languages. Such areas must contain a linguistic French- or English-speaking minority of 10 per cent or be in an area where, if the minority is less than 10 per cent, the services were customarily available in both languages. The Act also creates the office of the Commissioner of Official Languages (language ombudsman), who is responsible for compliance with the Act. Finally, the Act encourages the provinces to follow suit.

The Act was the chief recommendation of the Royal Commission on Bilingualism and Biculturalism in 1967. While the most obvious public impact of the Act has been in the extension of the use of French, the most contentious issue for the Liberal Government was the impact of the Act on the federal public service. In the 1970's, the Government effectively reduced its goals for encouraging the use of French in the administration, and it encouraged the provinces to support second-language training. In political terms, the Official Languages Act has always had the support of all party leaders, but it has had little support among the non-francophone public. While the Act represented the general objectives of the federal Liberal Government to make French Canadians feel "at home" across Canada, French nationalism in the 1970's led to increasing unilingualism and pro-Quebec sentiment among French Canadians in that province. See *Bilingualism and biculturalism; Commissioner of Official Languages; Quiet Revolution*.

Official Opposition.   The party in the legislature which represents the alternative to the Government-of-the-day if it resigns following defeat in the legislature, or the likely alternative if the Government party is defeated in an election and resigns. Usually, but not necessarily, the official Opposition party holds the second-largest number of seats in the legislature. In 1921, the Progressives elected the second-largest number of MPs, but they refused to accept the role of official Opposition. Though the Liberals elected fewer members than the Conservatives in the 1925 federal election, the Liberal Government remained in office with the support of the third-ranking Progressives; the first-ranking Conservatives were the official Opposition.

All parties other than the Government party are generally known as "the Opposition," but the official Opposition party holds specific financial and procedural advantages over the other opposition parties. At the federal level, for example, the leader of the official Opposition has a publicly owned and financed residence and receives the salary of a cabinet minister. His or her office and party receive more money for research purposes than the other opposition parties; and, of great importance in parliamentary debate, the official Opposition party's questions, motions, and amendments to Government motions take precedence in debate over those of the smaller opposition parties.

Official Secrets Act (1939). Federal legislation which prohibits the private possession, distribution, and publication of information which is prejudicial to the interests of the state. The Act was passed in the pre-World War Two months of 1939, to deal with the activities of "foreign powers" in Canada.

As the Act stood in 1979, it did not define prejudicial information or "official secrets." Indeed, some sections of the Act, under which charges might be laid, did not require the demonstration of prejudice. The Act also allowed for trials on charges under it to be held *in camera* and included presumption in favour of the Crown. Prosecutions under the Act, however, could take place only with the approval of the attorney-general of Canada.

In 1978, charges were laid for the first reported time against an editor and publisher of a metropolitan newspaper. They were accused of publishing an allegedly secret report by the Royal Canadian Mounted Police on espionage activities in Canada. The defendants were found not guilty. In 1979, a conviction obtained in a secret trial of a person charged with unlawful and careless possession of documents was overturned.

In 1979, the House of Commons accepted a motion by Gerald Baldwin, a private member, to have a committee examine recent prosecutions under the Act, and to deny the cabinet any claim of crown privilege to limit the extent of the inquiry. The Conservative Government also introduced a freedom-of-information bill in 1979. However, both the parliamentary inquiry and the legislation died when Parliament was dissolved later that year.

There has been pressure from other sources to amend the Act. In 1979, the Law Reform Commission of Canada published a report which was critical of the broadly drafted Act. In the same year, the Canadian Civil Liberties Association recommended to a federal commission investigating the Royal Canadian Mounted Police that criminal sanctions be retained only on the disclosure of information that might reasonably be expected to "create a serious injury to the physical safety and defence of Canada." The Association would also require the relevant cabinet minister to establish the need to classify the material secret for safety and defence purposes. The group further recommended that reception of secret documents no longer be an offence. See *Freedom-of-Information Act.*

Oil, Chemical, and Atomic Workers Case, 1963.   A ruling of the Supreme Court on the political rights of trade unions, which illustrates the lack of constitutional clarity on civil liberties. In this case, the Supreme Court upheld an amendment to the British Columbia Labour Relations Act which prohibited unions from using for political purposes any funds contributed through a check-off or as a compulsory condition of union membership. This legislation had clear political motives, as Premier W.A.C. Bennett's Social Credit Government had recently been returned to office with a reduced majority, his losses being gains for the trade union-supported New Democratic party.

The majority (4-3) ruled that provincial legislatures could, under Section 91:13 of the British North America Act ("Property and Civil Rights"), attach conditions to the rights which trade unions had under provincial labour law for purposes of collective bargaining, including conditions affecting participation in federal and provincial elections. The legislation was not deemed invalid, as in the Alberta Press Bill and Quebec Padlock Law cases, because unions and their members remained free to support political parties.

Among the three dissenters on the court, only one argued that the preamble to the BNA Act, which granted Canada a constitution "similar in Principle to that of the United Kingdom," prevented either Parliament or provincial legislatures from enacting such measures. A second justice argued that the amendment was not legislation in labour relations, but in the political activity of unions, including activity in federal campaigns. A third dissenting judge observed that, as virtually all union funds came from members' dues, the legislation virtually prohibited unions from financially supporting a party. See *Alberta Press Bill Reference; Duff Doctrine; Padlock Law; Supreme Court.*

Ombudsman. A public officer, appointed by and responsible to the legislature, who investigates and reports on citizens' complaints about actions by the public administration. The concept, originally established in Scandinavia, has spread to many western parliamentary democracies, where it has been implemented in various ways. Canada's first ombudsman was appointed in Alberta in 1967. Ombudsmen now exist in most provinces. However, federal Liberal legislation to create a federal ombudsman died on the Order Paper in 1979. The federal Commissioner of Official Languages, the federal Commissioner of Human Rights (as well as the Information Commissioner as proposed in freedom-of-information legislation which died on the Order Paper in 1979) operate as ombudsmen in the context of their respective statutes.

In most models, the ombudsman has access to government files and may interview public servants. In the Scandinavian models, the ombudsmen may reverse administrative decisions. In the Canadian provincial, British, and New Zealand cases, the principle of parliamentary democracy is retained, and the ombudsmen may only make public recommendations to the legislatures. In Britain, the ombudsman may act initially only on complaints referred to that office by a member of Parliament.

Karl A. Friedman observes that, while the ombudsman originated as a legislative control device over the executive and the bureaucracy, the popular interpretation is that of the defender of the "little man" against seeming arbitrariness in large government bureaucracies. See his "The Public and the Ombudsman: Perceptions and Attitudes in Britain and in Alberta," *Canadian Journal of Political Science* 10 (1977), 497-525. See also D.C. Rowat, *The Ombudsman Plan: Essays on the World-wide Spread of an Idea* (Toronto: McClelland and Stewart Ltd., 1973); and his earlier *The Ombudsman: Citizen's Defender* (Toronto: University of Toronto Press, 1968).

One-party (single-party) dominance. A phrase denoting a party system with several parties, but with one party being historically dominant. For example, the House of Commons contained four party groups from 1935 to 1957, but Liberal majorities dominated the five parliaments during that 22-year period. One-party, or single-party-dominant, systems are prevalent currently at the provincial level. For example, the Conservative party has won office in Ontario in three-party elections since 1943, although the party has been in a minority position since 1975. The oldest one-party-dominant system is in Alberta. There, the United Farmers dominated a provincial multi-party system from 1921 to 1935. From 1935 to 1971, the Social Credit party dominated the system. Since then, the Conservative party has dominated Alberta's party system. See *Party system.*

Open-ended grants.   Federal payments provided conditionally to the provinces to finance their programmes, but without limiting the financial commitment of the federal government. Thus, federal-provincial agreements established a formula for subsidizing provincial expenditures without controlling the ultimate cost to the federal treasury. After 1965, the federal government moved away from open-ended financial commitments for such costly programmes as medical and hospital insurance and post-secondary education. First, the federal government placed limits on annual cost increases which it would subsidize; later it replaced some shared-cost conditional grant programmes with unconditional grants and equalized tax point abatements. See *Conditional grants; Federal-provincial tax-sharing agreements.*

Opening of Parliament.   The ceremonies attendant upon the beginning of a newly elected Parliament or a new session of a Parliament (in the provinces, the opening of the Legislature). Prior to a new Parliament, elected members of Parliament sign the roll and take an oath of office administered by the Clerk of the House, following their summons to Ottawa by the governor-in-council. Also prior to a new Parliament, the MPs elect a Speaker; and the Mace, the symbol of the Speaker's authority, is placed on the table in front of the Speaker. At the opening of a new Parliament or a session of Parliament, the Commons is then summoned to the bar of the Senate to hear from the governor general. Also in attendance are the senators and members of the Supreme Court. The diplomatic corps is present in the galleries of the Senate. The governor general's "Speech from the Throne" (in Quebec, the premier's "Inaugural Address") is a Government-drafted review of the state of the nation and the Government's programme, stated in general terms, for the next session of Parliament. The speech delivered, the members of Parliament return to the House of Commons to conduct their own business before turning to consideration, or debate, on the Speech from the Throne at their next sitting.

Opposition parties.   Parties in the legislature which do not constitute the Government-of-the-day. The rights and obligations of opposition parties in Canada are formalized in the parliamentary system of the provinces and the Parliament of Canada. See *Official Opposition.*

Opting-Out Formula.   See *Contracting Out.*

Order (Notice) Paper.   The common name for Order of Business and Notices, the daily agenda of the House of Commons and provincial legislatures. Items on the Order Paper when Parliament is dissolved or a session ended are said to have "died" on the Order Paper.

Order-in-council.   An explicit, written executive or legislative action determined by the cabinet and proclaimed in the name of the governor-in-council (lieutenant-governor-in-council at the provincial level). Federal executive actions by order-in-council include appointments of senators, diplomats, and certain judges and senior officials. Some dismissals may also be effected by executive order-in-council. The disallowance and reservation of provincial legislation, and the power of clemency, are other federal executive acts effected by order-in-council. Legislative actions of federal and provincial cabinets by order-in-council constitute delegated legislative power, which exists only when permitted under specific acts of the appropriate legislature. Such orders-in-council are legion; they range from matters of administrative routine to major political acts, such as the invocation of the War Measures Act by the governor-in-council and the reversal or modification of major decisions by administrative regulatory agencies. Normally, under the federal Regulations Act of 1950, federal orders-in-council must be published in the *Canada Gazette.* However, the governor-in-council may make exceptions of certain categories (by order-in-council), though such categories must be published and tabled in Parliament.

Organic law.   A statute which is considered part of the constitution, not because it is entrenched or difficult to amend, but because of its purpose and content. Thus, R. MacGregor Dawson cites the federal statutes which created the Supreme Court of Canada, created new provinces, and established the franchise as examples of Canadian organic law. Dawson also includes comparable provincial statutes as part of the organic law, as well as provincial and federal orders-in-council concerning constitutional matters which might be passed from time to time (*The Government of Canada* [5th ed., rev. by Norman Ward; Toronto: University of Toronto Press, 1970], 63-64).

P

Padlock Law (Switzman v Elbling and Attorney-General for Quebec, 1957).   A ruling of the Supreme Court on the constitutionality of Quebec's so-called Padlock Law (Act Respecting Communistic Propaganda [1937]), which prohibited the propagation of communism in Quebec. Specifically, the case concerned a tenant (Switzman) who was sued by his landlord (Elbling) for cancellation of his lease and damages on the grounds that the premises had been used illegally. The opinions of the justices illustrate the lack of jurisdictional clarity over civil liberties in Canada.

All but one of the justices declared the Act unconstitutional. Five of the eight in the majority argued that the provincial legislation violated Parliament's jurisdiction over criminal law (British North America Act, Section 91:27). Three of the justices dismissed the Padlock Law as a restriction of a fundamental civil liberty and, in the manner of the Duff Doctrine, a violation of the preamble to the BNA Act, which grants Canada a constitution "similar in Principle to that of the United Kingdom . . . ." One of these stated that the preamble denied both Parliament and provincial legislatures the ability to interfere with freedoms associated with parliamentary democracy. See *Duff Doctrine; Supreme Court.*

Pairing.   An agreement between a legislator of the Government and a legislator of an Opposition party that, for a specified period, neither will vote in a party-based division of the legislature. Thus, both legislators may be absent from the House without the relative strength of Government and Opposition being affected. Pairing, which is arranged (and cancelled) by the party whips, is very important in cases of minority governments or when Governments are in power with slim majorities, to avoid precipitate defeat of the Government. House procedures do not recognize pairing; and if an arrangement is broken in error, the vote stands. Often, a present but paired member who has not participated in the division will inform House, for the sake of the printed record, how he would have voted if he had not been paired.

Parachuting (candidates).   The determination of a party's candidate in a constituency by the party leadership rather than by a local constituency association. Parachuted candidates usually have tenuous links, if any, with the constituency. While party officials usually deny the effectiveness of parachuting candidates into a constituency, the practice is not unknown to most parties. Parachuting occurs when there may be a weak local organization, when the constituency is safe (that is, the election is likely to be won by the party parachuting the candidate), or when the party desires this particular person to be elected.

Parliament of Canada.   The Crown, the Senate, and the House of Commons (British North America Act, Section 17). Within the powers granted to it under the BNA Act, Parliament is supreme – that is, composed of the executive and the legislature, Parliament is itself beyond interference by any body. The term "Parliament" also refers to a particular form of the institution which exists following a general election. Thus, since 1867, there have been 32 parliaments. A House of Commons may last five years from the day of the return of the election writs; but the Crown's representative, the governor general, may dissolve Parliament and issue writs for a new election before the term expires (Section 50). Parliament must also meet for at least one session each year at the summons of the governor general (Section 20). Within the constitutional limits of the five-year term and one annual session, the summons and dissolution of Parliament are usually carried out on the "advice" of the prime minister, whose Government (cabinet) requires the support of the House of Commons to remain in office. Acts of Parliament require the approval of both houses of Parliament, and then royal assent, before becoming effective. While the prerogatives of Parliament are considerable, the reality is that of an institution much of whose behaviour is ritualistic and predictable and which is functionally inferior in terms of policy-making to the cabinet and the senior civil service. See *Crown; Cabinet; Governor General; House of Commons; Parliamentary privilege; Senate; Supremacy of Parliament.*

Parliamentary indemnity.   A traditional term for financial remuneration (now recognized as salaries) for members of Parliament, senators, and provincial legislators. In 1980, members of Parliament and senators received $30 600 a year as a sessional indemnity. In addition, MPs received a tax-free allowance of $13 500 and senators, one-half an MP's allowance. Under a statute passed in 1979, the salaries and allowances increase annually by 7 per cent or the annual rate of inflation, whichever is smaller. The allowance is larger for MPs from certain remote ridings. Ministers, party leaders, and other MPs and senators who have additional parliamentary or ministerial responsibilities receive additional salaries.

Parliamentary parties.   Parties, such as the federal Liberal and Conservative parties, whose origins were in the legislative environment in the nineteenth century. They are controlled by a small elite, which is usually in the legislature, and are assisted by selected officials, fundraisers and organizers. Such parties, while they have developed an extra-parliamentary organization among the public in the twentieth century, remain traditionally elite-dominated in terms of policy-making and campaign decision-making. The decision-making in parliamentary parties can be characterized as practical and manipulative, given the objective of such parties to achieve and retain electoral office. By contrast, movement parties, such as the New Democratic party, originate in society in times of social crisis; they possess an extra-parliamentary organization whose behaviour impinges on the leadership's ability to respond to the requisites for electoral gain. Movement parties are committed to a broad set of social goals, and often they are strongly committed to particular policy items; parliamentary party programmes are more difficult to predict and are subject to unexpected reversal. See *Brokerage politics; Conservative party; Liberal party.*

Parliamentary privilege (immunities).   Rights which the federal Parliament, the provincial legislatures, and each legislator individually possesses; these are rights with which no other body can interfere and without which legislators could not carry out their functions. The principle of parliamentary privilege in Canada derives from customary privileges acquired by the British Parliament and known collectively as the *lex et consuetudo Parliamenti.* The British North America Act recognizes parliamentary privilege (Section 18); and in 1868, a federal act was passed to grant Parliament the powers, immunities, and privileges possessed by the British Parliament. These can be increased by an act of Parliament, which would be a constitutional amendment.

The privileges of individual legislators include: immunity from arrest or imprisonment as a result of civil action while the legislature is in session; immunity from actions for libel for content of speeches in the legislature and publications prepared under the authority of the legislature; and exemption from jury duty during a session. Another parliamentary privilege is the right of committees to hear witnesses under oath.

The collective privileges of the legislatures involve the maintenance of order and discipline. It is the Speaker's responsibility to compel obedience from legislators. If repeated demands for order or withdrawal of offending remarks fail to bring a legislator to heel, the Speaker may "name" the offending legislator; that is, the Speaker may call the legislator by name, rather than "honourable member," and may have the sergeant-at-arms escort him or her from the legislature while it decides what disciplinary measures to exact. Disciplinary measures range from suspension for the day to expulsion from the legislature. The legislature may also refuse to admit a member who has been elected; the rejected member may stand again, be elected, and be refused admission again. Alleged breaches of privilege by members of the public may result in their appearance before the bar of the house to explain their behaviour. The legislature may punish such individuals by public reprimand or by imprisonment during the session of the legislature.

Parliamentary privilege is important in terms of a legislator's freedom of speech and freedom from arrest arising out of civil action. The courts have rebuffed recent attempts by some legislators to broaden parliamentary privilege to include refusal to participate in criminal proceedings – specifically, refusal to disclose the "confidential" source of information which they have presented in the legislature and which has led to charges. In 1979, the Ontario Court of Appeal ruled that, in a criminal proceeding, a court could not refrain from compelling a member of the provincial legislature to reveal the source of relevant and admissable information; nor could the Ontario legislature enact legislation to protect its members from being compelled by a court in a criminal case to disclose the existence, source, or content of a communication from an informant. In a dissenting view, Mr. Justice J.A. Weatherston wrote: "It has long been a major part of [a legislator's] responsibilities to intercede on behalf of his constituents who claim to be oppressed by government bureaucracy . . . . It must also be acknowledged now that members have assumed the responsibility of bringing alleged scandals in public administration to public attention. In all these cases, the member may rely on information given to him in confidence. His effectiveness as a member may depend on confidences given and received, and the courts should respect those confidences unless the public interest clearly compels a breach of them."

See W.F. Dawson, "Parliamentary Privilege in the Canadian House of Commons," *Canadian Journal of Economics and Political Science* 25 (1959), 462-70.

Parliamentary secretaries. Government members of Parliament appointed, under a federal statute, for two-year renewable terms to assist cabinet ministers in their work. Such appointments allow backbench MPs to gain some executive and administrative experience, and they allow the prime minister and senior ministers to gauge the abilities of such MPs. The appointment of parliamentary secretaries may also make the Government appear more representative of particular interests and help to keep ambitious backbenchers occupied.

While parliamentary secretaries may answer for their ministers in the House and in committees, the Opposition usually interprets such consistent action as an affront to the House. The parliamentary secretary can, with no parliamentary criticism, act on behalf of the minister outside the legislature – for example, receiving deputations from the public and fulfilling public engagements. However, parliamentary secretaries are not part of the cabinet and do not take the Privy Council oath. Therefore, they are not supposed to have cabinet documents and information, and they cannot deal with their ministers on a confidential basis. Therefore, in terms of a working relationship with a minister, a parliamentary secretary may find that he or she has a less efficacious relationship than the minister's personally selected executive assistants. In 1980, parliamentary secretaries received a salary of $5600 in addition to their regular parliamentary salary and allowance.

Parliamentary-cabinet system. A system of government which is parliamentary in that the Crown (or executive) and the legislature act as countervailing checks, but is cabinet government in that the Crown has ministers who are responsible to the legislature to carry out its affairs. In Canada, the Crown and its representatives (the governor general and the lieutenant-governors) have become largely a formal executive with few prerogative powers; the Crown virtually always acts on the advice of the ministers, the political executive, who must retain the confidence of the House of Commons (or provincial legislatures) to remain in office. By contrast, the constitution of France includes a parliamentary-cabinet system, but it gives considerable power to the elected president. Instead of a parliamentary-cabinet system, the United States has a congressional-presidential system under a constitution which enshrines the separation of powers. See *British North America Act; Responsible government; Supremacy of Parliament.*

On the development of the parliamentary-cabinet system in Canada, see J.R. Mallory, *The Structure of Canadian Government* (Toronto: Macmillan Co. of Canada Ltd., 1971), 7-20.

Parti Québécois. A French nationalist party in Quebec, created in 1968 from a union of several independentist groups; its objective is to establish "sovereignty-association" – that is, associate state status for Quebec on an equal basis with the government of Canada – or sovereign status for Quebec. In addition to being a vehicle of French nationalism in Quebec, the PQ is also a moderate left-wing party with a membership-based policy-making process and finances.

The PQ came to power in 1976, with 41 per cent of the popular vote. In 1970 and 1973, it received 23 and 30 per cent of the vote respectively. Its electoral success can be credited to the weakness of the incumbent Liberal Government and to a tactical decision to separate the question of "independence" from voting for the party in the election. The PQ promised a referendum on the question of sovereignty-association. In 1979, the Government announced the referendum for 1980 to give the Government a mandate to negotiate sovereignty-association; it published a white paper on sovereignty-association and the form of the question. The question promised that "No change in political status resulting from these negotiations" would be effected unless approved in "another referendum." See *Referendum; Sovereignty-association.*

On the PQ, see Vera Murray, *Le Parti Québécois: de la fondation à la prise du pouvoir* (Montréal: Cahiers du Québec/Hurtubise HMH, 1976). Also see several articles by Maurice Pinard and Richard Hamilton: "The Basis of Parti Québécois Support in Recent Years," *Canadian Journal of Political Science* 9 (1976), 3-26; "The Independence Issue and the Polarization of the Electorate: The 1973 Quebec Election," *Canadian Journal of Political Science* 10 (1977), 215-59; and "The Parti Québécois Comes to Power: Analysis of the 1976 Quebec Election," *Canadian Journal of Political Science* 11 (1978), 739-75. See also Edward McWhinney, *Quebec and the Constitution, 1960-1978* (Toronto: University of Toronto Press, 1979).

Party system. The totality of relationships among political parties and the public as communities of particular interests. In pluralist democracies, the party system is often described in terms of the number of parties. Thus, since 1935, Canada is said to have had a federal one- or single-party-dominant, multi-party system. Alberta historically has a one-, or a single-party-dominant, system; Ontario currently has a competitive multi-party system; most of the Maritime provinces have two-party systems. Totalitarian states often have a one-party or a pseudo-coalition party system.

There is considerable literature on the Canadian party system. See, for example, F.C. Engelman and M.A. Schwartz, *Canadian Political Parties: Origin, Character, Impact* (Toronto: Prentice-Hall of Canada Ltd., 1975); Hugh G. Thorburn (ed.), *Party Politics in Canada* (4th ed.; Toronto: Prentice-Hall of Canada Ltd., 1979); C. Winn and J. McMenemy, *Political Parties in Canada* (Toronto: McGraw-Hill Ryerson Ltd., 1976); and the bibliography in Richard J. Van Loon and Michael S. Whittington, *The Canadian Political System: Environment, Structure, and Process* (2nd ed.; Toronto: McGraw-Hill Ryerson Ltd., 1976), 527-36.

Passage (of legislation). The process by which a bill, once introduced in Parliament or a provincial legislature, is approved and becomes a statute. See *Legislation.*

Patriation (of the constitution). The transfer of the power to amend the Canadian constitution from the British Parliament to Canadian institutions, Parliament and the provincial legislatures. In 1949, on an address by the Canadian Parliament, the British Parliament amended the British North America Act to allow the Canadian Parliament to amend "the Constitution" except where it affects provincial jurisdiction, language and education rights, and the requirements that Parliament meet at least once a year and that a House of Commons not last more than five years (Section 91:1). The amendment of 1949 established a distinction between sections to be amended by the Canadian Parliament and those to be amended by the British Parliament on an address by the Canadian Parliament with, by convention, the consent of the provinces. There is some question whether Parliament can amend Canadian constitutional statutes, such as the act establishing the Supreme Court of Canada, without provincial support. In 1979, the Supreme Court ruled that Parliament could not unilaterally amend the BNA Act with respect to the role of, and representation in, the Senate – changes which would fundamentally alter the constitution.

The obstacle to patriation is not the British Parliament, but the inability of the eleven Canadian governments to agree on an amending formula dealing with those sections of the BNA Act not covered by Section 91:1. Several formulas for a Canadian amendment procedure – notably the Fulton-Favreau Formula (1964) and the provisions of the Victoria Charter (1970) – have been advanced; but none has received the support of all governments. In the patriation process, Canadian legislatures would either have to re-enact the British-based constitutional instruments as their own, or adopt a new constitution. It is the latter procedure that many provincial governments favour. See *Fulton-Favreau Formula; Victoria Charter.*

Patronage.   The appointment of individuals to honorific or authorita-
tive public positions, or the granting of business to an individual or a
group, on a discretionary basis. In a pejorative sense, political patronage usually refers to discretionary acts, without reference to merit and
competition; these are performed – by the Government-of-the-day – as
a reward for past service or an incentive for future service.

"Peace, Order and good Government."   The phrase in the preamble
in Section 91 of the British North America Act generally stating the
scope of the Canadian Parliament's legislative jurisdiction. A reading
of the preamble readily suggests that the intention of the "fathers" of
Confederation was to centralize political power in the Canadian federation and to place residual and emergency legislative powers in Parliament.

   In the process of interpreting the Act, the Judicial Committee of the
Privy Council systematically separated the "Peace, Order and good
Government" clause from the enumerated heads in Section 91. While
the decision in *Russell* v. *the Queen,* 1882, upheld the centralist view
of Parliament's role, the process of judicial review subsequently reduced the clause to a residual power to be exercised by Parliament
only in a time of great national emergency. In 1937, the Judicial Committee declared most of Prime Minister R.B. Bennett's "New Deal" legislation (introduced during the depression of the 1930's) to be *ultra
vires.* Thus, the clause was reduced from a justification for comprehensive residual legislative competence by the Parliament of Canada to a
justification for temporary comprehensive legislative competence only
in a national emergency such as war or insurrection. In place of the
"Peace, Order and good Government" clause, the Judicial Committee
effectively substituted the enumerated head under provincial powers,
"Property and Civil Rights" (Section 92:13), as the residual power
clause except in dire national emergency.

   Since the Supreme Court became the final court of appeal in 1949,
judicial interpretations have tended to strengthen the power of the federal government, at least in economic matters. The Court has replaced
the narrow emergency doctrine of the Judicial Committee with the notion of "inherent national importance" under the "Peace, Order and
good Government" and "Trade and Commerce" clauses. For example,
the Supreme Court has permitted the reassertion of federal authority
over aviation, the assertion of federal authority over western off-shore
mineral rights, and federal power to establish mandatory wage and
price controls. See *Judicial Committee of the Privy Council; Supreme
Court.*

Petro-Canada (Petro-Can).   A federal crown corporation established
in 1975 to increase Canadian presence in the petroleum industry. Petro-Canada is involved in exploration and drilling activities on leased
and owned land, and in the creation of reserves and sales in either sole
or joint ventures. It conducts research and development, especially in:
the technology of developing non-conventional oil resources of heavy
oil and tarsands; transportation of energy from remote and difficult lo-
cations; and developing new sources of energy. Petro-Canada also assesses foreign-based opportunities to acquire energy supplies for im-
port-dependent Canadian markets.

The role of the corporation in national oil policy has been hotly debated, especially since 1979, when Petro-Canada's takeover of Pacific
Petroleums Ltd. more than doubled the crown corporation's assets (to
$2.5 billion). This resulted in a promise from the Conservative leader
of the Opposition Joe Clark to "privatize" the corporation. In the general election of 1980 which he lost, Prime Minister Clark proposed that
Petro-Canada retain its mandate, but become a publicly traded corporation, with the Canadian government holding a controlling one-third of
the shares and the remainder widely distributed to Canadians. The
Liberal and New Democratic parties maintained their opposition to the
transformation of Petro-Canada from an instrument of national policy
to a profit-making company. See *National oil policy*.

Petro-Canada has a board of directors composed of a chairman, president, and up to 13 other people whom the governor-in-council appoints. The directors include senior civil servants as well as individuals from the private sector. Its head office is in Calgary.

Platform.   Policy proposals, often individually termed "planks," announced by political parties and candidates prior to and during an
election campaign; they are proposals to which the party is supposedly
committed if it forms the Government.

For Canadian party platforms, see D.O. Carrigan (ed.), *Canadian
Party Platforms, 1867-1968* (Toronto: Copp Clark Publishing, 1968).

Plurality.   The largest number of votes cast for one candidate in an
election with more than two candidates, but which is not a majority of
the votes cast. All provincial and federal elections in Canada operate
on the single-member constituency system with plurality win, or first-
past-the-post system. In multi-party elections, it is common for legislators to be elected with a plurality, but not a majority, of the votes cast.
As the votes for the defeated candidates do not have any electoral effect, the system results in discrepancies between the percentage of the

votes cast for the parties' candidates and the percentage of seats the parties hold in a legislature. See *Electoral system; Proportional representation; Single-member plurality electoral system.*

Policy (analysis; -making; public).   Decisions related to goal-determination and the selection of methods to achieve the goal. A policy may also be a single decision and a negative decision. The goal may be concrete, abstract, narrow, or general. The term "public policy" refers specifically to government decisions. Thus, for example, a single, negative, concrete, and narrow public policy would be a decision by the federal government not to legalize the non-medical use of certain drugs. An example of a complex, positive, abstract, and general public policy would be a government decision that Canada should become self-sufficient in energy. Usually, the term "public policy" is used in the latter sense, to define several decisions related to a general purpose.

"Policy-making" is the process involving various "actors" and institutions by which policies are determined and implemented. In specific cases, this may involve a set of activities including intergovernmental negotiations, cabinet consideration, legislative debate, interest-group lobbying, the regulatory process, and judicial review.

"Policy analysis" is a yet broader term which, in addition to the above, involves the examination of alternative models of decision-making and policies, using the tools of economics and administrative theory in addition to those of political science.

See David Braybrooke and Charles Lindblom, *A Strategy of Decision: Policy Evaluation as a Social Process* (New York: Free Press, 1970); Marsha A. Chandler and William M. Chandler, *Public Policy and Provincial Politics* (Toronto: McGraw-Hill Ryerson Ltd., 1979); G. Bruce Doern and Peter Aucoin (eds.), *The Structure of Policy-Making in Canada* (Toronto: Macmillan Co. of Canada Ltd., 1971); G.B. Doern and S.V. Wilson (eds.), *Issues in Canadian Public Policy* (Toronto: Macmillan Co. of Canada Ltd., 1974); and Richard Simeon, "Studying Public Policy," *Canadian Journal of Political Science* 9 (1976), 548-80. See also Richard W. Phidd and G. Bruce Doern, *The Politics and Management of Canadian Economic Policy* (Toronto: Macmillan Co. of Canada Ltd., 1978).

Political cabinet (federal Liberal party).   A device established by the federal Liberal party when in office during the 1970's to connect the cabinet and the party's executive. The political cabinet consisted of the cabinet, regional caucus chairmen, the party's president, and the national director. If the extra-parliamentary Liberal party had been a genuine membership-based organization, the political cabinet might have represented a source of party input to cabinet decision-making. It appears, however, that policy was discussed less often than party finance, organization, morale, and election prospects.

Political culture.   A set of orientations – that is, attitudes, beliefs, and values – toward the political process, held by members of a political system. A political culture is the result of the interplay of historic and contemporary factors in a process of socialization. It may contain sub-sets, or subcultures, based on cultural, geographic, and class differences. Political subcultures which are very distinct from the political culture of the larger political community may pose a threat to the integration of the larger community.

The functionalist notion of political culture is outlined in Gabriel Almond and Sydney Verba, *The Civic Culture* (Boston: Little, Brown and Co., 1965). See also J. Pye and S. Verba (eds.), *Political Culture and Political Development* (Princeton: Princeton University Press, 1965). Concerning Canada, see David J. Bellamy, Jon H. Pammett, and Donald C. Rowat (eds.), *The Provincial Political Systems: Comparative Essays* (Toronto: Methuen Publications, 1976), Part I; David J. Elkins and Richard Simeon, *Small Worlds: Parties and Provinces in Canadian Political Life* (Toronto: Methuen Publications, 1980); John Meisel, *Working Papers on Canadian Politics* (Montreal: McGill-Queen's University Press, 1973); Jon Pammet and Michael Whittington (eds.), *Foundations of Political Culture* (Toronto: Macmillan Co. of Canada Ltd., 1976); Mildred A. Schwartz, *Politics and Territory: The Sociology of Regional Persistence in Canada* (Montreal: McGill-Queen's University Press, 1974); Michael D. Ornstein, H. Michael Stevenson, and A. Paul Williams, "Region, Class and Political Culture in Canada," *Canadian Journal of Political Science* 13 (1980), 227–71; Richard Simeon and David J. Elkins, "Regional Political Cultures in Canada," *Canadian Journal of Political Science* 7 (1974), 397-437; and John Wilson, "The Canadian Political Cultures: Towards a Redefinition of the Nature of the Canadian Political System," *Canadian Journal of Political Science* 7 (1974), 439-83. See also David Bell and Lorne Tepperman, *The Roots of Disunity: A Look at Canadian Political Culture* (Toronto: McClelland and Stewart Ltd., 1979); and W. Christian and C. Campbell, *Political Parties and Ideologies in Canada* (Toronto: McGraw-Hill Ryerson Ltd., 1974).

Populism. A term describing a political movement which seeks in general terms to wrest government from the control of a centralized and sophisticated clique and to make it respond to the needs and interests of the "common people." Some politicians may also be described as populists, although their party may not be a populist movement.

Populist movements in Canada have been successful when led by charismatic individuals who could articulate regional grievances and exploit established social and political organizations and new techniques of communication such as radio and television. Examples of such populist movements have been: the Progressives in the 'teens and the 1920's; the Social Credit party in the 1930's and 40's; and the *Ralliement créditiste* in Quebec in the 1960's, led by Henry Wise Wood, William Aberhart, and Réal Caouette respectively. The fact that populist movements are vehicles of regional discontent tends to restrict geographically the extent of their electoral success and also make the movements leader-dependent.

John Diefenbaker, leader of the Conservative party from 1956 to 1967, is often described as a western populist. Diefenbaker developed a populist constituency within a party traditionally dominated by wealthy business personalities with an upper-class-oriented policy. See *Movement parties; Progressive movement; Ralliement des créditistes.*

Pork barrel. A term to describe large-scale political patronage offered to a community or private interests as a reward for, or incentive to provide, political support in the form of money, oranizational resources, or votes. The patronage, or "pork," has traditionally been government jobs or contracts for individuals; and public works such as bridges, post offices, and waterfront improvements for communities. In an era of complex and costly federal-provincial agreements for job retraining and industrial incentive programmes, government grants focussing on particular regions may also be identified as "pork."

Portfolio. A term used to describe ministerial responsibilities in a cabinet. For example, finance is the portfolio of the minister of finance. Collectively, the responsibilities are described as cabinet or ministerial portfolios.

Positive (negative) entitlement. A positive or negative figure indicating whether, in separate and specific revenue sources recognized in the Federal-Provincial Fiscal Arrangements Act, the per capita tax yields in each province are above or below the national average in those fields. If the total figure of all entitlements is positive (that is, the total provincial tax yield is lower than the national average), the province is entitled to an unconditional equalization transfer payment from the federal government to make up the difference. If the total figure is negative (that is, the total provincial tax yield is higher than the national average), the province is not entitled to a transfer payment. The definition of provincial revenue sources and tax fields is crucial to the result of the calculation. See *Federal-provincial tax-sharing agreements.*

Prairie Farm Rehabilitation Act (Administration) (PFRA). A federal programme established in 1935 to assist the rehabilitation of agricultural lands affected by the "dust bowl" conditions of the 1930's in the three prairie provinces. The PFRA is the oldest federal programme of regional development. In the past 40 years, the PFRA has developed approximately 100 community pastures on 2.5 million acres of marginal and submarginal land, most of which it operates. The PFRA is also responsible for the construction of large irrigation and water storage projects, as well as for technical assistance or financing of smaller on-farm water-related projects. The Act is administered in the Department of Regional Economic Expansion. See *Department of Regional Economic Expansion; Regional disparity.*

Premier. The head of a provincial cabinet, or Government, who is appointed by the lieutenant-governor of the province and remains in office as long as he or she has the confidence of the legislature. Thus, the premier is usually the leader of the party which has elected the most members to the legislature. The premier "recommends" the appointment of the cabinet, which acts formally as the lieutenant-governor's Executive Council. The premier's relationship to the lieutenant-governor, the cabinet, and the legislature is comparable to that of the prime minister to the governor general, the federal cabinet, and the House of Commons. See *Prime Minister.*

President of the Privy Council for Canada. A cabinet portfolio with no defined functions; thus, the prime minister assigns particular responsibilities to this cabinet minister. Under both Prime Ministers Joe Clark and Pierre Trudeau, the president of the Privy Council was made Government leader in the House, supervising the preparation of the legislative programme and acting as the Government's manager. The president of the Privy Council and Government House leader is also concerned with: co-ordinating department and agency responses to questions on the Order Paper, and motions for the production of papers; procedural reform, including the development of techniques to review subordinate legislation and statutory instruments; and the development of research facilities for members of Parliament.

President of the Treasury Board.   The cabinet minister who chairs and is responsible to Parliament for the federal Treasury Board. This particular designation derives from the Board's peculiar status since the early years of Confederation as a statute-defined committee of the Privy Council of Canada, rather than an ordinary cabinet committee. Until 1966, the minister of finance chaired the Board and its staff came from the department of finance. In 1966, however, the Board was established as a separate department of the federal government with its own minister, styled the president, and its own secretariat. The minister of finance is now a member of the Treasury Board. In 1979-1980, the Conservative cabinet included a minister of state for Treasury Board. See *Treasury Board; Treasury Board Secretariat.*

Press gallery.   A collective term for journalists and broadcasters who cover the activities of the legislature and government. Through a formal organization, accredited correspondents gain access to facilities provided by the Speaker of the legislature to cover political events on a daily basis. The press gallery is an important link between the politicians and the public who rely heavily on the mass media of communication for political information. Politicians themselves, both in Government and in Opposition, use the media to gauge public opinion and to create favourable impressions of themselves and their party. The status of the press gallery is recognized, for example, in its members' confidential access to copies of Government documents such as budgets and throne speeches before they are made public. They also have free movement in areas of the legislative buildings which are normally closed to the public, places such as the lobbies, the library, and restaurants. See *Mass media of communication.*

There is no academic work on the national press gallery. However, for an article on the legislative press gallery in Ontario, see Frederick J. Fletcher, "Between Two Stools: News Coverage of Provincial Politics in Ontario," in Donald C. MacDonald (ed.), *Government and Politics of Ontario* (Toronto: Macmillan Co. of Canada Ltd., 1975), 249-69.

Pressure groups.   Organized interest groups which seek to influence, or "pressure," political authorities for specific policies and decisions favourable to themselves. See *Interest groups.*

Prime Minister.   The head of the federal cabinet or Government-of-the-day, appointed by the governor general and retaining office as long as he or she clearly has the confidence of the House of Commons. Thus, the prime minister is usually the leader of the party which has elected the most members to the House. The prime minister chooses the cabinet, which acts formally in the name of the Queen's Privy Council for Canada, and submits the Government's resignation to the governor general when appropriate.

The power of prime ministers over their colleagues, as well as over the Opposition, lies in their relationship to the Crown. Only the prime minister has the prerogative to "advise" the governor-general on matters ranging from certain appointments to the dissolution of Parliament. The prime minister "recommends" appointments to and withdrawals from the federal cabinet. The prime minister also may organize the cabinet, the Privy Council Office, and the Prime Minister's Office largely without constraint, and may allocate responsibilities in the government. In some cases, parliamentary approval may be required for some reorganization, but other changes can be made without legislative approval – through an order-in-council, a minute of cabinet, or under delegated authority. The prime minister's usually effective control over most of the members of Parliament ensures any parliamentary approval that may be required. Other powers of "recommendation" which the prime minister has with respect to the Crown include such appointments as senators, chief justices, senior administrators, senior diplomats, and lieutenant-governors of the provinces.

The prime minister has been traditionally termed *primus inter pares* – first among equals. While cabinet ministers may be the prime minister's colleagues rather than subordinates, the prime minister clearly has powers which they individually or collectively do not possess. Having organized and appointed the cabinet, the prime minister determines its agenda and defines its consensus on issues. All members are subsequently compelled to share that consensus publicly or else resign. Cabinet ministers must have seats in Parliament, usually the House of Commons and their presence in the cabinet is sometimes a recognition by the prime minister of their status in the party and in the country.

The constitutional conventions of cabinet secrecy and collective ministerial responsibility also enhance the prime minister's power. Any minister wishing to diverge publicly from the prime minister's declared view of the Government's position must first resign from the cabinet. Furthermore, present and former cabinet ministers are forbidden by their Privy Council oath from disclosing cabinet business – though unattributed cabinet leaks are not unknown. Also by convention, neither the prime minister nor senior advisors in the Privy Council Office will appear before parliamentary committees. In 1979, however, Prime Minister Joe Clark became apparently the first prime minister to appear before a House committee, with the clerk of the Privy Council, to discuss his departmental estimates and answer questions concerning his office.

In the federal system, the prime minister can affect the direction of federal-provincial relations. Perhaps here the prime minister may be more aptly called *primus inter pares*. Each provincial premier holds power in his or her own right, and not at the behest of the prime minister. However, the prime minister, more than any provincial premier, is the focus of attention at federal-provincial conferences. The prime minister guides the agenda-setting prior to the meetings, and also chairs, guides, and attempts to define the consensus of the meetings. In general, the prime minister influences the pace and quality of federal-provincial relations in a way which can be matched only by some premiers on some issues. While the federal system constrains the prime minister in important respects, the process of federal-provincial consultation with the prime minister and federal cabinet at the centre can lead to the setting of federal priorities in areas of provincial or intergovernmental jurisdiction.

The prime minister's personality clearly determines the style and form of the Government. Ultimately, however, the degree of the Government's success will have an influence on the prime minister's power. The influence of Prime Minister John Diefenbaker over his cabinet was very different in 1962-1963 from what it was in 1957-1958. Diefenbaker, who was uncontested from within in 1958, led a cabinet in disarray in 1962-1963. The vagaries of electoral fortune aside, each prime minister seems to stamp a personal style upon the national politics of the day. For example, one often hears of the (William Lyon Mackenzie) King era, the (John) Diefenbaker and (Lester B.) Pearson years, and the (Pierre) Trudeau decade (the 1970's).

On the prime minister, see T. Hockin (ed.), *Apex of Power* (Toronto: Prentice-Hall of Canada Ltd., 1971); W.A. Matheson, *The Prime Minis-*

ter and the Cabinet (Toronto: Methuen Publications, 1976); and R.M. Punnett, The Prime Minister in Canadian Government and Politics (Toronto: Macmillan Co. of Canada Ltd., 1977). On the influence of the prime minister in the federal system, see Richard Simeon, Federal-Provincial Diplomacy: The Making of Recent Policy in Canada (Toronto: University of Toronto Press, 1972).

Prime Minister's Office (PMO).   The secretariat which is the political instrument of the prime minister and which keeps the prime minister informed on political developments in the country. It maintains contact with the extra-parliamentary segment of the party and provincial party organizations; and it arranges the prime minister's schedule of private appointments, public appearances, correspondence, public statements, and relations with the mass media. The prime minister determines the organization and role of the PMO, and its operations are therefore a reflection of the prime minister's personality and needs. The PMO is a public relations office for the prime minister, but it is also an important source of political counsel.

Under Prime Minister Pierre Trudeau in the 1970's, the PMO was headed by the principal secretary, with two assistant principal secretaries for policy and planning and for international relations. Especially in his early years as prime minister, Trudeau used this office to bring into his service people in whom he had confidence, but who did not hold prominent positions in the party or who were not in the House of Commons and therefore could not be in his cabinet. The PMO then included regional officers who reported on political developments – to the chagrin of some cabinet ministers and backbench Liberal members of Parliament, who saw the PMO moving into their areas of responsibility. The senior civil servants in government departments at the Privy Council Office also perceived the policy role of the PMO as a challenge to their traditional prerogatives. When Joe Clark was prime minister in 1979-1980, the key advisor from his staff when he had been leader of the Opposition served as head of the PMO. See Principal secretary/chief of staff.

See Colin Campbell and George J. Szablowski, The Super-Bureaucrats: Structure and Behaviour in Central Agencies (Toronto: Macmillan Co. of Canada Ltd., 1979); W.A. Matheson, The Prime Minister and the Cabinet (Toronto: Methuen Publications, 1976); and R.M. Punnett, The Prime Minister in Canadian Government and Politics (Toronto: Macmillan Co. of Canada Ltd., 1977). See also Thomas d'Aquino, "The Prime Minister's Office: Catalyst or Cabal? Aspects of the Development of the Office in Canada and Some Thoughts about its Future," *Canadian Public Administration* 17 (1974), 55-79; and Denis Smith, "Comments on 'The Prime Minister's Office: Catalyst or Cabal?'," 80-84.

Principal secretary/chief of staff.   The chief officer of the Prime Minister's Office and an important aid to the prime minister. Under Prime Minister Pierre Trudeau in the 1970's, the so-titled principal secretaries were: Marc Lalonde, who later became a cabinet minister; Martin O'Connell, who was a defeated cabinet minister and later returned to the House of Commons and the cabinet; Jack Austin, a former senior civil servant who was later appointed to the Senate; and James Coutts. When he was prime minister in 1979-1980, Joe Clark appointed William Neville, his chief of staff when he had been leader of the Opposition, to head the PMO under the title "chief of staff." In 1980, Coutts resumed his role as Trudeau's principal secretary. See *Prime Minister's Office.*

Private bills.   Non-government legislation introduced by private members; they are is designed to alter the law relating to some particular interest, to confer rights on or relieve the obligations of some person or group of people. For example, bills to incorporate private companies or to alter their charters are private bills. In Parliament, most private bills are introduced in the Senate. Bills which must receive the approval of the House of Commons are usually dealt with perfunctorily by that chamber. For other types of bills, see *Legislation.*

Private member.   A member of a provincial or federal legislature who is not a cabinet minister and who may be an Opposition party leader or designated critic, or otherwise a Government or Opposition backbencher. See *Backbencher.*

Private member's legislation (bill).   A type of public but non-government bill introduced by legislators who are not in the cabinet. Such bills, which cannot involve the expenditure of public money (a prerogative enjoyed only by ministers introducing public government bills), may concern any matter which falls within the jurisdictional competence of the legislature. Seldom does a private member's bill go beyond first reading – introduction and printing stage. Should the bill go further, it will likely be "talked out," that is, it will not be voted upon before the time allotted the debate has ended. Very rarely, a Government may allow a private member's bill to proceed, indicating support for the measure. The little time allotted to the lengthy list of private member's bills in most Canadian legislatures, and the Governments' reluctance to admit legislation other than their own to be of value, are the causes for the fate of most private member's bills. In a white paper on the reform of Parliament in 1979, the federal Conservative Government proposed procedural changes under which private members' bills might come to a vote in the House of Commons. The proposal would have allowed a motion supported by 60 MPs to force a vote or to extend the debating time for a bill.

The importance of private member's legislation is the opportunity it gives backbenchers on both sides to introduce measures they consider important; and, though not passed by the legislature, the bill in printed form may be distributed to interested groups in the public and to civil servants for consideration. The private member's bill may thus be a vehicle for bringing an important issue to public attention and maintaining it high on the public agenda in the hope that eventually a Government will commit itself to the measure. Such is the origin, for example, of federal freedom-of-information legislation, which Conservative MP Gerald Baldwin personally promoted for many years and which the brief Conservative Government introduced in 1979 and which the Liberals promised in 1980.

On private member's bills, see Stewart Hyson, "The Role of the Backbencher: An Analysis of Private Members' Bills in the Canadian House of Commons," *Parliamentary Affairs* 27 (1974), 262-72.

Privy Council.   The common name for the Queen's Privy Council for Canada, a formal advisory body to the Crown, established under the BNA Act (Section 11); the governor general appoints members to the Privy Council on the advice of the prime minister. Membership, which is for life, includes mostly former and present federal cabinet ministers, provincial premiers, and former speakers of the House and Senate. A recent exception to these categories of appointment was that in 1979 of Stanley Knowles, a long-time CCF-New Democratic MP, who was being honoured as a parliamentarian. By convention, those members of the Privy Council who "advise" the Crown form a committee which is identical to the federal cabinet. Thus, the cabinet, which has no statutory basis, acts formally as a committee of the Privy Council through orders-in-council issued in the name of the governor-in-council. See *Cabinet.*

Privy Council Office (PCO).   The prime minister's government department headed by the clerk who, since 1940, has been designated secretary to the cabinet. In 1974, Parliament created a Federal-Provincial Relations Office headed by a secretary to the cabinet for federal-provincial relations; it took on responsibilities which had been in a division of the PCO. The Privy Council Office is a central executive agency responsible for co-ordinating the activities of cabinet and cabinet committees and for liaison with government departments and agencies on cabinet matters. The PCO provides secretarial and other support systems, including the preparation and presentation of documents, for interdepartmental committees. It ensures conformity of submission for approval by the cabinet with policy and legal requirements; examines, edits, registers, and arranges for the publication of statutory regulations; and it generally advises concerning the prime minister's prerogatives and responsibilities in the organization of the federal government. Traditionally, the Privy Council Office advises the prime minister on senior appointments in the public service which are outside the purview of the Public Service Commission.

Under Prime Minister Pierre Trudeau in the 1970's, the PCO was divided into two divisions, Operations and Plans. Each division was headed by a deputy secretary and contained a number of secretariats to assist the prime minister and cabinet. The PCO staffs each cabinet committee except the Treasury Board, which has its own secretariat. The secretariats prepare support material and the agenda for each committee and maintain committee records.

The PCO is clearly the site of considerable independent political influence, though providing what is ostensibly neutral support services. For example, it was disclosed in 1978, during the investigation of allegedly illegal security activities by the Royal Canadian Mounted Police, that the PCO had initiated the scrutiny of the financing of the *Parti Québécois* in the early 1970's. The PCO was allegedly unaware of the means by which the examination was carried out.

The PCO has been the focus of criticism by those who complain of the inordinate influence of the bureaucratic "mandarinate" in the federal government. One of those critics was Opposition MP Joe Clark. After he became prime minister in 1979, Clark replaced the clerk of the PCO, and the secretary for federal-provincial relations resigned. Also in 1979, Clark apparently became the first prime minister to appear before a House committee with the clerk of the Privy Council to discuss his estimates. When he returned to office in 1980, Prime Minister Pierre Trudeau recalled the earlier clerk of that position. See *Clerk of the Privy Council; Federal-Provincial Relations Office.*

On the PCO and other central agencies, see Colin Campbell and George J. Szablowski, *The Super-Bureaucrats: Structure and Behaviour in Central Agencies* (Toronto: Macmillan Co. of Canada Ltd., 1979). On the two PCO secretaries and Joe Clark's criticisms, see J.R. Mallory, "The Two Clerks: Parliamentary Discussion of the Role of the Privy Council Office," *Canadian Journal of Political Science* 10 (1977), 3-19.

Progressive Conservative party. See Conservative party.

Progressive movement (party). A political movement, composed mostly of farmers and some small businessmen close to the agricultural community, in the Canadian prairie West in the late 'teens and 1920's. The political consciousness of western farmers had been rising steadily during the first two decades of the century. High tariffs which successive federal Governments imposed to protect eastern commercial interests compounded the natural problems of farm life. Through co-operative action, farmers became conscious of their particular interests and of their weaknesses in the disciplined parliamentary system which made their few MPs in Ottawa powerless.

The momentum for independent political action, which had been delayed by World War One, resumed in 1919-1920. In 1919, T.A. Crerar resigned from the federal Union cabinet to sit with eight other MPs as an independent. The federal Liberal party selected an Ontario Liberal closely associated with business to succeed Wilfrid Laurier, and the party reaffirmed its commitment to tariff protection. A general strike took place in Winnipeg. A coalition of the United Farmers of Ontario, Labour, and independent MLAs formed a minority government in Ontario; and the United Farmers of Alberta decided to contest the next provincial election. In 1920, the Progressive party was formed out of basically a Manitoba group, led by Crerar and dedicated to parliamentary politics, and a group from Alberta led by Henry Wise Wood which was dedicated to replacing the party system with a form of occupational group representation. In the House of Commons, eleven MPs designated themselves the National Progressive party and chose Crerar as their leader.

In the general election of 1921, the Progressives elected the second-largest group of MPs, and the Liberals formed a minority government. Wood's anti-party sentiment dominated the Progressive caucus, and the 61 MPs refused to form the Opposition. The United Farmers of Alberta formed the Government of Alberta that same year, and factional division within the federal party-movement was never healed. By 1922, Crerar had resigned the leadership, and the federal party was in disarray. In the general election of 1925, the Progressives held a crucial position in another house of minorities, but that Parliament was short-lived. After 1926, the party ceased to be an important organization.

The "shades" of the Progressive party in western Canada persist 60 years later. In the 1930's, Progressives drifted into alliances which resulted in the formation of the Social Credit party and the Co-operative Commonwealth Federation (CCF), now the New Democratic Party. Since John Bracken, a former Progressive premier of Manitoba, was leader of the federal Conservative party in the early 1940's, it has been styled the Progressive Conservative party. John Diefenbaker's leadership of the party from 1956-1957, however, is in large part responsible for that party's benefiting from the populist legacy of Progressivism. Meanwhile, the federal Liberals have retained a central-Canadian bias in leadership, policy, and electoral fortunes, and have little support in western Canada.

On the Progressive party, see W.D. Morton, *The Progressive Party in Canada* (Toronto: University of Toronto Press, 1950); and Paul F. Sharp, *The Agrarian Revolt in Western Canada* (Minneapolis: University of Minnesota, 1948).

"Property and Civil Rights."   The enumerated head in Section 92 of the British North America Act; it allocates legislative jurisdiction in that area to the provincial legislatures (:13). This power has gained primacy over the "Peace, Order and good Government" phrase in Section 91 as the seat of residual power (or comprehensive legislative authority) except in extreme national emergency. When the Judicial Committee of the Privy Council over time determined that the "Peace, Order and good Government" clause was subordinate to the enumerated heads of Sections 91 and 92, the provinces gained, because 92:13 ("Property and Civil Rights in the Province") was capable of inclusive meaning. Thus, as a result of judicial review, residual power was in a sense moved from the jurisdiction of Parliament to that of the provincial legislatures. The Supreme Court became the final judicial arbiter of the constitution in 1949, and it has since tended to sanction the federal government's use of the "Peace, Order and good Government" and "Trade and Commerce" (91:2) clauses in matters of "inherent national importance." See *Judicial Committee of the Privy Council*; *"Peace, Order and good Government"*; *Supreme Court*.

Proportional representation.   An electoral system which results in a close approximation between the number of seats held by the political parties in a legislature and their percentage of the popular vote in the election. For example, a party which wins 40 per cent of the popular vote would invariably hold close to 40 per cent of the legislative seats under proportional representation. Variants of proportional represent- ation systems, in which electors vote for a list of party candidates in multi-member constituencies, are used in many European countries and in Israel.

The single-member constituency system with plurality wins is the electoral system used in federal and provincial elections. Discussions about proportional representation arise because, under the established system, there is usually a discrepancy – and on occasion a gross dis- crepancy – between the percentage of votes won and the percentage of seats subsequently held by a party. For example, following the federal election of 1979, the Conservatives formed a Government with 22 seats more than the Liberals, but with 4 per cent less of the popular vote. Only the *Parti Québécois* is committed to changing the electoral sys- tem. While in opposition, it elected seven members (6%) with 23 per cent of the vote in 1970 and six members (6%) with 30 per cent of the vote in 1973. In 1976, it formed the Government, winning 71 seats (65%) while increasing its vote to 41 per cent.

In 1979, the PQ Government published a green paper on the reform of the electoral system; it included a discussion of proportional repre- sentation as one of three alternatives to the present system. The green paper noted that a regional proportional representation system would result in electors having "several members, larger ridings, governments that are numerically not as strong as before, and a greater risk of minor- ity governments" (*One Citizen, One Vote: Green Paper on the Electoral System* [Quebec: Ministry of State for Electoral and Parliamentary Re- form, April 1979], 106). Also in 1979, the federal Task Force on Cana- dian Unity recommended the introduction of an element of propor- tional representation into the federal electoral system (*A Future Together: Observations and Recommendations,* [Ottawa, 1979]). See *Electoral system; Single-member plurality electoral system.*

Proprietary corporations.   The type of federal crown corporation which is responsible for the management of lending or financing oper- ations, or for the management of commercial or industrial operations, involving the production of goods or dealing in goods and the supply- ing of services to the public. Some proprietary crown corporations are required to operate without parliamentary appropriations. Proprietary corporations operate under the crown corporation part of the Financial Administration Act except where another act pertaining to a particular corporation takes precedence.

Many proprietary corporations compete with private corporations, and thereby acquire protection from parliamentary scrutiny and exemptions from personnel management prerogatives of the Public Service Commission. The annual reports of these corporations (unlike agency corporations, for example) need only include information required of private companies under the Companies Act. See *Crown corporation.*

On proprietary and other types of crown corporations, see C.A. Ashley and R.G.H. Smails, *Canadian Crown Corporations* (Toronto: Macmillan Co. of Canada Ltd., 1965).

Prorogation of Parliament.   The ceremonial termination of a session of Parliament by the governor general, acting on the "advice" of the prime minister. Prorogation brings all parliamentary business to an end. Bills remaining on the Order Paper "die" and must be re-introduced as new items in a subsequent session. On the "advice" of the prime minister, the governor general may proclaim the dissolution of Parliament following the prorogation of any session within the five-year term of the House of Commons. However, a request for prorogation and dissolution following a brief first session of a Parliament might, under some circumstances, be cause for the exercise of the Crown's prerogative to deny such a request. See *Crown prerogatives; King-Byng Dispute.*

Provincial autonomy (rights).   The scope of independent, legislative competence enjoyed by the provincial legislatures in the Canadian federation under the distribution of powers outlined in the British North America Act and adjudicated by the courts. Provincial régimes have jealously guarded their rights and sought to enlarge them since Confederation. Although Quebec is usually a province with powerful representatives and movements for provincial rights for cultural reasons, many anglophone provinces have been governed by provincial-rights-oriented régimes. The careers of many provincial premiers (perhaps beginning with Oliver Mowat of Ontario in the early decades of Confederation and currently including Peter Lougheed of Alberta) have been constructed on opposition to the federal government. Federal leaders have also come to power as proponents of provincial rights.

Wilfrid Laurier in 1896, John Diefenbaker in 1957, and Joe Clark in 1979 came to power opposing government parties long associated with centralization and insensitivity to provincial interests.

Debate over provincial autonomy and rights has involved not only jurisdictional disputes but also the financial arrangements within the federation, which have given the greatest power of taxation to the federal government. Moreover, the uneven distribution of resources within the provinces makes the taxing power of some provinces less valuable in revenue yield than others. The history of provincial autonomy and rights debates has involved the sometimes meritorious, and other times "pork barrel," financial arrangements that have been proposed and effected from time to time between the federal and provincial governments. Conditional federal grants, especially in the areas of education and health, which impinge upon areas of provincial authority and upset provincial budgetary priorities have enhanced the suspicion of provincial governments towards the federal government in recent years. See *Distribution of powers; Federal-provincial tax-sharing agreements; Judicial Committee of the Privy Council; Supreme Court.*

Public accounts committee. A standing committee of the House of Commons which is responsible for post-auditing government expenditures, primarily by examining the auditor general's annual report to Parliament. Provincial legislatures have a standing committee to perform a comparable task. As in other House of Commons committees, membership in the approximately 20-member committee is roughly proportional to party representation in the House. However, unlike other parliamentary committees, an Opposition member of Parliament has chaired this committee since 1957. In addition, the auditor general and the auditor general's staff assist the committee in its post-audit scrutiny. The auditor general's report and presentation to the committee are often more effective in attracting public attention than the committee's own report to the House. The public perceives the auditor general as an independent officer of Parliament, while the committee's activity is naturally partisan. The House receives the committee's report, which is usually ignored by the Government; the auditor general's report, however, is often the subject of parliamentary questions and debate and is widely reported to the public in the mass media.

At a conference on government auditing which the auditor general sponsored in 1978, the chairman of the Commons committee on public accounts, Conservative MP Ronald Huntington, said the committee could only review the broad issue of expenditure control. He recommended that comprehensive, cyclical audits by the auditor general be reviewed by additional House committees and that a new estimates committee be created to review major spending proposals. Huntington also recommended that the public accounts committee receive greater status, a separate budget for research and investigation, research staff, office space, and its own committee room. See *Auditor General.*

Public bills.   Bills introduced in a legislature either by the Government or a private member which are intended to be of general application to society. Government-sponsored public bills comprise most of the legislation introduced and are referred to as government bills, while those sponsored by private members are called private members' bills. Public bills may deal with any matter which falls within the competence of the legislature, but only Government-sponsored measures may involve the expenditure of money. See *Legislation; Private member's legislation.*

Public service (administration).   The public bureaucracy, also referred to as the civil service, which is characterized in Canada by large, well-defined hierarchical administrative units; it is staffed in large part by career officers ("civil servants") who work under an oath of secrecy. The federal public service includes several types of institutions. These are: government departments headed by deputy ministers and their assistants; several types of crown corporations; and central structures such as the Privy Council Office, the Federal-Provincial Relations Office; the Treasury Board Secretariat, and the Public Service Commission. Regulatory agencies, such as the Canadian Radio-television and Telecommunications Commission and the Canadian Transport Commission, are also part of the public service. Provincial public bureaucracies contain similar organizations.

    Theoretically, the public service is subject to general legislative authority and specific cabinet direction in applying and enforcing current policies and developing new policies. Because of the large size of the public service, there are concerns about its independence in terms of actual policy-determination and the lack of effective cabinet control of policy-implementation and financial expenditures. The cabinet theoretically controls the public service and is accountable to the legislature for the administration. In terms of policy, the cabinet committees and the Prime Minister's Office in recent years have been designed to act as counterweights to independent policy-making tendencies within the public service. However, the cabinet's secretariat, the Privy Council Office, is part of the bureaucracy. The budgetary process which is centred in the Treasury Board is also designed to control financial demands from the bureaucracy. However, the effectiveness of the Board is debatable; and again, the Treasury Board Secretariat itself is part of the public administration. In 1979, Parliament established the Office of Comptroller-General, responsible to the Treasury Board for the implementation of financial management controls within the public service.

In carrying out administrative duties under delegated authority, public officials often exercise considerable discretion in departments and regulatory agencies. In some cases, an aggrieved individual has no recourse to an independent judicial review of an administrative decision. In such cases, the only recourse may be an appeal to the cabinet, which operates informally and in secret.

The extent of rule-making within the public service, the principle of secrecy which makes public documents confidential unless declared public, and the apprehension about arbitrary bureaucratic decisions (including allegedly illegal behaviour, as in the case of the security services division of the Royal Canadian Mounted Police in the 1970's) have led to demands for federal and provincial freedom-of-information legislation to make public service documents more accessible to the public, and to the creation of ombudsmen to investigate complaints against decisions of public bodies. The federal Conservative Government's freedom-of-information legislation died on the Order Paper in 1979. In 1980, the Liberal Government promised to introduce its own measure.

Since the 1960's, collective bargaining legislation in several jurisdictions has altered the collegiality within the public service, at least at the mid- and low-level ranks. Public service unions, once virtually non-existent, are now among the largest unions in Canada. (See entries under many of the topics mentioned above.)

On the public administrations in Canada, see W.D. Kernaghan (ed.), *Public Administration in Canada: Selected Readings* (3rd. ed.; Toronto: Methuen Publications, 1977) and *Canadian Cases in Public Management* (Toronto: Methuen Publications, 1977); and T.J. Stevens, *The Business of Government: An Introduction to Canadian Public Administration* (Toronto: McGraw-Hill Ryerson Ltd., 1978). On the central agencies in particular, see Colin Campbell and George J. Szablowski, *The Super-Bureaucrats: Structure and Behaviour in Central Agencies* (Toronto: Macmillan Co. of Canada Ltd., 1979).

Public Service Commission.   The federal agency responsible to Parliament which staffs a large part of the federal public service under the Public Service Employment Act. The three-member Commission, appointed by the governor-in-council for ten-year renewable terms, appoints qualified persons to and from within the public service. It hears and makes decisions on appeals against staffing decisions, investigates and rules on allegations of discrimination and political partisanship, and operates staff development programmes. The creation of its predecessor, the Civil Service Commission, in 1908 introduced the principle of merit into a service that had been run on a partisan patronage basis. The merit principle has been modified since then, notably in the Official Languages Act of 1969, to encourage the development of a bilingual federal public service. In 1978, 26 per cent of the 279 207 federal civil servants employed under the Public Service Commission were francophones, a slight drop from 1977 (27 per cent of 282 788 employees). Comparable commissions exist in all the provinces.

The Public Service Commission "covers" approximately one-half of the federal public servants. Many senior civil servants hold their positions at the "pleasure" of the Government-of-the-day, while many federal departments, crown corporations, and other government bodies have the authority to hire personnel themselves. Also, the Treasury Board, which negotiates with civil servants on salary and working conditions, is responsible for some personnel management policy and administrative efficiency.

In its annual report to Parliament in 1978, the Commission proposed that senior staffing in the public service – which is now the prerogative of the cabinet, the Privy Council Office, and Treasury Board – be put under the jurisdiction of the Public Service Commission. The report argued that centralizing senior staffing would help increase scope for variety and advancement beyond that possible in any one department.

Public Service Staff Relations Board (Act).   A federal body which determines bargaining units and agents, hears complaints of unfair practices, and is generally responsible for the administration of collective-bargaining legislation in the public service which comes under the Public Service Staff Relations Act. The Board includes a full-time chairman, vice-chairman, and at least three deputy chairmen; they hold office for up to ten years. In addition, there are between four and eight part-time members, equally representing "employer interest" and "employee interest," appointed for up to seven years. The governor-in-council makes all appointments under provisions of the Public Service

Employment Act. The Board reports to Parliament through a minister who does not sit on the Treasury Board, the cabinet committee which deals with personnel management. See *Canada Labour Code; Canada Labour Relations Board*.

Quasi-judicial decisions.   Decisions made within the public administration, which are based upon discretionary power held under delegated legislative authority from Parliament and need not be made solely in accordance with laws and regulations. Discretionary quasi-judicial decisions are based on considerations of public policy and the public interest. The chief advantage of quasi-judicial power is the flexibility possessed by the decision-makers in the administration of complex regulatory matters. The chief disadvantage is that there is often limited recourse to the courts on appeal of such decisions; and, while discretionary power does not necessarily lead to arbitrary power, it introduces the suspicion of arbitrariness and weakens the principle of rule of law. Parliament and the courts remain, however, as overseers of the administrative process and the use of quasi-judicial power. See *Delegated power; Regulatory agencies (regulations); Rule of law*.

Quasi-party system.   C.B. Macpherson's description of the party system in Alberta in the 1920's and 1930's, which in his view was developed and sustained by a single-class society with a "quasi-colonial" status in relation to the metropolitan, or core, area of the country. The lack of internal social cleavages and the dependence upon a one-crop economy leads to the creation of indigenous mass-movement parties committed to specific notions of political and economic change – in the Canadian West, the Social Credit party in Alberta and the Co-operative Commonwealth Federation (CCF) in Saskatchewan. See *Agrarian socialism*.

See *Democracy in Alberta: Social Credit and the Party System* (Toronto: University of Toronto Press, 1953). Macpherson's analysis can be compared with Seymour Martin Lipset's account of "agrarian socialism" in *Agrarian Socialism: The Co-operative Commonwealth Federation in Saskatchewan* (Berkeley: University of California, 1950). See the exchange between Macpherson and Lipset in *Canadian Forum*, November and December, 1954, and January, 1955.

Quebec Act (1774-1791).   A British parliamentary act pertaining to the defeated French colony. The Act defined the territory of the conquered colony and the rights of its subjects. It extended the western boundaries to include land between the Ohio and Mississippi Rivers, granted freedom of worship to Roman Catholics, and sanctioned the retention of French civil law until altered by the colony. Criminal law was British. A Proclamation of 1763 to the British governor in Quebec had called for the establishment of a legislative assembly. However, the assertiveness of colonial assemblies to the south, coupled with doubt that the French majority in Quebec wanted an assembly, led instead to a provision in the Act for only an appointed legislative council. The Quebec Act may be seen as reactionary in that it reversed the trend toward representative government in British North America. On the other hand, the tolerance of the Act towards French-Canadian society might be seen as enlightened. When the American Revolution took place, Quebeckers did not participate. The Constitutional Act replaced the Quebec Act in 1791. See *Constitutional Act.*

Quebec Conference (Resolutions) (1864).   A conference of colonial representatives from Canada, Nova Scotia, New Brunswick, Prince Edward Island, and Newfoundland. It endorsed the principle, agreed upon a few months earlier at Charlottetown, of a federation or "legislative union" of all the colonies under the Crown. As a counterweight to centripetal forces, the new constitution would have a strong bicameral Parliament and inferior provincial legislatures. The Conference, which lasted only three weeks, resulted in 72 resolutions outlining such a union, including a resolution to obtain "the sanction of the Imperial and Local Parliaments" for the union.

The consensus achieved at Quebec, however, did not last. Only the Canadian legislature approved the resolutions and requested the British government to implement them. Prince Edward Island and Newfoundland repudiated the proposed union. The Government of New Brunswick was defeated on the question in an election; and the Nova Scotia Government avoided a division in the assembly to escape the same fate. The Canadians convinced the British of the value of the union, and they in turn applied pressure to bring about partial Maritime approval and participation. At a conference in London in 1866-1867 attended by delegates from Canada, New Brunswick, and Nova Scotia, the Quebec Resolutions were revised and some substituted. The Quebec and London resolutions were the basis for the British North America Act, which came into effect on July 1, 1867.

For a discussion of the Charlottetown, Quebec, and London conferences, see R. MacGregor Dawson, *The Government of Canada* (5th ed., rev. by Norman Ward; Toronto: University of Toronto Press, 1970), Chapter Two.

Question period. The occasion in the proceedings of the legislature when the Government is required to respond to oral and written questions from private members, usually Opposition legislators. The time devoted to questions varies in legislatures. In the House of Commons, for example, there is a daily 45-minute period for oral questions, while responses to written or starred questions are tabled and printed in *Hansard*. Though the question period is well established elsewhere in Canada, the procedure was introduced in the legislature of British Columbia only in 1972.

The oral question period is a highlight of legislative debate. Both Opposition members and Government ministers prepare carefully for the event, which is supposed to focus on urgent matters and elicit information from the Government. The Opposition's strategy is to embarrass the Government by forcing it to respond to interrogatory charges defined on the Opposition's terms. The Government's strategy, by contrast, is to respond briefly without appearing too disdainful. No debate is permitted during the period; but the "supplementary questions" allow a member an opportunity to cross-examine a minister who has evaded his or her question or to enter a brief riposte in *Hansard*.

The effectiveness of question period for the Opposition is measured by the amount of interest aroused in the press gallery on particular questions. The press may pick up some matters in interviews with Government and Opposition MPs in the lobbies following the question period. If the public shows an interest in a certain line of questioning, the Opposition will pursue the matter in subsequent question periods, and the relevant minister will have his or her senior civil servants prepare responses for further questions.

The question period is one of few occasions in a legislature when the Opposition should have a tactical advantage over the Government. While the questions may elicit information, the potential loser in the exchange is the Government, whose ministers may be seen to be evasive or ignorant. With the support of the senior officials, however, a minister should be well prepared for questions from a less well-briefed Opposition member. Question period generally keeps a Government attentive, and occasionally matters of ministerial or administrative recklessness are disclosed.

Quiet Revolution. A popular term for the totality of events in Quebec in the 1960's, when the provincial strategy for the survival of French society changed from a traditional, conservative, and defensive nationalism to a modern, aggressive nationalism, using the state as the chief instrument for change. The Quiet Revolution is associated in particular with the Liberal Government of Jean Lesage from 1960 to 1966 and with the slogan "*Maîtres chez nous.*" The return to office of the more traditional *Union nationale* from 1966 to 1970 did not reverse the direction of change. Numerous "separatist" movements came into being, and in 1968 several merged to form the *Parti Québécois* under former Liberal minister René Lévesque.

While the Quiet Revolution led to new demands upon the federal government and applied new strains to Confederation, it had dramatic effects within French society in Quebec. These included the growth of post-secondary educational institutions, expansion of the public sector, intellectual fervour manifested in the arts, increased militancy among trade unions, and the decline of the Roman Catholic Church as a social and political force.

The federal government's response to the Quiet Revolution is associated with Lester Pearson's Liberal Government from 1963 to 1968 and Pierre Trudeau's first Government in particular from 1968 to 1972. The federal government acceded to Quebec's concerns about financial and administrative autonomy in the formula for contracting, or opting, out of shared-cost federal-provincial programmes. It promoted constitutional reform and a policy to increase bilingualism in the federal public service and to strengthen the position of French minorities outside Quebec. See *Bilingualism and biculturalism; Parti Québécois; Sovereignty-association.*

For a bibliography on French Canada, including references on the Quiet Revolution, see Richard J. Van Loon and Michael S. Whittington, *The Canadian Political System: Environment, Structure, and Process* (2nd ed.; Toronto: McGraw-Hill Ryerson Ltd., 1976). See also Dale Posgate and Kenneth McRoberts, *Quebec: Social Change and Political Crisis* (Toronto: McClelland and Stewart Ltd., 1976); and Edward McWhinney, *Quebec and the Canadian Constitution, 1960-1978* (Toronto: University of Toronto Press, 1979).

Quorum. A specific number of members of a legislative body required to be present before it can meet and conduct business. In the legislatures and their committees, the Government party whip is responsible for ensuring that enough Government MPs are available to establish a quorum should the Opposition seek to embarrass the Government by challenging the existence of a quorum and forcing the legislature or committee to adjourn. The quorum for Parliament established under the British North America Act is 20 MPs for the House of Commons, including the Speaker (Section 48), and 15 senators including the Speaker for the Senate (Section 35).

R

Radio-Canada.   The French-language section of the Canadian Broadcasting Corporation, with production facilities located in Montreal. See *Canadian Broadcasting Corporation.*

Ralliement des créditistes.   The Quebec section of the federal Social Credit party, which experienced its greatest electoral successes in the 1960's and outlived the anglophone section of the federal party in electoral importance. The party grew increasingly weaker during the 1970's and failed to win a seat in the 1980 election. Despite national pretensions, the federal Social Credit party in the 1970's was the Quebec organization.

The Social Credit emerged in Quebec in the 1940's as the *Union des Electeurs*. In 1962, when Social Credit could elect only two members each from British Columbia and Alberta, the *Ralliement* (led by Réal Caouette) won 26 seats in Quebec, second to the Liberals' 35. Like Social Credit earlier in the West, the *Ralliement* under Caouette was an indigenous and populist movement, responding to the economic and social grievances among the rural and small-town population. The *Ralliement* also benefited from the lack of any other alternative to the dominant Liberal party.

After 1962, friction developed not unexpectedly between the Quebec and western sections of the federal party, whose formal leader was one of the western MPs. Eventually, the federal Conservative party displaced the Social Credit party in the West, leaving the *Ralliement* as the major electoral force in the party. Since 1965, the *Ralliement* has alternated between alliance and separation from anglophone Social Crediters. The existence of the *créditiste* MPs from Quebec was based largely on their personal appeal and the weakness of the Conservative and New Democratic parties in Quebec. In 1979, under Fabien Roy, the party won only six seats and 14 per cent of the popular vote in Quebec. In 1980, it failed to win any seats and obtained 5 per cent of the popular vote in Quebec. See *Third parties; Social Credit party.*

Readings.   Stages of legislative approval required for the passage of bills. See *Legislation.*

Recall.   A device by which electors may remove someone from elective office. The recall was associated with the delegate theory of representation, which would ensure that the legislator represented the interests of his or her constituents. Recall had support particularly among the United Farmers parties and the Progressive movement in the early twentieth century. Manitoba experimented with recall, and Alberta had a Recall Act until 1937. There is no provision for recall currently in any provincial or federal elections act. See *Delegate theory of representation.*

Reciprocity.   The elimination of protective tariffs and other customs duties between countries and the establishment of free trade. The issue of protection versus free trade traditionally distinguished the federal Conservatives from the federal Liberals, although the differences were more symbolic than real. The Conservatives were associated with protection, largely as a result of the National Policy of Sir John A. Macdonald in the 1880's; the Liberals have been associated with reciprocity and free trade, generally as a result of the proposed agreement with the United States which resulted in Liberal defeat in 1911. Reciprocity was popular in western Canada, where the protective tariff on manufactured goods was seen to benefit eastern interests to the detriment of westerners.

Reconstruction party.   A political party created in 1935 by H.H. Stevens, formerly a prominent minister in Prime Minister R.B. Bennett's Conservative Government. Stevens was concerned about the level of profits being made by retail stores and packing houses during the depression. His frequent attacks on business when in cabinet resulted in rebukes from the prime minister. Stevens resigned from the cabinet and was appointed to head a royal commission on price spreads and mass buying. Later, when Bennett seemed reluctant to deal with the royal commission's recommendations for coping with unfair competition and profiteering, Stevens resigned from the party and formed the Reconstruction party – whose platform, of course, included the recommendations of Stevens' royal commission.

The party contested only the election of 1935, when it received 8.7 per cent of the popular vote – almost as many votes as received by the Co-operative Commonwealth Federation (CCF) and twice as many votes as the Social Credit party (both of which were also contesting a federal election for the first time). The party, however, won only one seat, Stevens', while the CCF won seven seats and the Social Credit 17.

The fate of the Reconstruction Party is a lesson to elite members of parliamentary parties who would abandon their party of power for a solo exercise in party politics. The fate of the party also demonstrated the bias of the electoral system against parties with diffused national support. The party had won over 10 per cent of the vote in Nova Scotia, New Brunswick, and Ontario, but failed to win any seats in those provinces. See *Electoral system; Fragment parties; Single-member plurality electoral system.*

Red Tory (-ism). A concept to describe those whose sympathy for collectivist public policy associated with state intervention in the economy and society seems to be based, not on liberal notions of progress or the egalitarian values of social democracy, but on a traditional conservative or Tory value of obligation inherent in a hierarchical society which is necessary for the preservation of the social order. Thus, George Grant, writing from such a perspective, has said: "There is confusion in the minds of those who believe in socialism and the emancipation of the passions. It is surely difficult to deny that greed in some form is a desire of man qua man and is not simply produced by the society of scarcity. If this is so, to emancipate the passions is to emancipate greed. Yet what is socialism, if it is not the use of government to restrain greed in the name of social good? In actual practice, socialism has always had to advocate inhibition in this respect. In doing so, was it not appealing to the conservative idea of social order against the liberal idea of freedom?" (*Lament for a Nation: The Defeat of Canadian Nationalism* [Toronto: McClelland and Stewart Ltd., 1965], 58-59). Reprinted by permission of the Canadian Publishers, McClelland and Stewart, Toronto.

Gad Horowitz has argued that the existence of a "Tory streak" in English-Canadian political tradition has made the anglophone political culture different from that in the United States. For example, he writes, the Conservative party is "a business oriented party." The "primary component of the ideology" of such a party is "liberalism," but "Tory ideology does *help* to account for the fact that a British or Canadian as distinguished from an American right-wing, business-dominated, conservative party has been capable of mounting statist projects" ("Notes on 'Conservatism, Liberalism, and Socialism in Canada,'" *Canadian Journal of Political Science* 11 [1978], 392-93, emphasis in the original).

For Horowitz's original statement, see "Conservatism, Liberalism, and Socialism in Canada: An Interpretation," *Canadian Journal of Economics and Political Science* 32 (1966), 143-71. See also Rod Preece, "The Anglo-Saxon Conservative Tradition," *Canadian Journal of Political Science* 13 (1980), 3-32.

Redistribution (electoral).   The periodic defining of federal and provincial constituency boundaries to take into account population growth and shifts that have taken place since the previous redistribution. Redistribution takes place every decade and usually results in the creation of additional constituencies; it usually involves the reduction of seats in some parts of the jurisdiction and an increase elsewhere. See *Electoral Boundaries Readjustment Act.*

Redistributive policy.   Public policy designed to allocate wealth on an egalitarian basis. Debate over redistributive issues are class-related. Those supporting redistribution are on the left of the class cleavage, and those opposing redistribution are on the right. Debate in this century, and especially since the depression of the 1930's, has focussed on the role of the state or public sector in conscripting private wealth and economic power to provide basic welfare services. One means of doing this is through the tax system. Another is through the statutory power of government to nationalize certain industries or to create public corporations to compete with private companies and modify their behaviour – and to regulate the economy generally through fiscal and monetary policies and regulatory commissions in the administration.

In the 1970's, serious criticism developed concerning the size of government involvement at all levels in the Canadian economy. The criticism was particularly powerful because it included left-wing critics, who argued that there was no necessary connection between the size of the public sector, the regulatory influence of the state, and the distribution of personal wealth in society. Indeed, some alleged that redistributive state policies had reinforced the unequal distribution of wealth. While the lower strata of society benefited from the welfare state, the middle and upper levels appeared to acquire proportionately greater benefits. Massive investments of public funds in university education since World War Two, and government-sponsored medical care programmes instituted in the 1960's, are two cases which suggest that public programmes are not necessarily progressive, and may indeed be regressive. See *Class cleavage.*

For an analysis of redistributive policy and Canadian political parties, see Douglas McCready and Conrad Winn, "Redistributive Policy," in C. Winn and J. McMenemy, *Political Parties in Canada* (Toronto: McGraw-Hill Ryerson Ltd., 1976), 206-27. On social development policies in Canada, see Marsha A. Chandler and William M. Chandler, *Public Policy and Provincial Politics* (Toronto: McGraw-Hill Ryerson Ltd., 1979), 178-252.

Reference.   A judicial decision on a question of legislative jurisdiction referred to the courts by a provincial or the federal government. The reference may facilitate federal-provincial agreement on the particular matter and avoid subsequent litigation on actual legislation. A concern about this procedure is that, as references become instruments in federal-provincial negotiations rather than definitive judicial verdicts, the Court may be seen to be involved in political negotiations rather than independent adjudication. Recent references from the federal government to the Supreme Court concerned jurisdiction over west coast off-shore mineral rights and the ability of Parliament to amend unilaterally the constitution of the Senate. Important earlier references include decisions on Prime Minister R.B. Bennett's "New Deal" legislation in 1937. See *Judicial Committee of the Privy Council; New Deal; Supreme Court.*

Referendum.   A means of submitting a policy, constitutional question, or proposed legislation to the electors. The device is contrary to the principle of the supremacy of Parliament. In the United States, however, approximately 20 state and many municipal legislatures use the referendum to settle policy and constitutional questions; and citizens have the right to petition for an obligatory referendum on a legislative enactment or on the failure to enact legislation. In the case of legislative inaction, the popular demand for a referendum is called an initiative. Australia uses the referendum for constitutional amendments. Switzerland employs the procedure for a wide range of policy.

Canadians have only limited experience with referendums. The Progressive party in the early twentieth century supported the institution of the referendum in the American manner. National referendums have been held in Canada only twice, in 1898 and 1942 (under enabling legislation), on prohibition and conscription. In both cases, results were not binding, and the referendums represented dilatory behaviour on the part of the federal Governments. The vote in 1942 – actually defined as a plebiscite – to release the Government from its anti-conscription election pledge two years earlier was designed to avoid effective resolution of a seriously divisive issue.

Two referendums were held in Newfoundland in 1949 on the question of union with Canada. Newfoundlanders barely rejected Confederation in the first referendum and accepted it in the second.

In the election of 1976 in Quebec, the successful *Parti Québécois* promised a referendum on the question of Quebec's independence. Two years later, the Quebec legislature passed enabling legislation generally allowing referendums. In 1979, the PQ Government published the question – which asked for a mandate to negotiate sovereignty-association – and held the referendum in 1980. The question included a promise to hold a second referendum to obtain approval before effecting any negotiated "change in political status." The enabling legislation of 1978 required the creation of two umbrella committees by members of the national assembly to control participation and expenditures during the referendum campaign. Also in 1978, the federal Liberal Government countered with legislation, which subsequently died on the Order Paper, to allow for non-binding national or provincial votes on questions related to "political and judicial institutions and processes." According to the Government, this bill was designed, not in response to Quebec's proposed referendum, but as part of a constitutional amending formula should one or more provincial governments oppose an amendment. The federal legislation did not propose umbrella committees as in the Quebec legislation; but it would have restricted private spending in a campaign, placed no restrictions on federal and provincial political party involvement, and provided for partial public reimbursement to parties and registered referendum committees for expenses.

Regina Manifesto. The basic document of the Co-operative Commonwealth Federation (CCF), adopted in Regina in 1933; it committed the party to public ownership of industries and government planning to create "democratic self-government, based on economic equality." The Manifesto declared that "the principle regulating production, distribution, and exchange will be the supplying of human needs and not the making of profits. We aim to replace the present capitalist system, with its inherent injustice and inhumanity, by a social order . . . in which economic planning will supersede unregulated private enterprise and competition . . . ." The document asserted that no CCF government would "rest content" until it had "eradicated capitalism and put into operation the full programme of socialized planning . . . ." The members of the League for Social Reconstruction drafted the document, and the CCF executive revised it before it was adopted by the party. See *League for Social Reconstruction*.

Regional disparity.   The discrepancy between the levels of natural, industrial, and personal wealth in different parts of the country. The disparity in wealth, especially as it is defined in geographic terms, has fostered the development of a powerful geographic cleavage in Canadian politics. For example, in the early half of the twentieth century in the prairie West, the combination of geographic and class-related discontent led to the development of indigenous mass political movements.

Federal-provincial tax-sharing agreements since World War Two have been designed to "equalize" the revenue of provincial governments in Canada in order to provide comparable public services to the population. Since the 1960's, specific federal policies for regional development have included the Agricultural Rehabilitation and Rural Development Act (1961), the Fund for Rural Economic Development (1966), and the Regional Incentives Development Act (1969). The federal and provincial governments signed comprehensive general development agreements in 1973 to co-ordinate federal programmes for the development of particular provinces and regions under the aegis of the federal Department of Regional and Economic Expansion, which was created in 1969.

Debate persists over federal development strategy in so-called "designated regions." For example, is social capital invested in retraining workers preferable to capital investment in new plants and machinery? Is the commitment of public capital and the direction of private capital into low-income regions a better strategy than the promotion of labour retraining and subsequent emigration to high-productivity areas of the country? Given the legitimacy of national objectives, to what extent and cost should national public enterprises be compelled to sustain regional objectives? See *Department of Regional Economic Expansion; Federal-provincial tax-sharing agreements; Geographic cleavage.*

On public policy to deal with regional disparity, see T.N. Brewis, *Regional Economic Policies in Canada* (Toronto: Macmillan Co. of Canada Ltd., 1969); Marsha A. Chandler and William M. Chandler, *Public Policy and Provincial Politics* (Toronto: McGraw-Hill Ryerson Ltd., 1979), especially Chapters 5, 6, and 7; Allan G. Green, "Regional Economic Disparities," in Lawrence H. Officer and Lawrence B. Smith (eds.), *Issues in Canadian Economics* (Toronto: McGraw-Hill Ryerson Ltd., 1974), 354-70; and R. W. Phidd, "Regional Development Policy," in G. Bruce Doern and V. Seymour Wilson (eds.), *Issues in Canadian Public Policy* (Toronto: Macmillan Co. of Canada Ltd., 1974), 166-202.

Regionalism. A term used objectively to indicate distinctive areas within a larger spatial unit, and normatively to indicate a positive or negative impact of such distinctiveness in the larger unit. In Canada, for example, the country is divided into several regions for purposes of representation in the Senate under the British North America Act; the provinces are autonomous political units in the federal state which may individually or collectively constitute regions; and several provinces contain regional urban municipalities. On a normative level, governments have sought to overcome socio-economic regional disparities, while in cultural terms regionalsim has tended to be viewed as a positive force, notably by French Canadians and westerners. See *Cultural duality; Geographic cleavage; Political culture; Quiet Revolution; Regional disparity.*

On the importance of regionalism in Canadian politics, see David J. Elkins and Richard Simeon, *Small Worlds: Parties and Provinces in Canadian Political Life* (Toronto: Methuen Publications, 1980); and Mildred A. Schwartz, *Politics and Territory: The Sociology of Regional Persistence in Canada* (Montreal: McGill-Queen's University Press, 1974). See also Donald E. Blake, "The Measurement of Regionalism in Canadian Voting Patterns," *Canadian Journal of Political Science* 5 (1972), 55-81. For an analysis of the relationship of effects of region and class on political attitudes, see Michael D. Ornstein, H. Michael Stevenson, and A. Paul Williams, "Region, Class and Political Culture in Canada," *Canadian Journal of Political Science* 13 (1980), 227–71.

Regulation 17 (Ontario, 1912). A provincial regulation which severely restricted the use of French in education in Ontario schools. This anti-French measure was particularly objectionable because there were sizeable French communities in the province, especially in the Ottawa Valley along the Ontario-Quebec border, including the national capital. The dispute over Regulation 17 was one of several disputes around the turn of the century over minority rights in education which were "protected" in the British North America Act (Section 93) but had been under attack since passage of the Manitoba Schools Act in 1890. See *Manitoba schools question.*

See *Report of the Royal Commission on Bilingualism and Biculturalism,* 2 (Ottawa, 1968), 47-53.

Regulatory agencies (regulations). Public boards which are created and operate under authority delegated by a particular statute to regulate, supervise, and administer public policy and "advise" the government on new policy. A regulation enacted by a regulatory agency has the force of law. Thus, many agencies sit as courts of record, examining witnesses under oath, compelling the production of papers, and enforcing the agencies' orders. Important and well-known federal regulatory agencies include the Atomic Energy Control Board, the Canadian Radio-television and Telecommunications Commission, the Canadian Transport Commission, and the National Energy Board.

The delegated power which regulatory agencies possess may be judicial and quasi-judicial – that is, judicial in that the statute or regulations of the agency determine the decision; and quasi-judicial in that the agency may exercise discretion in making its decision. The fact that agencies may establish and enforce regulations, and exercise quasi-judicial functions, creates considerable scope for abuse of delegated power.

Particular statutes set out the procedure for appeal to the courts or the cabinet of the decisions of each regulatory agency. The regulatory agencies do not operate according to uniform procedures, but they must have publicly known procedures; however, federal and provincial cabinets which traditionally operate in secret, have no publicly acknowledged procedures for dealing with appeals.

In 1979, the Economic Council of Canada published an interim report on the effect of government regulation in the economy. The Council said that widespread deregulation was not advisable; but regulation by federal and provincial governments discourages the economic integration of the country and inhibits technical change in private business. The Council recommended an assessment of economic costs and benefits of new regulations before they are implemented, as well as periodic review of existing regulations. To protect the independence and impartiality of the agencies and the regulatory process, the Council also recommended public funding of public-interest groups and the abolition of appeals to cabinets (*Responsible Regulation* [Ottawa: 1979]).

Douglas G. Hartle, of the Institute for Policy Analysis at the University of Toronto, has recommended that regulatory agencies be created in two categories. One category of agencies would be advisory, and the second category would be decision-making. He would abolish the cabinet's power to override decisions of the second category. The independence of these commissions would be spelled out in legislation; and, if a Government found it necessary to oppose a decision, it would do so by introducing legislation in Parliament. Thus, the cabinet's intervention in the regulatory process would be a public matter debated by Parliament (*Public Policy Decision-making and Regulation*

[Montreal: Institute for Research on Public Policy, 1979]). See *Delegated power; Rule of law.*

On the regulatory process, see also G. Bruce Doern (ed.), *The Regulatory Process in Canada* (Toronto: Macmillan Co. of Canada Ltd., 1978).

Remedial legislation. Legislation which the federal cabinet may introduce on its own or in response to appeals to the governor-in-council, to protect denominational schools established in a province at the time of union. Section 93 of the British North America Act gives the provinces the right to legislate on education providing they do not violate the established rights of a Protestant or Roman Catholic minority in the province. Remedial legislation, however, represents an explicit limit on provincial rights; and, as a result, the courts rather than the federal government have become the guardian of sectarian minority education rights. Remedial legislation introduced by the Conservative Government to deal with the anti-French and anti-Catholic Manitoba Schools Act of 1890 failed to pass in the face of Liberal opposition. The Liberals nonetheless appeared to win on the issue in Quebec, where they posed as defenders of provincial rights. In 1978, the federal Liberal Government refused to introduce remedial legislation to counter the provisions of Quebec's Official Language Act, which affect English-language education in the province. See *Manitoba schools question; Bill 101 (Charter of the French Language).*

Renewed/Restructured federalism. Terms devised in the late 1970's to describe various options for constitutional reform in opposition to the sovereignty-association proposals of the *Parti Québécois.* The federal Liberal Government described its proposals in the constitutional amendment bill of 1978 as "renewed federalism." Other proposals by the Liberal party of Quebec under Claude Ryan since 1977 have generally been referred to as "renewed federalism" (see *A New Canadian Federation* [1980], published by the party's constitution committee). In 1979, the federal Task Force on Canadian Unity described its proposals as "restructured federalism." See *Federalism; Sovereignty-association; Task Force (. . . on Canadian Unity).*

Representation by population. The determination of representation in a legislature according to the size of the population. The phrase "Rep by Pop" was a political slogan of Reformers such as George Brown in Canada West (Lower Canada, Ontario) in the 1850's, when the census of 1851 showed that the population of Canada West had become larger than Canada East (Lower Canada, Quebec). In the Act of Union of 1840, which reunited Upper and Lower Canada in the Province of Canada, Canada East had equal representation in the assembly with Canada West, although until 1851 the former's population was larger.

In Confederation, the British North America Act established representation by population in the House of Commons. Representatives for Canada East had agreed to "Rep by Pop" in the new House of Commons in return for permanent sectional balance in the appointed Senate, with an equal number of senators from Quebec, Ontario, the three Maritime provinces combined, and the four western provinces combined (Sections 21, 22, 40). In 1952, a minimum number of seats was guaranteed in the federal Representation Act to sparsely populated provinces and the territories.

Representation Commissioner. The federal officer responsible for preparing alternative proposals for electoral boundary changes to the Electoral Boundaries Commissions following each decennial census. The commissioner is a member of each of the provincial boundaries commissions and reports on behalf of the commissions to the House of Commons through the Speaker. The commissioner also reviews methods of registering voters and methods of absentee voting in federal elections. The commissioner is appointed by a resolution of the House of Commons, and can be removed only by a resolution of both the House and Senate. See *Electoral Boundaries Readjustment Act (redistribution)*.

Representative government. A political system with provisions for a legislature which is representative of the population. The phrase is usually a reference to the eighteenth- and nineteenth-century forms of government in the British colonies. Representative government existed in the British colonies in America in the eighteenth century, when the British-appointed governor received the opinions of an appointed legisative council and an elected legislative assembly.

The Quebec Act (1774) required the governor of that colony to establish an appointed legislative council but not an elected assembly, which was "at present inexpedient." Provisions for elected assemblies then came with the creation of Upper and Lower Canada by the Constitutional Act of 1791. The institution of representative government was of little consequence, as the decisions of the assemblies were only advisory to the governor and his appointed Executive Council. The Executive Councils of Upper and Lower Canada, for example, were drawn from society's elite (known as the Family Compact and the Château Clique). Representative government acquired significant meaning in British North America only with the granting of responsible government, which required the governor to select executive advisors from those who had the support of the legislative assembly. See *Responsible government*.

Representative theory of representation. A theory of representation according to which members of a legislature are elected to represent views which are in the national interest, even though they may conflict with the interests of their particular areas or the view of the majority of their constituents. Thus, in the representative theory, members are to exercise their own personal judgment and not be bound by previous commitments to individual or group interests. This theory is consistent with the provisions of parliamentary government, which hold parliament to be a supreme assembly of representatives from all regions of the province or country freely debating and determining public policy. The theory runs counter to the delegate and occupational group theories of representation, and against such populist inhibitions on legislators and parliaments as recall and referendum. This theory is enforced federally by the Canada Elections Act, which makes it illegal for any candidate for the House of Commons to sign a document which would "prevent him [or her] from exercising freedom of action in Parliament . . . , or to resign . . . if called upon to do so by any person . . . or association. . . ."

In practice, the disciplined party system compromises the representative theory. Most candidates for election to the House of Commons and the provincial legislatures stand on behalf of political parties, and they can be relied upon to support their party in the legislature. It was this reality, combined with the perceived insensitivity of the established parliamentary parties' leadership to the interests of western farmers, that gave rise to the delegate and occupational group theories of representation in Canada in the early twentieth century and to demands for the introduction of the institutions of recall and referendum. See *Delegate theory of representation; Recall; Referendum*.

Reservation (of legislation). Powers possessed in the early years of Confederation by the governor general to reserve certain classes of bills for the "Queen's Pleasure" (that is, for approval or disallowance by the British Government); power similarly possessed by the lieutenant-gov-

ernors, under the British North America Act, to reserve provincial bills
for the pleasure of the governor-in-council (that is, the federal cabinet).
The imperial conference in 1926 and a conference in 1929 declared British interference in the legislation of the dominions to be unconstitutional, although the disallowance power in Section 56 of the British North
America Act remains "on the books." Sections 56 and 90, which allow
for reservation and disallowance of provincial legislation, are effectively inoperative. Federal reservation and disallowance powers were
consistent with the intentions of the "fathers" of Confederation to create
a federal, but centralized, union. However, many of the cases of reservation by lieutenant-governors were embarrassing to the federal cabinets,
including the most recent case in Saskatchewan in 1961. Moreover, the
trend of federal-provincial relations in the twentieth century, assisted
by judicial decisions, has been in the opposite direction. In a reference
sought by the federal Government in 1938, the Supreme Court declared
the powers of reservation and disallowance to be unimpaired (Disallowance and Reservation Case). However, recent proposals for constitutional amendments, such as the ill-fated Victoria Charter (1971), have
contained no provision for reservation and disallowance. See
Disallowance; Victoria Charter.

See John T. Saywell, *The Office of Lieutenant-Governor: A Study in
Canadian Government and Politics* (Toronto: University of Toronto
Press, 1957). On the most recent case of reservation, see J.R. Mallory,
"The Lieutenant-Governor's Discretionary Powers: The Reservation of
Bill 56," *Canadian Journal of Economics and Political Science* 27
(1961), 518-22.

Residual power.   A comprehensive grant of legislative authority to
one particular level of government in a federation, exclusive of those
areas in which authority has been explicitly assigned. In Canada, the
"fathers" of Confederation clearly intended Parliament to possess residual power; as outlined in Section 91 of the British North America Act:
Parliament would legislate "for the Peace, Order and good Government
of Canada, in relation to all Matters not coming within the Classes of
Subjects ... assigned exclusively to the Legislatures of the Provinces."
The "fathers" then listed federal powers under enumerated heads "for
greater Certainty, but not so as to restrict the Generality of the foregoing
...."

Through judicial review, the Judicial Committee of the Privy Council
managed to frustrate the clear intentions of the "fathers" by elevating
the enumerated head outlining provincial jurisdiction with respect to

"Property and Civil Rights in the Province" (92:13) to a position superior to that of the general clause in Section 91. By the turn of the century, the Judicial Committee had separated the general clause and the enumerated heads of Section 91 and declared the enumerated heads of both Sections 91 and 92 to take precedence over the "Peace, Order and good Government" clause except in dire national emergencies. Thus, the all-inclusive enumerated head "Property and Civil Rights in the Province" acquired superior status; and residual power came to rest largely with the provincial legislatures. The Supreme Court became the final judicial arbiter of the constitution in 1949. Since then, it has tended to broaden the federal government's emergency use of "Peace, Order and good Government" in matters of "inherent national importance." See *Judicial Committee of the Privy Council*; *"Peace Order and good Government"*; *"Property and Civil Rights"*; *Supreme Court.*

Resource rents and royalties. In economics, rent is the surplus above normal returns that accrue to a factor of production in conditions of inelastic, or fixed, supply. "Resource rents" is a term used to describe the additional surplus revenue which accrues in an imperfectly competitive world (when, for example, the price for oil rises); it is surplus to costs and profits required to encourage further investment of capital, labour, and supplies. Resource royalties are taxes which owner-governments impose on the resource developer; they are fixed to quantities of the extracted resource, that is, $X for each barrel of oil. The political debate is largely over how this surplus revenue or rent from increased prices in oil ("windfall profits") is to be captured and shared between the resource-owning provinces and the federal government.

The intergovernmental debate in Canada over who should appropriate resource rent matches the resource-rich provinces (which can recover the rent through manipulation of the royalties system in their provinces) against some resource-poor provinces and the federal government, the latter being able to recover the rent through corporation tax and to redistribute some of it through equalization grants.

Resource income is included in provincial revenues for the purpose of calculating provincial entitlements to federal equalization payments. Increased resource revenues for a few provinces since 1973 have resulted in distortions when calculating equalization grants from the federal treasury to the "have-not" provinces. Ontario, for example, which has one of the highest provincial levels of per capita income, has come close to qualifying for equalization payments. In attempts to cope with the "windfall" revenues to the oil-producing provinces, the federal Liberal Government threatened not to allow royalties paid to the provincial governments as income deductible from corporate income which was taxable by the federal government. In 1975, Parliament also enacted legislation permitting the federal Government to set prices for oil and natural gas in the event of disagreement with the resource-owning provinces. See *National oil policy; Natural resources.*

See Anthony Scott (ed.), *Natural Resource Revenues: A Test of Federalism* (Vancouver: University of British Columbia Press, 1976); Marsha A. Chandler and William M. Chandler, *Public Policy and Provincial Politics* (Toronto: McGraw-Hill Ryerson Ltd., 1979), 253-71; and John Weir, "Trade and Resource Policies," in C. Winn and J. McMenemy, *Political Parties in Canada* (Toronto: McGraw-Hill Ryerson Ltd., 1977), 228-49.

Responsible government. The requirement by convention of the Canadian constitution that the Government remain in office only as long as it has the support of the legislature. Thus, the governor general (lieutenant-governors in the provinces) usually appoints as prime minister (premier) the acknowledged leader of the largest party represented in the House. In turn, the prime minister will recommend the appointment of party supporters in the legislature (or soon to be in the legislature) as members of the cabinet – the effective part of the governor general's Privy Council (the lieutenant-governor's Executive Council). Should the Government lose a major vote in the House, the prime minister will ask the governor general to dissolve Parliament and issue writs for an election, or the prime minister must resign. Should an election result indicate doubtful long-term support for the prime minister in the new House, the prime minister still has the right to meet the House within a reasonable time to seek its confidence. Responsible government came to Nova Scotia, New Brunswick, and Canada in 1848, and to Prince Edward Island in 1851.

On the non-statutory introduction of responsible government in British North America in the nineteenth century, see R. MacGregor Dawson, *The Government of Canada* (5th ed., rev. by Norman Ward; Toronto: University of Toronto Press, 1970), 9-19.

Restrictive Trade Practices Commission. A federal commission established under the Combines Investigation Act; it reports to the minister of consumer and corporate affairs on possible illegal business activities, such as combines and price-fixing. The governor-in-council appoints the three-member Commission, which reviews evidence submitted by the director of investigation and research in the department. The Commission may receive further information from people involved; following a formal hearing, it makes recommendations to the minister on the material and the effects of disclosed practices on the public interest. In turn, the minister may refer the matter to the attorney-general of Canada for legal proceedings. Whether the Government acts or not, it must publish the Commission's reports within thirty days of their receipt. See *Combines (anti-combines legislation)*.

Returning officer (district) (DRO).   The principal electoral officer in a constituency, appointed by the chief electoral officer, who is responsible for the direction and supervision of the administration of a general election or by-election. The duties of the DRO include: the training of enumerators and poll clerks; the establishment of polling stations; the registration of voters, and the publication and distribution of the voters' lists and their revisions; the administration of advance polls, and the polling on election day; the counting and official reporting of the vote; and the care of the ballots cast and unused ballots. Political parties and the public may call upon the DRO for clarification of the provisions of the Elections Act.

Riding.   An informal term for constituency, a legislative district. See *Constituency*.

Rowell-Sirois Royal Commission on Dominion-Provincial Relations (1937-1940).   A royal commission which the federal government established unilaterally to examine and make recommendations on the distribution of powers and the financial relationship between the federal and provincial governments. Its evidence and report constitute an important study of the basis of Confederation, which set the stage for major restructuring of federal-provincial relations following World War Two.

In brief, the Commission recommended a transfer of functions and a shifting of taxation power to the federal government and the creation of grants to the provinces on the basis of need, to equalize the tax revenues of the provinces. Thus, every province could "provide for its people services of average Canadian standards and . . . thus alleviate the stress and shameful conditions which now weaken national unity and handicap many Canadians . . . without resort to heavier taxation than the Canadian average, to provide adequate social, educational, and de-

240The Language of Canadian Politics

velopmental services" (*Report of the Royal Commission on Dominion-Provincial Relations*, 2 [Ottawa: 1940], 125,86). Specifically, the Commission recommended that the provinces give up personal income and corporation taxes and succession duties, and that the federal government assume all provincial debts and accept responsibility for relief of the unemployed and a proposed old age pension. The federal government would pay an adjustment grant to "have-not" provinces.

The Rowell-Sirois report was presented to Parliament in 1940 and discussed at the Dominion-Provincial Conference in 1941. Although the report itself met with considerable provincial opposition, many of its proposals were effectively introduced on a piece-meal basis during the 1940's.

On the Commission and its report, see R. MacGregor Dawson, *The Government of Canada* (5th ed., rev. by Norman Ward; Toronto: University of Toronto Press, 1970), Chapter 6; and Donald V. Smiley, *Canada in Question: Federalism in the 70's* (2nd ed.; Toronto: McGraw-Hill Ryerson Ltd., 1976), 117-20.

Royal assent.   Approval by the Crown's representative (the governor general, or the lieutenant-governor of a province) given to legislation passed by the legislature. By convention, royal assent has become a formality. The date on which assent is given is endorsed on every act, becomes part of the act, and is the date on which the act takes effect unless other provisions for its proclamation are contained in it. See *Crown prerogatives; Reservation*.

Royal Canadian Mounted Police (RCMP).   The federal law-enforcement agency created in 1873 which enforces criminal and provincial law in all provinces except Quebec and Ontario, and operates also in the Yukon and Northwest Territories. The RCMP is a civil force, trained and organized in a para-military fashion. The principal officers are appointed by the governor-in-council. They include: a commissioner and three deputy commissioners (criminal operations, administration, national policy service), and a director general for the security service division. Only the head of the security service division is a civilian; by tradition, the others are career officers in the force.

In 1978-1980, a federal royal commission chaired by Judge David McDonald investigated allegations of wrongdoing by the RCMP during the 1970's. Matters referred to the McDonald Commission included: a break-in at *Parti Québécois* headquarters and the theft of membership lists and financial documents (1973); 400 break-ins without warrants by the criminal investigations branch, mainly in British Columbia (since 1970); penetration of the New Democratic party's "Waffle" faction (1970-1973); the electronic surveillance of at least one member of Parliament (1977); unauthorized, widespread mail openings (1950's-1976); the burning of a barn in Quebec (1972); theft of dynamite (1972); use of forged documents (1971); widespread monitoring of election candidates (since the 1950's); and the use of violence in recruiting informants (early 1970's in Quebec). From1970 to 1977, a special unit existed within the RCMP headquarters to authorize "disruptive operations" or "dirty tricks," regardless of legality or propriety. Some of the above items were also being investigated in the late 1970's by a Quebec inquiry (Keable Commision). Also under investigation in Ontario (Krever Commission) was the inspection of confidential files (widespread since 1970).

One of the objectives of the McDonald inquiry was to ascertain the degree of ministerial culpability in these events. There was liaison among the Royal Canadian Mounted Police, senior civil servants, and three solicitors general during the 1970's. It appears, however, that communications were characterized partly by distrust between the civilians and the police officers; but there also appeared to be a desire on the part of the police to protect their "cabinet boss" from having embarrassing information, and an equal desire on the ministers' part to keep from possessing it. While the RCMP officers testified to the McDonald Commission that they had informed their ministers of various activities, the three former solicitors general each testified that they had not been informed.

In 1977, the solicitor general told the House of Commons that steps were being taken to bring the security service division of the RCMP within the law and under cabinet control. Two years later, however, the head of security service told the McDonald Commission that there were still no "formalized briefings or range of specifics to be brought to the attention of a new ... minister."

On the activities of the security service division of the RCMP, see Jeff Sallot, *Nobody Said No: The Real Story About How Mounties Always Get Their Man* (Toronto: Lorimer, 1979); and John Sawatsky, *Men in the Shadows: The RCMP Security* (Toronto: Doubleday Canada Ltd., 1980).

Royal commission.   An inquiry into some special matter of public interest, in the case of federal commissions under the Inquiries Act or another statute. Not all commissions of inquiry are designated "royal";

but, apart from the prestige afforded by the name, any other commission of inquiry may have as much authority. A royal commission may be composed of one or several members. While commissioners may be appointed on the basis of their abilities, Governments are also careful to choose people who are likely to be sympathetic to their aims. Some reports of royal commissions may have fairly immediate impact in terms of government legislation; other reports may help to create a climate of public opinion favourable to the later implementation of comparable proposals. In general, the appointment of a royal commission commits a Government to doing something about a particular policy area sooner or later. Important federal royal commissions have included the Rowell-Sirois Royal Commission on Dominion-Provincial Relations (1937-1940), the Glassco Royal Commission on Government Organization (1960-1962), and the Laurendeau-Dunton Royal Commission on Bilingualism and Biculturalism (1963-1967).

For a bibliography on royal commissions, see Richard J. Van Loon and Michael S. Whittington, *The Canadian Political System: Environment, Structure, and Process* (2nd ed.; Toronto: McGraw-Hill Ryerson Ltd., 1976), 555-56.

Royal Commission on Bilingualism and Biculturalism (1963). A federal commission of inquiry formed by the Liberal Government of Lester B. Pearson in 1963 to investigate the status of French Canadians and the use of French in Canada. The co-chairmen were André Laurendeau, editor of the Montreal daily *Le Devoir*, and Davidson Dunton, president of Carleton University. The Commission was appointed during the period of the Quiet Revolution in Quebec, when French society was clearly undergoing important internal changes and expressing a more assertive nationalism than in the past. The Royal Commission also sponsored a considerable amount of social science research into questions related to culture, language, the economy, and government.

There was little surprise about, and all-party support for, the Commission's major recommendation that English and French be declared the official languages of Parliament, the federal administration, and the courts. The Commission also recommended that these language rights be entrenched and extended through the provinces. (On language, the British North America Act only requires the use of French and English in Parliament, the Quebec legislature (that is, the government), and the federal and Quebec courts [Section 133].) The Commission recommended the application of language rights across the country by establishing "bilingual districts" in areas where linguistic minorities represented 10 per cent of the population. The major recommendations of the Commission were included either in the federal Official Languages Act of 1969 or in the federal Liberal Government's proposed Charter of Human Rights (Bill of Rights).

While the support of federal party leaders for the "B and B" (bilingual and bicultural) policy has been unanimous, there has been little sympathy for it in English-speaking Canada. Moreover, the federal Liberal Government during the 1970's reduced its goals for administrative bilingualism. Meanwhile, nationalist opinion among francophone Quebeckers has become scornful of the "B and B" concept of Canada. See *Bilingualism and biculturalism; Bill 101 (Charter of the French Language); Official Languages Act; Parti Québécois; Sovereignty-association.*

Rule of law.   The principle of "legal equality, or the universal subjection of all classes to one law administered by the ordinary courts" (A.V. Dicey, *Introduction to the Study of the Law of the Constitution* [10th ed.; London: The Macmillan Company, 1961], 193). While the exact meaning of the rule of law is not stated in statutory form, it is a customary principle of the constitution; it restricts arbitrary authority and requires the law of government to be stated precisely and to be subject to adjudication by the courts. The practice of parliamentary delegation of discretionary executive and legislative authority, especially since the 1940's, has tended to remove officialdom from such judicial scrutiny. See *Delegated power; Regulatory agencies (regulations).*

Russell v. The Queen (1882).   A decision by the Judicial Committee of the Privy Council which upheld the comprehensive power of Parliament to legislate on a matter not enumerated under the power of the provincial legislatures in Section 92 of the British North America Act, under the "Peace, Order and good Government" clause of Section 91. Specifically, the federal Temperance Act provided for local prohibition subject to local option. The ruling was an early (and soon to be undermined) decision upholding the comprehensive legislative authority, or residual power, of Parliament. One year later, the Court ruled that the Russell Case was not relevant, when it adjudicated another case involving the liquor trade and established the so-called Aspect Doctrine.

Eventually, the Judicial Committee restricted the residual power to national emergencies only. Attempting to reconcile the Court's view of Parliament's power under the "Peace, Order and good Government" clause in 1925 with the decision in *Russell* v. *The Queen*, Viscount Haldane wrote that the Court in 1882 must have considered drunkenness a pestilential "menace to the national life" – though the act in question provided for local option (*Toronto Electric Commissioners* v. *Snider*, 1925). Since 1949, the Supreme Court has tended to sanction broader legislative jurisdiction for Parliament. See *Aspect Doctrine; Judicial Committee of the Privy Council; Supreme Court.*

S

Safe seat.   An electoral district which tends to elect the candidate of the same political party, regardless of the candidate and the electoral fortunes of the party elsewhere.

Saumur v. *Quebec and Attorney-General for Quebec, 1953.*   A ruling of the Supreme Court concerning the freedom of religious expression; it illustrates the lack of jurisdictional clarity on civil liberties. In this case, a Jehovah's Witness challenged the validity of a bylaw of Quebec City, which prohibited the distribution on the streets of books or pamphlets without police permission. Saumur claimed that the bylaw, enacted under provincial legislation which chartered Quebec City, was unconstitutional. He argued that it violated the preamble of the British North America Act, which granted Canada a constitution "similar in Principle to that of the United Kingdom," and also violated a pre-Confederation Canadian statute on freedom of worship which the Quebec legislature had re-enacted in 1941.

Although the Court ruled 5-4 that the bylaw could not prevent Saumur from distributing the pamphlets, only four justices in the majority denied provincial jurisdiction on the matter. The fifth justice declared the bylaw unconstitutional because it violated the Quebec statute. Not surprisingly, the Quebec *Union nationale* premier, Maurice Duplessis, had the legislature amend the Act to exclude the distribution of Jehovah's Witness pamphlets from its provisions. Three justices held that freedom of religious expression was a provincial matter under Section 92:13 ("Property and Civil Rights"); four held that the BNA Act removed jurisdictional competence from the provinces, citing the preamble to the Act. Some justices associated themselves with the Duff Doctrine, and others with the criminal law power of Parliament (Section 91:27) and the protection of educational rights of religious minorities (Section 93). See *Duff Doctrine; Supreme Court.*

Science Council. A federal crown corporation created in 1966 to assess and make recommendations to the government on Canada's scientific and technological resources, including: the adequacy of scientific and technological research and development in Canada; priorities in that area; long-term planning for the development and utilization of appropriate labour skills; and co-operation among government, the universities, and the private sector in encouraging science and technology in Canada. The Council initiates, and the designated minister may request, studies and/or inquiries related to any of these areas. In addition to its annual report to the House of Commons, the Council may publish its studies and reports. The governor-in-council appoints the 25-member Council, which is aided by a small professional and administrative staff.

In 1978 and 1979, the Council criticized the lack of research and development activity in Canada due to technological imports through multinational corporations; and it described a decline in Canadian manufacturing leading to de-industrialization. The Council advocated a goal of "technological sovereignty" for government, industry, and labour. The Council recommended the regulation of technological imports as a "defensive perimeter around the work of repair, reconstruction and enhancement of Canadian manufacturing, keeping out foreign technology and other factors of production" that operate against Canada's objectives and allow the entry of technology that would help the recovery process. At the same time, the Council recommended government action to increase the capacity of the economy to develop and absorb technology (*The Weakest Link: A Technological Perspective on Canadian Industrial Underdevelopment* [Ottawa, 1978]).

Scrutineer. A representative of a candidate who is allowed to oversee the administration of a poll, including the counting of ballots, in a general or by-election. Each candidate in a constituency is allowed to designate one person to be in attendance at each polling station during the poll and the count, and to report the unofficial count to the party.

Secrecy. A dominant feature by convention, and reinforced by statute, of the operation of cabinet government and the public administration in Canada. All members of the Privy Council (effectively the federal cabinet), for example, are bound by oath to "keep close and secret all such matters as shall be treated, debated, and resolved on in Privy Council, without publishing or disclosing the same or any part thereof, by Word, Writing or any otherwise to any Person out of the same Council, but to be such only as be of the Council." Thus, all documents which may be construed as relevant to treatment, debate, and resolution by cabinet are confidential. In practice, all government documents are confidential unless made public. Upon entering the federal or provincial public service, an employee swears that he or she will not without authority disclose or make known matters that come to his or her attention during employment.

Private citizens are held to secrecy by statute. Various provisions of the Criminal Code of Canada deal with offences such as breach of public trust, theft, and even treason. The federal Official Secrets Act (1939) is the major statutory device which describes the offence of possessing or communicating "documents or information" entrusted in confidence, or possessing information while believing it to be illegally obtained. The Act provides for public or secret trials and punishment by fine and/or imprisonment. In addition, a cabinet may require secrecy in a particular matter. This occurred in 1976; the federal Liberal Government passed an order-in-council approving a regulation of the Atomic Energy Board which made it illegal to disclose material relating to "conversations, discussions, or meetings" that took place during a specific time "in respect of the production of uranium." One year later, another order superseded this one, making it permissible to discuss information that had already been made public in the United States about Canada's role in the establishment of a cartel of uranium-producing countries. Otherwise, the ban remained in effect.

In 1979, the federal Conservative Government introduced freedom-of-information legislation and promised changes to the Official Secrets Act, which would have modified the traditional secrecy of cabinet government in Canada. The legislation died on the Order Paper; but in 1980, the Liberal Government promised to introduce a similar measure. See *Freedom-of-Information Act; Official Secrets Act.*

Secretariat. The executive/administrative department of a government body; it is responsible for the development and implementation of policy, though ostensibly in an advisory and administrative support role to the particular government body. In reality, the senior officials of such secretariats are among the most influential of government officials. At the federal level, for example, the Privy Council Office, the Federal-Provincial Relations Office, and the Treasury Board Secretariat are central executive/administrative secretariats for the cabinet and the Treasury Board. See *Federal-Provincial Relations Office; Privy Council Office; Treasury Board Secretariat.*

Secretary of State (Department of). A federal cabinet portfolio, established in 1867. Its earliest responsibilities included: official correspondence with the provinces; the Northwest Mounted Police; and the public service. Currently, the Department deals with programmes and policies related to the arts in Canada, federal education policies and programmes in support of national objectives, the acquisition of citizensip, encouragement of bilingualism, and matters of state protocol and ceremony. The secretary of state reports to Parliament for several bodies including the Canadian Broadcasting Corporation, the National Film Board, the National Museums of Canada, the National Library, and the Public Archives.

Secretary of State for External Affairs (Department of External Affairs). A cabinet portfolio created in 1909 concerned with foreign affairs. These included: the supervision of relations between Canada and other countries and in international organizations; the gathering and evaluation of information relating to international relations; the negotiation of treaties and agreements; and the protection of Canadian interests abroad and assistance to Canadians abroad.

Traditionally a senior portfolio, the Department of External Affairs is a large administrative unit in Canada and abroad. In Ottawa, the Department in 1976 included regional, functional, and administrative bureaus and several operational units. Four regional bureaus administered twelve geographical divisions. Seven functional bureaus included twenty divisions: for example, the Bureau of Economic and Scientific Affairs comprised the divisions of aid and development, commercial policy, scientific relations and environmental problems, and transportation, communications, and energy. There were also the bureaus of: legal affairs; defence and arms control affairs; public affairs; United Nations affairs; and co-ordination relating to the Commonwealth, federal-provincial co-ordination, and francophone institutions divisions. Four administrative bureaus were responsible for security and intelligence, personnel, finance and administration, and communication. The department also includes such structures as a policy analysis group, an interdepartmental committee on external relations, and special advisers. The International Joint Commission reports to the secretary of state for external affairs and to the United States's secretary of state. See *Interdepartmental committees; International Joint Committee.*

Sections 91 and 92 (British North America Act).   The sections of the
British North America Act which outline in large part the distribution
of legislative powers between Parliament (Section 91) and the provincial legislatures (Section 92). It is fundamentally the adjudication of
these two sections by the courts that, for most of Confederation, has determined the scope of legislative power (and, implicitly, cabinet power) of the two levels of government. In particular, debate has centred on
the extent of residual power resting with the federal government as a
result of the "Peace, Order and good Government" clause in the preamble of Section 91 and the scope of provincial competence under the
enumerated head "Property and Civil Rights in the Province" in Section 92 (:13). The courts have also adjudicated the scope of Parliament's authority under Section 91:2, "The Regulation of Trade and
Commerce." See *Declaratory power; Judicial Committee of the Privy
Council; Natural resources; "Peace, Order and good Government";
"Property and Civil Rights"; Spending power; Supreme Court; "Trade
and Commerce" power.*

Senate.   The appointed upper house of the Parliament of Canada.
Acting on the "advice" of the prime minister, the governor general appoints senators, who remain in office until 75 years of age unless they
become disqualified. There are a maximum of 112 positions in the Senate, divided into four representative divisions by the British North
America Act: Ontario (24 senators); Quebec (24); the Maritime provinces (24); the western provinces (24); Newfoundland (6); Yukon (1);
and Northwest Territories (1), with provision for four or eight more
members representing equally the first four divisions. The regional representation indicates the major objective of an upper house in a federation – to represent regional interests.

There are formal (in accordance with the BNA Act) and informal
qualifications for a seat in the Senate. To qualify formally, one must be
a Canadian, at least 30 years old, hold residence in the relevant division, and hold unencumbered real property worth at least $4000. A
senator is disqualified by failure to attend two consecutive sessions,
loss of Canadian citizenship, ceasing to meet the residence and property qualifications, being adjudged bankrupt, or upon conviction of a
criminal offence. No one can hold a seat in the Senate and the House of
Commons at the same time. However, an informal but most important
political qualification for a "summons" to the Senate is the favour of
the Government, notably the prime minister. Traditionally, Senate appointments are rewards for party service and represent a publicly re-

munerated office from which senators may continue to perform organizational, fund-raising, and election campaign activities for their party.

Though it possesses legal powers almost as great as the House of
Commons, the "fathers" of Confederation clearly intended the Senate
to be inferior to the House. Not only is the Senate not representative;
but supply and revenue bills may be introduced only in the House, and
by convention the Government is responsible only to the House. Rarely
are there cabinet ministers in the Senate other than the Government
leader. In forming his cabinet in 1980, however, Prime Minister Pierre
Trudeau included one senator from each of the three westernmost
provinces following an election in which no Liberal candidates were
elected from those provinces. In 1979-1980, Joe Clark had several senators with important portfolios in his cabinet. This was done to satisfy
the need for French-Canadian representation in his cabinet, and included one candidate who had failed to win a seat in the Commons in
the election.

Like the House of Commons, the Senate is organized into Government and Oppostion ranks and must approve legislation on three readings before it receives royal assent. The examination of legislation
there is often perfunctory. The House of Commons must concur in any
amendments made by the Senate to legislation it has already approved.
Though created in part as a moderating influence in the legislative
process, the contemporary Senate will usually do little to impede the
Government or insult the House, which would result in agitation to
abolish or at least "reform" the Senate.

Supporters of the Senate see its value in the legislative process
mainly in the investigation of proposed legislation before its actual introduction to Parliament, and in its longer-term examination of particular policy areas. Recent studies of the latter sort include examination
of the mass communication media (the Davey Committee) and of poverty (the Croll Committee). Joint committees with the House of Commons have also examined constitutional reform (1970-1972) and the
requirement for freedom-of-information legislation to reduce the degree of secrecy within the government. There is a standing joint committee which scrutinizes statutory instruments and other regulatory instruments.

The Senate is probably best known for its examination of government policy and legislation and for private bills pertaining to business
and finance in the committee on banking, trade, and commerce. However, many senators – and particularly those on the banking committee
– hold positions with private companies; thus, they may have associa-

tions with people who have holdings in private companies, or may be connected with law firms that represent clients who do business with the government. Consequently, there have been reasons to cite some senators for "informal" conflict-of-interest. Because conflict-of-interest provisions in the Senate and House of Commons Act are largely outmoded or inoperative, members are relatively free to determine their own degree of private interest on a public or private bill before them and to behave according to their own ethical standards. Freedom-of-Parliament legislation may be introduced to control the private business affairs of parliamentarians.

In 1978, the federal Liberal Government proposed an amendment to make the Senate more representative of regional and binational interests and more active as legislative body. The proposal for a so-called House of the Federation received little support, and the entire constitutional reform bill died on the Order Paper. In 1979, the Supreme Court ruled that Parliament could not unilaterally amend the British North America Act to effect fundamental changes affecting representation in, and the role of, the Senate. Traditionally, the New Democratic party (like its predecessor, the Co-operative Commonwealth Federation) has opposed the existence of the upper house and recommended its abolition.

For a recent study of the Senate, see Colin Campbell, *The Canadian Senate: A Lobby from Within* (Toronto: Macmillan Co. of Canada Ltd., 1978).

Senior civil servants.   A common term for the senior policy-makers in the public service of Canada and the provinces. While there is no exclusive definition for the term, deputy ministers and those with deputy minister rank, assistant deputy ministers, and directors in government departments are usually considered to be senior civil servants; chief officers of important crown corporations and members of important regulatory agencies may be termed senior public servants. The Government-of-the-day effectively appoints most senior civil servants. Some are easily removed; others are career officials, whose appointments are "protected" by a public employment statute, or they are officials with term appointments and can be removed before their terms expire only by a vote of the legislature.

The phrase is often used pejoratively. Because of the tendency of long-term party rule in some Canadian jurisdictions, senior civil servants individually develop a permanent role and collectively develop a pattern of influence which results in their having power over their political masters in the cabinet. Their full-time devotion to administration and their control over information flow give them advantages in influencing the ministers – who are part-time administrators with important political duties in the cabinet, the House, their party, and their constituency, and who often hold their portfolios for reasons other than their expertise in the field.

A common explanation for the weakness of John Diefenbaker's Conservative Government from 1957 to 1963 is his failure to replace certain senior civil servants who had been appointed during the preceding Liberal régime (from 1935 to 1957) with people more sympathetic to the new Government. However, the Conservative Government was seriously embarrassed when it sought to remove the governor of the Bank of Canada for espousing publicly opinions contrary to those of the Government. (For an account of the so-called "Coyne Affair," see John T. Saywell, *Canadian Annual Review for 1961* [Toronto: University of Toronto Press, 1963].) When the federal Conservatives came to power in 1979, after 16 years of Liberal rule, Prime Minister Joe Clark replaced the secretary to the cabinet (clerk of the Privy Council), but retained most of the other deputy ministers, all of whom were appointees of a Liberal Government.

Separate schools (parochial, dissentient). Tax-supported denominational schools at the primary and secondary levels of education, usually a reference to those operated by the Roman Catholic Church in predominantly Protestant provinces. The British North America Act gives jurisdiction in education to the provinces, and it protects "Separate or Dissentient" systems of education established before union from prejudicial provincial action. The Act provides for an appeal from any "Protestant or Roman Catholic Minority" to the governor-in-council on any prejudicial decision and for "remedial Laws" by Parliament (Section 93). Nonetheless, since the 1890's, federal governments have preferred to leave disputes over the provincial denominational schools to the directly interested parties and the courts. See *Bill 101 (Charter of the French Language); Manitoba schools question.*

Separation (separatism). The common term for secession which was associated with various movements in Quebec in the 1960's, some of which merged to form the provincial *Parti Québécois* in 1968. The strategists in the PQ abandoned the word for the more positive "independence" and later abandoned that word for the more complex and perhaps more strategically appealing "sovereignty-association." In the early 1970's, a vote for the PQ was a vote for separation; but prior to the 1976 election, the PQ separated electoral support for it from the question of independence, on which it promised a referendum. When in office, the PQ redefined the referendum as a mandate for the PQ government to negotiate sovereignty-association with the rest of the country and seek approval of negotiated changes in a second referendum. See *Sovereignty-association.*

Separation of powers.   A division of political functions which distinguishes legislative, executive, and judicial duties; on the assumption that these functions should not be assigned to a single body, institutional specialization may be created in which each body acts as a check against the other two. For example, separation of powers is part of the United States constitution; the president, the Congress, and the Supreme Court, each acting in its own sphere, represents a check against the others. Canada, by contrast, has a parliamentary-cabinet system in which one can distinguish the three institutions, but in which the legislature is supreme. The Government comes from the legislature and is responsible to it, and judicial review is limited. See *British North America Act; Judicial review; Responsible government; Supremacy of Parliament.*

Shadow cabinet.   A collective term for the critics in each of the opposition parties, particularly those in the official Opposition, who might comprise a real cabinet should the party come to power. In small opposition parties, members may be designated critics for several portfolios. In large opposition parties, the chairmen of caucus policy committees are usually designated critics in relevant policy areas. As leader of the Opposition in 1979, Pierre Trudeau created a parliamentary advisory committee composed of the caucus committee chairmen. In addition to these 29 designated critics, Trudeau also named 19 other MPs, not on the advisory committee, as critics.

Shared-cost programmes.   Government programmes provided by one level of government, usually the provinces, using money provided by the other level, usually the federal government. Shared-cost programmes help governments which have the jurisdictional obligation but lack the financial resources to provide programmes and maintain a nation-wide standard of public service. In the mid-1970's, the Privy Council Office listed 98 items under conditional grants and payments relating to shared-cost programmes and activities. The bulk of federal assistance, however, was directed to hospital and medical insurance, post-secondary education, and the Canada Assistance Plan (welfare assistance).

Shared-cost programmes have existed since the first decade of the twentieth century, but the present system originated with the Wartime Tax Agreement of 1941. The tax-sharing agreement is periodically re-negotiated as the Federal-Provincial Fiscal Arrangements and Established Programmes Financing Act. In these negotiations, the provincial strategy is to acquire as many federal funds with as few federal strings as possible. In the 1960's, Quebec "opted out" of certain shared-cost programmes and received financial compensation under the Established Programmes (Interim Arrangements) Act. In 1977, the federal government terminated the costly shared-cost programmes, representing 50 per cent of provincial expenditures in hospital and medical insurance and in post-secondary education. In place of the unlimited subsidy, the federal government granted equalized tax point abatements unattached to particular programmes. See *Conditional grants; Contracting out; Federal-provincial tax-sharing agreements.*

Single-member plurality electoral system. The electoral system currently used in all provincial and federal elections in Canada, also known as the "first-past-the-post" system. The winner is the candidate who receives at least one vote more than his or her nearest opponent. Thus, when there are more than two candidates, the winners often have a plurality, but not a majority, of the votes cast. The votes of the defeated candidates have no electoral effect; and when there are many three-or-more-candidate contests, a discrepancy develops between the popular vote percentages for the parties and their percentage share of seats in the legislature. Such discrepancies may be gross and systematic and lead to demands for some form of proportional representation. See *Electoral system; Proportional representation.*

On the impact of the current electoral system on the party system in Canada, see Alan C. Cairns, "The Electoral System and the Party System in Canada, 1921-1965," *Canadian Journal of Political Science* 1 (1968), 55-80; J.A. Lovink, "On Analyzing the Impact of the Electoral System in Canada," *Canadian Journal of Political Science* 3 (1971), 497-516, and Cairns's reply, 557-21; and Richard Johnston and Janet Ballantyne, "Geography and the Electoral System," *Canadian Journal of Political Science* 10 (1977), 857-66.

Social Credit party.   A populist movement party which arose in the Canadian West in the 1930's, particularly in Alberta; it developed a following in British Columbia in the 1950's, and in Quebec in the 1960's. The movement was successful in part because its leaders were compatible with regional societies and could effectively articulate the economic and social grievances of the regions. The party, however, could never integrate these several regional support bases, specifically the West and Quebec, into a national political force. The party has been successful in Alberta and remains a major force in British Columbia politics, while in Quebec it maintained nominal representation in the House of Commons until 1980 and minor activity in provincial politics.

The Social Credit party originated in Alberta, a province with a history of militant agrarian activism, under the leadership of evangelist William ("Bible Bill") Aberhart; it defeated the United Farmers of Alberta in 1935. Social Credit remained in power – for many years under the leadership of Aberhart's evangelist-politician protégé Ernest Manning – until 1970. It now forms the official Opposition to the Conservatives, with a handful of seats. In 1979, the provincial party's name was changed to the Alberta Party.

The Social Credit monetary theories were secondary to the charismatic, populist leadership in explaining the success of Social Credit. The theory of Social Credit was the so-called "A + B Theorum" of Major C.H. Douglas, a British army engineer. According to the theory, there is always a discrepancy between the costs of production and the purchasing power of individuals. A Social Credit Government would supplement individuals' purchasing power through direct grants. The Supreme Court declared attempts to effect Social Credit legislation in Alberta in the 1930's to be unconstitutional. Subsequently, the party persisted as a populist conservative party. Post-World War Two prosperity, occasioned in particular by the discovery of oil in the province, reinforced the conservatism of the Social Credit Government party.

In British Columbia, the party came to power in 1952 under the leadership of W.A.C. Bennett, an ebullient small-town, small businessman who had failed earlier to win the leadership of the provincial Conservative party. Bennett and the party held office until 1972. Under his son's leadership, the party returned to power in 1975. From 1935 to 1958, Social Credit had minor representation from Alberta and British Columbia in the House of Commons. The party elected no members in the Conservative landslide of John Diefenbaker in 1958.

In 1962, the party – which had had an organization in Quebec since the 1940's called the *Union des Electeurs* – elected 26 MPs under the leadership of Réal Caouette, another dynamic, small-town, small-businessman politician. The Quebec members and the four-MP western wing of the party were never integrated; and, as the western party finally disappeared from the House, the *Ralliement des créditistes* membership in the House of Commons also dwindled eventually to five MPs in 1979 and no seats in 1980. The *Ralliement* has played a minor role in provincial elections in Quebec since 1970. See *Ralliement des créditistes; Third parties.*

On the Social Credit movement in Alberta, see John A. Irving, *The Social Credit Movement in Alberta* (Toronto: University of Toronto Press, 1959); and C.B. Macpherson, *Democracy in Alberta* (Toronto: University of Toronto Press, 1953). On the role of Social Credit in British Columbia, see Martin Robin, "British Columbia: The Company Province," in Martin Robin (ed.), *Canadian Provincial Politics: The Party Systems of the Ten Provinces,* (2nd ed.; Toronto: Prentice-Hall of Canada Ltd., 1978), 28-60.

Socialism.   An cross-national set of values according to which the system of economic production, distribution, and exchange should be controlled (through public ownership and regulation) to achieve egalitarian goals rather than permitting individual aggrandizement through competition. Individual fulfillment, according to the theory, would be realized in the attainment of the collective welfare.

The implementation of socialist values in practice has resulted in the development of many "schools" and groups. In the late nineteenth and early twentieth centuries, the Canadian left included many sectarian groups. In 1921, the Communist party of Canada was founded on the Leninist model, appropriating for itself the role of official interpreter of Marx. Since then, the party has existed as a legal and illegal organization, remaining loyal to the policies of the Communist Party of the Soviet Union and undergoing the tensions and schisms that Communist parties have experienced elsewhere outside the Soviet bloc. Many democratic socialists – advocating gradualist, non-violent and parliamentary tactics to achieve socialist objectives – eventually coalesced in the Commonwealth Co-operative Federation in 1933.

The CCF experienced modest, but for socialists unsatisfactory, levels of success in some provinces. During the post-World War Two prosperity, the CCF underwent a transformation similar to that experienced by other western socialist parties. The CCF had been a hotbed of intellectual activity, especially evident in the output of the League for Social Reconstruction. As a political force, it formed the Government of Saskatchewan in 1944 and became an important electoral factor in Ontario and British Columbia. However, it was never a strong federal force except as its policies might have been taken over by other parties in office when the CCF showed signs of becoming popular. In the 1950's, the ideological rhetoric of the CCF and its policies of nationalization were exchanged for a more moderate brand of socialism, emphasizing the managerial or regulatory powers of government. The New Democratic party issued forth from this process in 1961, modelling its policies less on the British Labour party (which had been an important model for the CCF) and more on the Scandinavian social democratic parties. The NDP has remained influential in Ontario, Saskatchewan, and British Columbia; it has developed strength in Manitoba and, to some extent, in Nova Scotia and Newfoundland. However, the party remains a relatively minor federal force, winning 16 to 20 per cent of the popular vote in general elections. See *Co-operative Commonwealth Federation; New Democratic party.*

On the CCF-NDP, see Ivan Avakumovic, *Socialism in Canada: A Study of the CCF-NDP in Federal and Provincial Politics* (Toronto: McClelland and Stewart Ltd., 1978). On the origins of the Communist party, see Ivan Avakumovic, *Communism in Canada: A History* (Toronto: McClelland and Stewart Ltd., 1975); and William Rodney, *Soldiers of the International: A History of the Communist Party of Canada, 1919-1929* (Toronto: University of Toronto Press, 1968). On the "contagion from the left" thesis, see William M. Chandler, "Canadian Socialism and Policy Impact: Contagion from the Left?" *Canadian Journal of Political Science* 10 (1977), 755-80.

Solicitor General.   The federal cabinet minister responsible for the Royal Canadian Mounted Police, prisons and reformatories, parole, and remissions. The department has four branches: policy planning and programme evaluation, which includes a federal-provincial working group; police and security planning and analysis, which includes contingency planning for violent acts associated with international terrorism and social unrest; research and systems development, and communication and consultation for both internal and public purposes.

In the 1970's, the most contentious aspect of this portfolio involved the creation and work of the security planning and analysis branch and the activities of the security service division of the Royal Canadian Mounted Police following the so-called "October Crisis" of 1970. In 1978-1980, a federal royal commission investigated alleged wrongdoings by the security service division of the RCMP and the roles of three successive solicitors general in the events. See *Royal Canadian Mounted Police.*

Sovereign, The.   The person on whom the Crown is constitutionally conferred, symbolizing Canada's status as a constitutional monarchy and the incumbent's status as Canada's head of state in whom formal executive power is vested. In most cases, the sovereign's executive authority is delegated to the representative, the governor general, who is appointed on the prime minister's recommendation. The Crown in Canada is not divisible; the sovereign has one Privy Council, the effective part of which is the federal cabinet; there are also ten Executive Councils, effectively the provincial cabinets appointed by the provincial lieutenant-governors. Each set of "advisers" operates under the adjudicated provisions of the British North America Act. All legislation must receive royal assent and be proclaimed to be effective. All judicial functions are also conducted in the name of the sovereign. Canadian honorary awards are also conferred in the incumbent's name. The sovereign in Canada is also recognized as the head of the Commonwealth, a voluntary association of sovereign states, formerly British colonies or trusts, and associated states. See *Crown prerogatives; Governor General; Letters Patent; Lieutenant-Governor.*

Sovereignty-association.   The objective of the *Parti Québécois* in restructuring Quebec's relationship with the rest of Canada: to achieve national sovereignty in an economic association with Canada. A sovereignty-association as defined by the PQ in 1979 would involve a two-nation association which would include: a common currency but a reorganization of central bank functions (monetary policy) into community institutions with a joint central board; a free-trade zone with a common external tariff but with each community free internally to protect its agriculture, with temporary programmes to aid industrial development, and with each country allowed to give preference to its nationals when making purchases; and freedom of movement of citizens, with special arrangements for immigration and job employment between Canada and Quebec. Seats on the proposed central monetary board would be allocated on the basis of the "relative size" of the Quebec and "Canadian" economies. The monetary board, however, would devolve to central banks in each state the roles of public debt management and government banker. Differences between the two states would be referred to the Quebec-Canada council of ministers.

The constitutional device associating Canada and Quebec would be a treaty establishing four community agencies. A Quebec-Canada council of ministers would be the central institution. It would be served by: a secretariat called the commission of experts; the monetary board which has been mentioned above; and a court of justice with equal representation of the two states, which would adjudicate on differences arising from the treaty and acts of the association. See *Parti Québécois; Referendum.*

Sovereignty-association was defined first at a convention of the *Parti Québécois* in 1979; the definition later refined in a Government white paper, *Quebec-Canada: A New Deal – the Quebec Government's Proposal for a New Partnership between Equals: Sovereignty-Association.*

Speaker (of the House). The presiding officer of a legislative chamber. The elected members of Parliament choose a Speaker for the House of Commons from among themselves prior to the opening of Parliament following each general election and for the duration of that Parliament. In practice, the prime minister usually nominates (seconded by the leader of the Opposition) an MP who assumes the position by acclamation. The Speaker is usually a Government MP. In the brief Parliament of 1979-1980, however, the position was held by an Opposition Liberal MP who had held the post in the previous Parliament. The Speaker enforces the rules and maintains the rights and privileges of the House. He or she is also responsible for the management of the House, and sits with four ministers as the commissioners of internal economy to control the administrative affairs of the House. Because the position requires a thorough knowledge of rules and precedents and the individual requires the respect of members, and because a constituency is denied an active participating MP while the person is Speaker, there have been attempts to make the position a permanent appointment not contingent on holding a seat in the House of Commons. The appointment and functions of speakers of the provincial legislatures are similar to those of the Speaker of the House of Commons. The governor-in-council appoints the Speaker of the Senate, who serves for the term of the Parliament. The duties of the Senate's Speaker are similar to those of the Speaker of the House; but because the Senate is rarely the site of extensive partisan debate, the position is less demanding. See *House of Commons; Parliamentary privilege (immunities).*

Special Joint Standing Committee of the Senate and the House of Commons on the Constitution of Canada (1970-1972). A 30-member joint parliamentary committee which held public hearings on constitutional reform and issued a final report, with informal minority reports being issued by five members. The official "majority report" supported the constitutional amending formula proposed in the abortive Victoria Charter (1971), greater provincial jurisdiction over social policy and federal jurisdiction over economic policies, and a six-month suspension power for the Senate over legislation from the House of Commons (Ottawa: Information Canada; 1972).

Two French-Canadian members of Parliament, one Liberal and one Conservative, issued their own report supporting recognition in a new constitution of Quebec's right to self-determination. Two New Democratic party MPs issued a report supporting the interdelegation of legislative powers between individual provincial governments and the federal government, and power for Parliament to act unilaterally in a national economic emergency. Senator Eugene Forsey, a co-chairman of the Committee, defended the existing constitution in the Senate (Martial Asselin and Pierre de Bané, *Minority Report*, Ottawa, [Mimeo], March 7, 1972; Andrew Brewin and Douglas Rowland, *Minority Report* [Mimeo], March 1972; and the Senate *Debates*, March 23–29, 1972, 222-25, 263-71, 278-86). See *Victoria Charter*.

Special status. An objective sought in a new constitution recognizing that Quebec, the historic homeland of French-speaking Canadians and the only province with a French majority, is a distinctive province and should be treated differently from the others. The demand is usually associated with the provincial Liberal Government of Jean Lesage during the Quiet Revolution of the 1960's. However, the Lesage Government spoke of "*statut particulier*" only in 1965, during its last year in office. Then, according to Donald V. Smiley, Government statements could be read either as a reference to recently acquired status as the sole province having contracted out of federal-provincial shared-cost programmes with financial compensation, or as a generalized demand for jurisdiction wider than that of the other provinces (*Canada in Question: Federalism in the Seventies* [2nd ed.; Toronto: McGraw-Hill Ryerson Ltd., 1976], 169-70). Later premiers Daniel Johnson (*Union nationale*, 1966-1970) and Robert Bourassa (Liberal, 1970-1976) walked the fine line between the "older" Quebec demands for a revised federalism and "new" demands for a constitution recognizing the existence of two nations. In fact, by 1966, Quebec had achieved informal special status in Confederation, being the sole province to have opted out of the shared-cost programmes under the Established Programmes (Interim Arrangements) Act of 1965. This action ended federal controls and increased Quebec's share of personal and corporation taxes. See *Contracting out; Quiet Revolution; Sovereignty-association.*

Speech from the Throne.   The governor general's address in the Senate with senators, members of Parliament, and the judges of the Supreme Court present; it opens sessions of Parliament. In all the provinces but Quebec, the lieutenant-governors read the Speech from the Throne to the provincial legislatures. In Quebec, the premier delivers an Inaugural Address in the national assembly in the presence of the lieutenant-governor. The prime minister (premier) and cabinet prepare the Speech from the Throne. It generally reviews the state of public affairs from the Government's perspective and provides a general outline of its legislative priorities in the coming session. At the next sitting of the legislature, a general "throne speech debate" takes place on a Government motion commending the governor general (lieutenant-governor) for the address.

Spending power.   In Canada, the power of the federal government to make payments to people, institutions, and governments for purposes on which Parliament does not have the constitutional power to legislate. The legislation under which funds are allocated must fall within Parliament's jurisdiction. Spending power has been the basis of the federal government's role since 1945 in conditional grant and equalization programmes, designed to create national standards of public service. Federal spending power is based in the broad powers of taxation given Parliament (British North America Act, Section 91:3, "The raising of Money by any Mode or System of Taxation") and the right to make laws relating to "The Public Debt and Property" (Section 91:1A), which has been interpreted to include the Consolidated Revenue Fund.

Constitutional experts disagree in their interpretations of the decisions of the Supreme Court and the Judicial Committee of the Privy Council concerning spending power. No government, however, has sought further clarification from the courts since the 1930's. Successive federal Governments have asserted Parliament's spending power, and provincial Governments (with the exception of Quebec) have simply criticized the use of such power – particularly in the creation, modification, and termination of shared-cost programmes. See *Conditional grants; Federal-provincial tax-sharing agreements.*

See Pierre Elliott Trudeau, "Federal-Provincial Grants and the Spending Power of Canada" (1969), quoted in part in J. Peter Meekison (ed.), *Canadian Federalism; Myth or Reality* (2nd ed.; Toronto: Methuen Publications, 1971), 216-34.

Standing (select, special) committees (of the House).   Standing committees are permanent committees of a legislature. They include specialist committees named after major government departments and others to deal with matters such as public accounts, miscellaneous estimates, miscellaneous private bills, procedures and organization, and privileges and elections. In Parliament, there are also joint standing committees of the House and Senate on parliamentary matters. From time to time, a legislature may establish a special committee, or Parliament a special joint committee of both Houses, to study select matters.

Membership on House of Commons committees varies; but is usually a maximum of 20, with party representation proportional to that in the legislature. The chairmen of all House committees, except the committee on public accounts, are usually Government members. Ministers are not normally members of standing committees; but their parliamentary secretaries may be appointed to the relevant committee to act as a watchdog on party colleagues. Membership on committees is temporary, and there is often a high turnover. Employees of the legislature serve as staff to the committees; but there are no committee secretariats to perform research duties or carry out questioning of witnesses, as in the United States congressional committee system.

The major function of House committees is to scrutinize Government legislation following second reading, including supply and ways and means legislation. The committees usually meet only in the capital city. Thus, parliamentary committees and those of large provinces effectively restrict their reservoir of potential witnesses to representatives of organized or well-financed interest groups who can afford to travel to the capital, or to maintain permanent representatives (lobbyists) there. The committees decide whom to call as witnesses and, following the hearings, what recommendations to submit to the legislature in the form of amendments to bills. In the case of a committee scrutinizing legislation, the relevant minister is usually the first and last witness before a committee. At his or her last appearance, the minister may review the testimony of witnesses and indicate the sort of amendments to the legislation which the Government is willing to accept. Government members on the committee may move such amendments and be prepared to oppose contrary amendments. On supply

bills, the committees are effectively limited. This is because the witnesses called to support departmental estimates are ministers, accompanied by officials in the departments who have already managed the
more onerous hurdles of interdepartmental and cabinet committees and
Treasury Board (or its counterparts in the provinces) and its secretariat;
and they now have the support of cabinet. At this stage, however, the
minister and accompanying officials are operating for the first and only
time in public, and the committee may be a forum for general criticism
of Government programmes as well as a rare occasion for holding a minister accountable for every estimated expenditure in his or her department (on the post-audit function of the legislature, see *Public Accounts
Committee*).

Standing or special committees may also act in a pre-legislative or
extra-legislative function, investigating public opinions on policy
areas or general policy questions. However, such investigations are
rare; they depend on the support of the Government, especially when
it controls a majority in the legislature, to create such committees with
appropriate terms of reference and resources.

Occasionally there have been requests, usually from Opposition
MPs, to give legislative committees the resources necessary to develop
effective scrutiny of Government legislation. The necessary resources
cited are permanent membership, research staff, reduction (if not the
abolition) of party discipline in committees, the resources to conduct
hearings across the country, and time. Supporters of a more effective
committee system, however, would also have to find legislators who
would be interested in long-term committee membership. These legislators would have to be: willing to devote more time to policy areas
and questions which were of little, if any, direct relevance to the interests of their constituents; willing to spend less time on constituency
matters; willing to ignore party strictures during committee hearings
which would be in place later in the legislature; and willing to work
largely without public recognition, as committee hearings are usually
poorly covered by the mass media.

In a white paper on the reform of Parliament in 1979, the short-lived
federal Conservative Government had recommended some reforms to
the committee system. It proposed that, on a motion supported by 50
MPs, at least ten from each of two political parties, the House of Commons could authorize a committee investigation. Although recommendations from such an inquiry would not be binding on the Government, it would have to respond to the report within three weeks. Under
the proposed changes, however, only five investigations could be held

concurrently. Also, the research budgets would have to be approved by the House's commissioners of internal economy – the Speaker and four cabinet ministers.

On committees, see C.E.S. Franks, "The Dilemma of the Standing Committees in the Canadian House of Commons," *Canadian Journal of Political Science* 4 (1971), 460-76; T.A. Hockin, "The Advance of Standing Committees in Canada's House of Commons," *Canadian Public Administration* 13 (1970), 192-202; and J.R. Mallory, "The Use of Legislative Committees," *Canadian Public Administration* 6 (1963), 1-14. See also Michael M. Atkinson and Kim Richard Nossal, "Executive Power and Committee Autonomy in the Canadian House of Commons: Leadership Selection, 1968-1979," *Canadian Journal of Political Science* 13 (1980), 287–308.

Standing Orders.   The codified rules of procedure of the legislature; in the House of Commons, for example, the rules are enforced by the Speaker, the deputy speaker, and the deputy chairman of committees. A legislature is the guardian of its own affairs; and, although the Speaker settles points of order on the basis of precedents, a legislature may revise its standing orders. The disciplined party system in Canadian legislatures helps the Speaker in enforcing the rules. Each party's House leader and whip arrange, as best they can in a partisan atmosphere, the business of the legislature and the order of members speaking. The revision of Standing Orders often becomes a matter of partisan debate – as changes which the Government proposes, which are designed to make the legislature more "efficient," usually mean less time for the Opposition to debate Government measures. For example, there was acrimonious debate in the House of Commons in 1969 when the Government successfully passed S.O. 75(A), (B), and (C) to allow the Government to limit debate (impose closure) unilaterally.

Stare Decisis.   The rule of precedent in judicial decisions. By convention, lower courts are bound by decisions of higher courts in deciding similar cases, while a court may choose to ignore its own precedents. For example, as a constitutional court, the Judicial Committee of the Privy Council could, and the Supreme Court may ignore its own precedents, although arguments referring to earlier decisions may be persuasive.

Statistics Canada.   A federal agency established in 1918. It is responsible for the census of Canada and for collecting, analyzing, and publishing statistical information relating to the social, economic, industrial, commercial, agricultural, and financial activities and conditions in Canada. Statistics Canada is also responsible for collaborating with other government departments for the publication of statistical information based on government activities, and for developing integrated social and economic statistics pertaining to Canada and each of the provinces. Not all statistical information gathered by the government, either voluntarily or by statute, is made public. The principal officers of Statistics Canada include: the chief statistician of Canada and six assistant chief statisticians for business statistics, household and institutional statistics, economic accounts and integration, statistical services, marketing service, and the census.

In 1979, the cabinet authorized investigations of Statistics Canada's management practices, technical and statistical production, and alleged malpractices in reporting certain statistics. The findings of these investigations were to be studied by a group which included the clerk of the Privy Council, the secretary of the Treasury Board, and the comptroller-general.

Statute (act).   A bill which has passed three readings in each parliamentary chamber (or a provincial legislature) and received royal assent. See *Legislation*.

Statute of Westminster (U.K., 1931).   An Act of the British Parliament giving effect to resolutions of the imperial conferences of 1926 and 1930. These declared the autonomy of the dominions (Canada, Australia, New Zealand, and South Africa) from British legislation and created the constitutional basis of the contemporary Commonwealth. The Act declared: that the Colonial Laws Validity Act (by which dominion legislation was void if it conflicted with British statutes) no longer applied to the dominions; that the British Parliament would not invalidate future acts of dominion parliaments; that no act of the British Parliament would affect a dominion unless it had requested and consented to it; that dominion parliaments could enact laws with extra-territorial effect; and that the Colonial Courts of Admiralty Act (1890) and the Merchant Shipping Act (1894) no longer applied to the dominions. At Canada's request, a clause was included which exempted the British North America Act and amendments from the Statute of Westminster, so that the BNA Act could not be amended solely by the Canadian Parliament. (Through an amendment of the BNA Act in 1949, the Canadian Parliament acquired the power to amend some sections of the Act [see *British North America Act*].) The Act gave statutory sanction to a resolution of the imperial conference of 1926 that "They [the dominions] are autonomous Communities within the British Empire, equal in status, in no way subordinate to one another in any aspect of their domestic or external affairs, though united by a common allegiance to the Crown, and freely associated as members of British Commonwealth of Nations...." See *Commonwealth*.

Statutory instruments. Any order, rule, regulation, commission, warrant, proclamation, or other government device which has the power of law. Such instruments are the output of executive and administrative bodies exercising delegated legislative authority. Since 1947, federal instruments have had to be published in the *Canada Gazette* within seven days of the making of the rule. If certain instruments are to be exempted from publication, the Government must publish the category of exemption. It is the responsibility of the clerk of the Privy Council to maintain the record of all federal regulations.

Although the instruments are published, there remains the problem of adequate legislative scrutiny of delegated legislation. At the federal level, the joint Senate-House of Commons Committee on Regulations and Other Statutory Instruments is responsible for ensuring that statutory instruments do not exceed authority delegated by Parliament. There is serious doubt, however, that this committee can effectively scrutinize all instruments. See *Delegated power; Regulatory agencies (regulations)*.

Subordinate legislation. Another term for delegated legislation. See *Delegated power; Regulatory agencies (regulations); Statutory instruments*.

Supplementary estimates. Government requests for additional funds to meet financial needs puportedly unforeseen when the main estimates were drawn up and presented to the legislature. When tabled in the legislature, the supplementary estimates are immediately referred to standing committees, with dates stipulated for their return. The first supplementary estimates for a fiscal year are usually dealt with in the House of Commons in the supply period ending not later than December 10; final supplementary estimates are dealt with in the March 26 period. See *Budgetary process; Estimates*.

Supply bill.   The informal name for an appropriation act, that is, Government legislation to appropriate funds with which to finance specified government operations. In Parliament, the Government may introduce supply bills only in the House of Commons. Government departments and agencies may spend money only for purposes authorized in an appropriation act. See *Budgetary process; Estimates.*

Supply period (allotted days; Opposition days).   Time allocated in the legislative timetable for the debate of supply bills. In the House of Commons, there are 25 days in the three supply periods (ending not later than December 10, March 26, and June 30) and three days for supplementary estimates, during which Opposition motions take precedence over all Government supply motions. On these so-called allotted days, or Opposition days, the Opposition may put forward motions of no confidence in the Government. With the exception of the mover and seconder, MPs are limited to 20-minute speeches. Such days are rare occasions in the House timetable, when the Opposition can determine the subject of debate on which the Government must defend itself. Prior to adjournment on the last allotted day, the Speaker puts the question to dispose of business related to supply. The House then votes on the supply bills before it.

Supremacy of Parliament.   The unlimited power to enact legislation. The supremacy of the Canadian Parliament and provincial legislatures is limited by the British North America Act, under which legislative power is distributed between the two levels of government. Until the constitution is patriated, or domiciled, the Canadian Parliament also shares power formally with the British Parliament (and, by convention, with the provinces) on amending various parts of the British North America Act. (See *British North America Act.*) No Parliament or provincial legislature may pass legislation binding a subsequent Parliament or legislature. Parliament or a provincial legislature may alter previous statutes and non-statutory common law practice by passing an Act. The courts, therefore, may declare legislation unconstitutional only if it violates the distribution of power under the BNA Act. Otherwise, should a federal or provincial Government feel that the courts have interpreted constitutionally acceptable legislation inappropriately, it may introduce legislation in Parliament (or the provincial legislature) amending the act to clarify its meaning – or, indeed, to prevent judicial review of matters under the act.

Supreme Court.   The superior court of Canada. It exercises exclusive and ultimate appellate civil and criminal jurisdiction in Canada. It has jurisdiction to consider matters referred to it by federal or provincial governments, and matters conferred on it by federal statute. Parliament established the Court under the Supreme Court Act of 1875; and, since 1949, its judgments have been final in all cases. Before then, the Judicial Committee of the Privy Council in London exercised final appellate powers except in criminal cases. The governor-in-council (effectively the federal cabinet) appoints the Court's chief justice and eight puisne judges. A judge ceases to be on the Supreme Court when 75 years of age or if removed by the governor-in-council on a joint resolution or address of Senate and the House of Commons. Three of the nine judges must be from the Quebec bench or the bar. An appointee must be, or have been, a superior court judge in a province or a barrister with at least ten years' experience.

The Supreme Court sits in Ottawa in three annual sessions, hearing appeals for which it has granted leave or on a constitutional reference where permitted by law. The Supreme Court usually hears appeals on criminal cases only in the case of a capital offence. When hearing appeals from Quebec, at least two of the sitting judges must be from that province. Either three or five judges may constitute a quorum in particular cases.

Since the Supreme Court became the final court of appeal in 1949, observers have sought to determine patterns on decisions relating to federal-provincial power (especially in the determination of federal jurisdiction over national economic policy under the "Trade and Commerce" clause in Section 91:2 of the British North America Act, and on civil liberties). Unlike the Judicial Committee, the Supreme Court publishes dissenting or minority views. Thus, the court can be analyzed judge by judge and case by case. With the development of executive federalism in the 1960's, the courts have been used less by the governments for decisive resolution of jurisdictional disputes. However, governments have referred constitutional questions to the Court (for example, the Court confirmed Parliament's jurisdiction over western offshore minerals; has ruled on the power of provincial marketing boards; and denied Parliament the power to amend unilaterally the British North America Act with respect to the role of, and representation in, the Senate); and the federal government joined at least one private case involving provincial legislation as a co-plaintiff (on Sasktchewan legislation regulating the production and pricing of potash). The Court has tended to strengthen the role of the federal government in national economic policy, replacing the narrow national emergency doctrine with the notion of "inherent national importance." For example, in the 1970's, in addition to confirming federal authority over western off-shore mineral rights, the Supreme Court found against Saskatchewan in the Potash case, as well as in another case concerning a provincial tax and royalty surcharge on oil which would have taxed the post-1973 windfall profits at 100 per cent, but for the provincial treasury. Also, the Court sanctioned the federal government's mandatory wage and price control programme in the 1975-1978 period.

On civil liberties, the direction of the Court has been more divided, showing evidence of a liberal-conservative split. Liberal judges have affirmed the criminal law power of Parliament, or the Duff Doctrine, which would protect civil liberties from both jurisdictions and give priority to the preamble to the British North America Act ("a Constitution similar in Principle to that of the United Kingdom") to protect free speech in a parliamentary democracy; the conservatives have granted jurisdiction to provincial legislatures under Section 92:13 ("Property and Civil Rights in the Province"). For three examples, see *Saumur v. City of Quebec and Attorney-General for Quebec*, 1953, *Switzman v. Elbling and Attorney-General for Quebec*, 1957 – the so-called Padlock Case, and *Oil, Chemical, and Atomic Workers International Union v. Imperial Oil Ltd. and Attorney-General of British Columbia*, 1963. For decisions on appeals based on the Canadian Bill of Rights (1960), see *Drybones v. The Queen*, 1970, and opinions expressed on the Lavell-Bedard Case (*Attorney-General of Canada v. Lavell*, 1974). See *Bill of Rights; Drybones Case; Lavell-Bedard Case; Oil, Chemical, and Atomic Workers Case; Padlock Law; Saumur v. Quebec.*

The appointment of Bora Laskin to the Court in 1970 and his subsequent appointment, only three years later, to chief justice strengthened the centralist and liberal groups on the Court; but they also renewed debate on the appointment procedure. Traditionally, the appointment procedure has been criticized because (on the assumption that other qualifications were met) judges or lawyers with backgrounds in the Government party were given advantage over those with different partisan backgrounds. Currently, however, the federal Government's monopoly has been criticized on the basis that, since the Supreme Court is in part a constitutional court, provincial governments should be involved in the appointment process. In 1978, the federal Liberal Government's short-lived constitutional amendment bill proposed formal, all-region representation on the Supreme Court, as well as a procedure by which to attempt to obtain provincial agreement to federal appointments, and necessary approval for appointments by a revised Senate containing provincial appointees.

On the rulings of the Supreme Court, especially relating to federal-provincial power and civil liberties, see Peter H. Russell, "The Supreme Court's Interpretation of the Constitution from 1949 to 1960," and "The Supreme Court since 1960," in Paul W. Fox, *Politics: Canada* (4th ed.; Toronto: McGraw-Hill Ryerson Ltd., 1977), 523-36 and 536-46. See also R.I. Cheffins and R.N. Tucker, *The Constitutional Process in Canada* (2nd ed.; Toronto: McGraw-Hill Ryerson Ltd., 1969).

Surveillance (function of Parliament). Short of bringing down the Government, the chief function of Parliament (and provincial legislatures) is to scrutinize Government executive and administrative action, using a number of procedural instruments. These devices include question period, supply debates (especially so-called Opposition days in the House of Commons), motions to adjourn for emergency debates, and general debates (for example on the Speech from the Throne and budgets). The surveillance function of Parliament is also manifested in the detailed examination of Government bills and statutory instruments in committees. Theoretically, the Crown represents the national interest and the legislature represents the individual, competing interests. Thus, Parliament's constitutional role is to exercise close watch over, and respond critically to, initiatives of a strong executive, now effectively the prime minister and his cabinet. Its role is not, as in republican theory, to be itself the source of political initiative. See *Estimates; House of Commons; Question Period; Responsible government; Standing (select, special) committees (of the House).*

T

Task Force (. . . on Canadian Unity). An investigative body established by a government to obtain information and make recommendations on policy matters. The use of task forces is one way of obtaining non-government advice for possible implementation in legislative form. A task force may be a less formal body than a royal commission, but it will have a staff and budget to carry out research. Clearly, the work of the force is a function of its terms of reference, members, and financial resources.

In 1978-1979, a federal Task Force on Canadian Unity, co-chaired by former Ontario premier John Robarts and former federal Liberal minister Jean-Luc Pépin, held hearings, sponsored research, and made recommendations for constitutional reform (described as restructured federalism). The Task Force recommended that language rights in the provinces be left to the provincial legislatures rather than be entrenched in the constitution. This recommendation ran counter to the federal Liberal Government's strategy from 1969 to 1979 and gave approval to Quebec's position, though not its actual legislation. Otherwise, the Task Force supported a bilingual federal government, a recommendation which was consistent with federal policy. The Task Force also recommended a new distribution of powers between the two levels of government, minimizing overlap and reducing federal power while strengthening provincial power. Recommendations also included introducing an element of proportional representation into the electoral system in federal elections and the replacement of the Senate with a Council of the Federation appointed by the provincial Governments; the Council would have legislative power of varied degrees related to specific kinds of legislation and would involve the provinces effectively in the federal legislative process. The Task Force further recommended provincial power to rule on federal appointments to the Supreme Court and certain major federal regulatory agencies such as the National Energy Board. (*A Future Together: Observations and Recommendations* [Ottawa: The Task Force on Canadian Unity, 1979]).

Tax abatement and Tax points.   In federal-provincial fiscal arrangements, a tax point is a percentage point of personal income taxes. Beginning with the Established Programmes (Interim Arrangements) Act (1965), the federal government compensated Quebec, which contracted out of shared-cost programmes, by abating or reducing its personal income tax up to 20 per cent, or up to 20 equalized tax points. There were cash transfers between the two governments to make up the difference between the yields of the abated taxes, or tax points, and the amount the provincial government would have received as a conditional grant in the programmes. If the equalized abatement provided more than the federal contribution to the programme would have been if the province had not opted out, the federal government recovered the money. If the equalized abatement fell short, the federal government would make an additional payment to the non-participating government. Equalized tax points were the basis of federal transfer payment in agreements in 1967 and 1972, and in the federal Fiscal Arrangements and Established Programmes Financing Act of 1977. See *Federal-provincial tax-sharing agreements.*

Tax expenditures.   Potential revenue to the government foregone as a result of tax-incentive schemes. Governments use favourable tax regulations to encourage individuals and private companies to act in particular ways. Such incentives constitute indirect public spending, or tax expenditures. In 1979, the short-lived federal Conservative Government included tax expenditures in its "envelope" system in the budgetary process. Ministers in the inner cabinet were to be responsible for maintaining ceilings on spending for programmes in particular policy areas; and the amount of revenue foregone through tax expenditures was included with direct public spending. According to a report of the federal Department of Finance in 1979, tax expenditures associated with 190 tax exemptions, deductions, write-offs, and special incentives totalled $32 billion. The report noted, however, that the figures were incomplete and that no attempt had been made to evaluate the effectiveness or utility of each item of expenditure (*Government of Canada Tax Expenditure Account* [Ottawa: 1979]). See *Budgetary process.*

Tax rental agreements (payments).   Federal-provincial agreements under which the provincial governments agreed to abandon their power to levy taxes in such fields as corporate and personal income tax in return for financial compensation. Under the Wartime Tax Agreements of 1941, all provinces entered agreements (though under war conditions, the federal government could have acted unilaterally) to abandon the fields until 1946 in return for a calculated tax rental payment. A tax rental payment scheme existed until 1957, after which there were "tax-sharing agreements" and currently "fiscal arrangements acts." See *Federal-provincial tax-sharing agreements.*

Territory (territorial government).   A region in Canada that does not have provincial status and which is governed by a federally appointed commissioner and a council under an act of Parliament. In 1979, the federal Conservative Government introduced responsible government to the Yukon Territory; it transferred executive power from the commissioner to an Executive Council, or cabinet, composed of members from the 12-member territorial council. In the Northwest Territories, a council of four appointed members and ten elected members advises the Territories' commissioner. The legislative responsibilities of the two commissioners-in-council are somewhat analogous to those of the provinces under Section 92 of the British North America Act. The federal government, however, retains control over lands, natural resources, taxation, and claims of native rights in these matters.

Third parties.   Political parties other than the Liberal and Conservative parties, which have come into existence since Confederation;
though they have displaced either or both of the "old" parties in some
of the provinces, they have not done so at the federal level. Thus, such
groups as the New Democratic and Social Credit parties have been
termed "third parties." Various explanations exist for the rise of so-
called "third parties" in Canada. The parliamentary, federal, party, and
electoral systems, and the cleavage structure each contribute to the development of "third parties":

The parliamentary system contributes because the focus of general
elections is the numerous constituency contests. The election of only a
few members gives some legitimacy and credibility to new movements.
Under the rules of the House of Commons, a group with 12 MPs receives public funds for a leader's salary, additional office space, research facilities and staff, and procedural "rights" in being recognized
in question period and during debate.

The federal system contributes because small movements articulat-
ing regional or localized grievances may find success in the provincial
legislatures, and may actually come to form provincial Governments
and exercise considerable influence in federal-provincial relations.

The disciplined party system contributes because it demands conformity from backbenchers, thus potentially alienating regional representatives who cannot alter policy of established parties to suit the interests of their region.

The electoral system contributes because it disproportionately rewards parties with concentrated sectional support.

The cleavage structure contributes because it reinforces those cleavages with regional or localized communities of interest, such as French
Canadians in Quebec (bicultural cleavage) and westerners (the geographic cleavage) and minimizes cleavages with continental or widespread communities of interest, such as the class cleavage.

Examining the rise of the *Ralliement des créditistes* in Quebec in the
1960's, Maurice Pinard suggests that third parties develop in times of
discontent when a single party has dominated electoral politics in a
large area for a long time. Thus, the long period of Liberal dominance
in federal politics led aggrieved rural Quebeckers to conclude that the
alternate parliamentary party, the Conservative party, was not a credi-
ble choice. The third-party *Ralliement* led by Réal Caouette, an indigenous populist movement, provided such an alternative in the 1960's
(*The Rise of a Third Party: A Study in Crisis Politics* [Englewood Cliffs:
Prentice-Hall, 1971]). See also Graham White, "One-Party Dominance

and Third Paries: The Pinard Theory Reconsidered," *Canadian Journal of Political Science* 6 (1973), 399-421; André Blais, "Third Parties in Canadian Provincial Politics," 422-38; and Pinard, "Third Parties in Canada Revisited," 439-60.

Pinard's explanation seems to apply also to the case of the Social Credit party ousting the United Farmers of Alberta in 1935. However, C.B. Macpherson suggests that the one-crop agricultural economy of the prairies at that time created a "colonial" society in relation to central Canada and resulted in practically universal electoral support for a party representing the interests of the single-class society in Alberta and a "quasi-party system" (*Democracry in Alberta: Social Credit and the Party System* [Toronto: University of Toronto Press, 1953]). See *Quasi-party system.*

Examining the Co-operative Commonwealth Federation in Saskatchewan, Seymour Martin Lipset argues that the one-crop agricultural economy there led to the creation of co-operative organizations and a class of experienced and relatively well-off activists who transferred their experience and energies to the CCF. Consequently, the CCF became a successful and entrenched political party in that province (*Agrarian Socialism: The Co-operative Commonwealth Federation in Saskatchewan* [Berkeley: University of California Press, 1950]). See *Agrarian socialism.*

Throne Speech, debate on.   A debate on a Government motion commending the governor general (lieutenant-governor in the provinces) for his or her address opening the session of Parliament (provincial legislature – except in Quebec, where the debate is on the premier's Inaugural Address). The debate in the House of Commons lasts eight days, with the Opposition parties moving amendments referring to some alleged deficiency in Government policy. Debate is wide-ranging and, apart from the initial remarks by the parties' chief speakers, is a rare opportunity for backbench members to address the House on matters of import to them and their constituents.

Tory.   A popular reference to the Conservative party and its supporters (moreso in central Canada and the Maritimes than in the West). In pre-Confederation Canada, Tories were generally in favour of maintaining the power of the governor and the appointed Executive Council against encroachments by the elected legislative assembly. Because Tories are often associated with the privileged colonial elites of church, state, and society, the term is also used pejoratively to refer to upper-class privilege. "Red Tories," by contrast, are in a normative sense considered to be more compassionate and concerned with public measures to curb excessive individual aggrandizement and deal with social distress. See *Conservatism; Conservative (Progressive Conservative) party; Red Tory.*

"Trade and Commerce" power. Legislative jurisdiction which Section 91:2 of the British North America Act gives Parliament, but which the Judicial Committee of the Privy Council denied as a source of broad legislative power. Since 1949, the Supreme Court has tended to restore legislative authority to Parliament under this enumerated head.

In its adjudication of "Trade and Commerce" power, the Judicial Committee distinguished between goods in intraprovincial trade and those in extraprovincial trade. However, the result made effective legislation by governments at both levels difficult. By contrast, the Supreme Court has interpreted "Trade and Commerce" power as a basis for important national economic policies by the federal government. On marketing, the Supreme Court declared interdelegation of powers between Parliament and a provincial legislature unconstitutional, but it permitted the delegation of power from one level to a regulatory body of another level.

In the 1950's, the Supreme Court introduced the notion of the "flow of trade," to replace the difficult categories of intraprovincial and extraprovincial trade, thus enhancing federal power under Section 91:2. Such federal power has implications for provincially owned natural resources. In 1977, for example, the Court declared two Saskatchewan acts to be in violation of federal "Trade and Commerce" power. The first was a tax and royalty surcharge on oil. It would have taxed post-1973 windfall profits at 100 per cent, but for the provincial treasury; it was declared to be an indirect, and therefore illegal, provincial tax. The second ruling overturned Saskatchewan's legislation to control the production, supply, and price of potash. See *Interdelegation Reference; Judicial Committee of the Privy Council; National oil policy; Natural resources; Supreme Court.*

For an opinion by Justice Bora Laskin in 1971 (appointed chief justice in 1973) which reviews the adjudication of the "Trade and Commerce" power, including the Judicial Committee's attenuation of federal power and the Supreme Court's restorative decisions, see *Attorney-General for Manitoba* v. *Manitoba Egg and Poultry Association,* 1971, the so-called Chicken and Egg Reference.

Transfer payment.   Any payment from one level of government to another (usually from the federal to the provincial governments), or directly to an individual from a government. Thus, conditional or unconditional grants, including equalization payments from the federal government, are transfers. Also, payments to individuals (for example, under Family Allowance, the Canada Assistance Plan, or the Canada Pension Plan) are transfer payments. See *Canada Assistance Plan; Canada (Quebec) Pension Plan; Conditional grants; Equalization grants; Federal-provincial tax-sharing agreements.*

Transferable vote (preferential ballot).   An electoral system no longer used in Canada. It allows the voter to rank candidates in single-member constituency elections according to his or her preference. Instead of marking the ballot in favour of a single candidate, the voter ranks candidates 1, 2, 3, and so forth. Should the count of first preferences not result in a candidate having a majority of the votes cast (that is, at least 50 per cent plus one), the last candidate is dropped from consideration and the second choices on ballots which listed that person's name as first choice are counted. This process continues until one candidate has a majority of the votes. The transferable vote, or preferential ballot, was used in provincial elections in Manitoba and Alberta in the early part of the twentieth century. It was used in the British Columbia general election in 1952. The system seems to have benefitted the Social Credit party in Alberta and in British Columbia, where its candidates received more second-choice support from Liberals, Conservatives, and CCFers (Co-operative Commonwealth Federation). It may have hurt the socialist CCF, which was an unsatisfactory preference for Liberals and Conservatives in particular.

Treasury Board.   A statutory federal cabinet committee (that is, formally a committee of the Queen's Privy Council for Canada). As Committee on the Expenditure Budget, it is responsible for recommendations to cabinet on the selection of programmes and projects and the appropriate allocation of funds to achieve Government objectives; as Committee on Management, it is responsible under the Financial Administration Act for administrative policy for financial management in the public administration, and for matters related to personnel, office space, supply, and contracts for services. In this respect, the comptroller-general reports to the Board, which was also responsible for dealing with the report in 1979 of the (Lambert) Royal Commission on Financial Management and Accountability in the Government of Canada.

The Treasury Board also negotiates for the Government in collective bargaining arrangements with public service unions and associations. The president of the Treasury Board chairs the Board. The Board also includes the minister of finance and four other ministers, whom the governor-in-council (effectively the prime minister) determines. The Treasury Board has an extensive staff, the Secretariat, a key central executive agency in the federal government. The Conservative cabinet of 1979-1980 included a Ministry of State for Treasury Board to assist the president of the Treasury Board. See *Auditor General; Budgetary process; Comptroller-General; Estimates; Treasury Board Secretariat.*

Treasury Board Secretariat (TBS).   A central staff agency in the federal government whose powers are based in the statutory authority of the Treasury Board. It deals with the determination of programme priorities and review of expenditures, administrative policy and organization of the public service, financial administration, personnel management, and official-languages policies in the public service.

On programme determination and expenditure review, the programme branch controls the budgetary cycle (when programme forecasts are reviewed and an expenditure plan is established) and estimates prepared for cabinet approval and submission to Parliament. The TBS here also examines new programme proposals. On administrative policy, the TBS develops and enforces rules on the acquisition and use of property ranging from office furnishings to computers. On the organization of the public service, the Treasury Board Secretariat has authority over classification at senior-management levels; it studies the effectiveness of organizational structures, for example, the relationship of "horizontal" ministries of state to the appropriate "vertical" departments of government. In this area, the Treasury Board Secretariat shares authority with the Privy Council Office and the Public Service Commission, two other central agencies. In financial administration, the Office of Comptroller-General exercises control over expenditures, accounting, and auditing procedures. The comptroller-general also conducts efficiency evaluations of programmes to determine their effectiveness in achieving policy objectives. Because the Treasury Board employs government personnel, the TBS deals with staff relations, compensation, benefits, and pensions. This branch, for example, negotiates collective agreements with public-service unions and associations. Finally, the Treasury Board Secretariat evaluates the implementation of provisions of the Official Languages Act (1969) in the federal public service. See *Auditor General; Budgetary process; Comptroller-General; Estimates; Treasury Board.*

For an article on the Treasury Board Secretariat by the then secretary, see A. W. Johnson, "The Treasury Board of Canada and the Machinery of Government of the 1970's," *Canadian Journal of Political Science* 4 (1971), 346-66; and by a former deputy secretary on budgetary and management controls generally in the federal administration, see Douglas G. Hartle, "Techniques and Processes of Administration," *Canadian Public Administration* 19 (1976), 21-33. For a description and analysis of the Treasury Board Secretariat and other central agencies in the federal government, see Colin Campbell and George J. Szablowski, *The Super-Bureaucrats: Structure and Behaviour in Central Agencies* (Toronto: Macmillan Co. of Canada Ltd., 1979).

Treaty power. The authority of the federal government to make commitments to other countries; this authority is tempered by the federal-provincial distribution of legislative power. The need to recognize the conditional nature of the federal power arises because Section 132 of the British North America Act grants treaty powers to the "Parliament and Government of Canada ... for performing the Obligations of Canada or of any Province thereof, as Part of the British Empire...." As Canada developed an international personality separate from that of the empire in the twentieth century, Section 132 became obsolete. Consequently, the Judicial Committee of the Privy Council declared that, if Section 132 did not apply, the power of the "Parliament and Government of Canada" depended on the distribution of legislative powers between the two levels of government. Thus, there was no such thing as "treaty Legislation," that is, legislative scope for the federal government in an area of provincial jurisdiction simply because Canada had committed itself to action in a treaty. Under Section 132, the federal government acquired power in areas unforeseen by the "fathers" of Confederation, in broadcasting and aeronautics (Radio Case, 1932, and Aeronautics Case, 1932), but was denied scope in labour legislation (Labour Conventions Case, 1937). In 1961, the Canadian government signed the Columbia River Treaty with the United States, but its implementation was delayed until the federal government and British Columbia reached an agreement in 1963. The treaty involved the development of a natural resource (a provincial responsibility under Section 92:5) in a project which the federal government was unwilling to declare "to be for the general Advantage of Canada or for the Advantage of Two or more of the Provinces" (92:10[c]). Since then, the federal government has continued to accept some provincial involvement in the negotiations of conventions and treaties, to ensure implementation.

In 1965, for example, Quebec and France signed an "entente" on education, a matter within provincial jurisdiction, in the context of an "umbrella" agreement between Canada and France. See *Judicial Committee of the Privy Council.*

Two nations ("deux nations"). A notion that, because Canada consists of "two founding nations," one French- and one English-speaking, a revised constitution should recognize jurisdictional equality between the "two nations," Quebec and the rest of Canada. The federal Conservative and New Democratic parties have at some time since the 1960's supported a form of the "two nations" theory. The federal Liberals have consistently opposed any formal distinction between Quebec and the remaining provinces. Informally, Quebec achieved "special status" in 1965 under the federal Liberal Government's Established Programmes (Interim Arrangements) Act. All provinces were given the option of withdrawing from federal-provincial shared-cost programmes with financial compensation, but only Quebec accepted the offer. Also, the federal Liberal Government in the 1970's allowed provincial governments to participate in international conferences on matters related to provincial jurisdiction as long as Canada retained a single international personality. Thus, in 1971, Quebec and the federal government concluded an agreement on participation in the international francophone Agency for Cultural and Technical Co-operation. Under the agreement, a Quebec official occupies one of Canada's two positions on the Agency's board of directors, and Quebec ministers or officials may attend Agency conferences to express Quebec's point of view on matters within provincial jurisdiction. The two governments divide equally the expenses of participation in the Agency.

Provincial parties in Quebec continue, however, to press for "self-determination" for Quebec, either in the "renewed" or "restructured" federalism proposed by the Liberals or in the "sovereignty-association" proposed by the *Parti Québécois.* See *Quiet Revolution; Renewed/Restructured federalism; Sovereignty-association; Special status.*

Two-party system. A party system in which there is a long-standing electoral competition between only two major parties. The use of this or other phrases to describe the competitiveness of a party system is somewhat arbitrary – except with reference to those countries where only one party is permitted by law. In Canada, the Atlantic provinces have the most obvious two-party systems, although in some of these provinces "third parties" may develop and become competitive. Party systems elsewhere in Canada may be described either as competitive multi-party systems or as one-party dominant multi-party systems. See *One-party dominance; Party system; Third parties.*

Two-tier cabinet. A political executive organized formally or informally into two groups, one of which is a small group of leading ministers which meets more often than the whole cabinet. From 1968 to 1979, Prime Minister Pierre Trudeau chaired a cabinet committee on priorities and planning, an informal executive committee of the cabinet. The short-lived federal Conservative Government of 1979-1980 contained a formalized, publicly acknowledged inner cabinet, which made decisions for which the entire cabinet was responsible. See *Cabinet; Cabinet organization; Inner cabinet.*

Ultra (Intra) Vires. A phrase which describes a statute of federal or provincial legislatures as beyond (within) their jurisdictional competence as determined through judicial review by the Judicial Committee of the Privy Council until 1949, and by the Supreme Court.

U

Unconditional grants (general-purpose transfer payments). Federal grants to provincial governments which are not designated for any specific expenditure programme and may be allocated by the recipient province in any fashion. The statutory subsidies provided for in Section 118 of the British North America Act were, in effect, unconditional grants. Currently, however, most unconditional grants are made under the equalization programme. "Have-not" provinces qualify for unconditional federal transfer payments under the programme. This provides a national standard of public services without creating an excessive tax burden for the residents. See *Conditional grants; Equalization grants; Federal-provincial tax-sharing agreements.*

Uncontrollable (statutory) expenditures. Public expenditures to which the government is committed by law. Shared-cost federal-provincial programmes, for example, have involved the federal government in financial support of costly provincial programmes in medical care and post-secondary education. Since the mid-1970's, the federal government has been modifying and renegotiating federal-provincial agreements to help alleviate the federal treasury of such costs. In its annual report in 1979, the Economic Council of Canada described the large federal deficits (created in part by uncontrollable, statutory expenditures) as one of several "deep-seated structural difficulties" in the Canadian economy. See *Conditional grants; Federal-provincial tax-sharing agreements.*

Unemployment Insurance (Commission).   A federal income-maintenance programme established during World War Two. In 1937, the Judicial Committee of the Privy Council declared a federal scheme for unemployment insurance to be a violation of provincial jurisdiction. In 1940, the British North America Act was amended to give jurisdiction unequivocally to the federal government (92:2A). One year later, a federal Unemployment Insurance Act was enacted to provide benefits to those who were unemployed and who had contributed premiums when employed. Under the Act, the governor-in-council appointed commissioners to administer the Act through several regional offices. The Act also allowed for appeals to independent referees by claimants. In 1977, the Unemployment Insurance Commission "merged" with the Department of Manpower and Immigration into one agency. The new agency, called the Canada Employment and Immigration Commission, forms one of the largest government operations in Canada. The minister responsible is the minister of employment and immigration.

As rates of unemployment have been consistently high since the 1960's, regulations pertaining to unemployment insurance are subject to constant political debate and government alteration. Some observers argue that the qualifications for unemployment insurance payments are too lax; others argue they are too strict. Some argue that the regulations ought to vary depending on the lack of employment opportunities from region to region. There have also been arguments over whether the scheme, which has become a general welfare programme, should be a strict insurance programme. Finally, these debates and the considerable cost in administering the programme have led some to argue that a negative income tax or minimum guaranteed income would be preferable as an income-maintenance programme.

Unicameral.   An adjective denoting one chamber in the legislative system as opposed to two (bicameral). All the provincial legislatures in Canada are unicameral, while the federal Parliament is bicameral by virtue of having the House of Commons and the Senate.

Union, Act of (1840).   The imperial statute which reunited Upper and Lower Canada from 1840 to 1867. Following the rebellions of 1837 in Upper and Lower Canada, the British government suspended the colonial constitutions and dispatched Lord Durham as governor to report on conditions. His two main recommendations were union and the granting of responsible government.

The Act made provision for union, but not for responsible government; the latter developed by custom and usage. The Act provided for a British-appointed governor, a legislative council appointed by the Crown for life, and an elected assembly of 84 members equally divided between Canada East (Lower Canada) and Canada West (Upper Canada). The Act consolidated the revenue of the two colonies. The Union thus favoured the initially less populous and financially less well-off English-speaking Canada West. Initially, only English was an official language of government; but the colony's legislature became bilingual out of functional necessity.

Though there was no statutory provision for responsible government, it was politically impossible for the governor to choose an Executive Council without considering the opinions of the assembly. During the early years of the Union, the governor's Council did have the support of the assembly. In 1848, a defeat of the Executive Council in the legislature on a non-confidence motion resulted in a change of Government, and responsible government was established. See *Lord Durham's Report; Responsible government.*

Union Government.   A coalition Government which was formed in 1917; it won the wartime election later that year, and it remained in in office until 1920. The coalition included Conservatives and English-speaking Liberals; however, it was essentially a Conservative administration created by Prime Minister Robert Borden, who had been in office since 1911. It ceased when Borden resigned and Conservative Arthur Meighen formed a Government. This has been the only coalition Government in Canadian federal history, other than the Confederation alliance in 1867. J. Murray Beck writes that, prior to the general election of 1921, "The Liberal-Unionists now had no choice but to go back to their old party on bended knee and, after a period of penance, be fully accepted, or to submerge themselves completely in the Conservative party. The latter had been left in a bad way by the non-partisan aura which had surrounded the Union government and which caused it to be . . . isolated from the electorate" (*Pendulum of Power: Canada's Federal Elections* [Scarborough: Prentice-Hall of Canada Ltd., 1968], 150).

Union nationale. A conservative, nationalist political party in Quebec; it originated in 1936 as an alliance of Conservatives and reform Liberals, in opposition to the corruption of the provincial Liberal régime. The UN was in power from 1936 to 1939, 1944 to 1960, and from 1966 to 1970. Initially a reformist party, the UN itself became an authoritarian régime in the 1940's and 1950's. It was known for its conservative defence of Quebec's historic rights and provincial autonomy under the British North America Act, and for its internal corruption. The party weakened, however, after the death (in 1959) of its dominant leader, Maurice Duplessis. The UN, whose base of support was in rural Quebec, returned to power under Daniel Johnston from 1966 to 1970. As a nationalist force, however, it has been eclipsed by the more aggressive and urban *Parti Québécois*. In 1976, the PQ came to power in part because the Liberal party lost votes to the now third-ranking *Union nationale*.

In federal politics, the Conservatives depended upon the UN organization from the 1940's to the 1960's. (Nonetheless, federal Liberal MPs and provincial UN members from the same area were well-disposed to "sweetheart" election deals; each would remain effectively neutral in the other's re-election campaign, to the detriment of their ostensible "allies" in the provincial Liberal and federal Conservative parties, respectively.) A former federal Conservative minister from Quebec in the 1960's has said the UN was responsible for ten of the eleven Conservative seats won in that province in 1957. UN leader Duplessis is reported to have even recruited candidates for the Conservatives, in addition to committing his party machine and government patronage to the effort (Pierre Sévigny, *This Game of Politics* [Toronto: McClelland and Stewart Ltd., 1963], 70-71, 204-05). Even more striking was the support extended the following year by Duplessis which helps to explain the election of 50 Conservative MPs from Quebec, a figure matched by Conservatives only in 1882.

In 1979, the UN leader, Rodgrigue Biron, announced that the party would dissolve itself in the hope of founding a new party "unifying all right-wing forces." Biron had advised Conservative Prime Minister Joe Clark of the plan, heightening expectation that the new party would be a provincial Conservative party, which has not existed in name since the 1930's.

On the *Union nationale* under Duplessis, see Herbert F. Quinn, *The Union Nationale: A Study in Quebec Nationalism* (2nd ed.; Toronto: University of Toronto Press, 1979).

Unitary state.   A political system in which a single parliament retains all legislative authority. By contrast, a federal system involves the distribution of legislative powers between autonomous levels of government which may also share certain legislative powers. The United Kingdom is an example of a unitary state, and Canada is an example of a federal state.

United Farmers of Alberta (Manitoba, Ontario).   Associations of farmers which became political parties in several provinces in the early twentieth century. The Alberta group was the most successful, holding office from 1921 to 1935. Henry Wise Wood was a major figure in the movement, which supported the notion of occupational group representation in legislatures rather than the conventional party system. The party sent Progressive MPs to the House of Commons during the 1920's, and it was one of the founding groups in the Co-operative Commonwealth Federation (CCF) in 1932-1933. In Ontario, the UFO formed a provincial Government in 1919 with the support of Labour and Independent members. D.C. Drury's Government was defeated in 1923. In Manitoba, the United Farmers formed a Government in 1922; but they were later swallowed by the Liberals, who remained in office as the Liberal-Progressive party until 1958.

Upper Canada.   A colony which existed in British North America from 1791 to 1840. Its seat of government was York, now Toronto. Under the Quebec Act of 1774, Quebec extended west to include land between the Ohio and Mississippi Rivers; the political system included provision for freedom of worship for Roman Catholics and for the use of the civil law on non-criminal matters unless changed by the colony. The American Revolution resulted in the migration of Loyalists to the western part of Quebec, around Lake Ontario and Lake Erie, as well as to the Maritime provinces. These newcomers to Quebec, who had experienced an atmosphere of relative political freedom, insisted on entirely British law and representative institutions. In 1791, the Constitutional Act divided Quebec into Upper and Lower Canada, creating representative institutions for both colonies and maintaining French civil law in Lower Canada. Following the rebellions in both Upper and Lower Canada, Lord Durham was dispatched as governor to investigate conditions in the colonies. He recommended union and responsible government. In 1840, the Act of Union reunited the two Canadas once again; this was, in part, in a vain attempt to absorb the French into the English-speaking community. See Lord Durham's Report; Union, Act of (1840).

Upper chamber.   In a bicameral legislature, the chamber which usually represents regional interests. It is less accountable to the electorate than the lower house, and is theoretically a conservative, moderating influence on the lower house. In Canada's bicameral Parliament, the upper house is the Senate, to which the governor general "summons" people (on the prime minister's "advice") to represent regional divisions as specified in the British North America Act (Sections 21-36). Elsewhere, upper houses may be elected for longer terms than representatives in the lower house (for example, the United States Senate) to represent state or provincial governments (for example, the Federal Republic of Germany's Bundesrat). Or they may be based on heredity and life appointments (for example, the British House of Lords). See *Senate.*

Urgent (emergency) debate.   Provisions in the rules of the legislature for an Opposition motion to adjourn the House to consider an urgent matter which cannot be dealt with immediately under the order of business. In the House of Commons, Standing Order 26 allows the Speaker to rule on the Opposition motion. If the ruling is favourable, the House may debate the motion at once or hold it over until the evening. There is no time limit for emergency debates; they may last into the night. Members are limited to 20-minute speeches, and the Speaker declares the motion to adjourn carried when he or she is satisfied that the debate has ended. While such emergency debates are rare, it is perhaps their selective use by the Opposition with the Speaker's approval that makes them effective criticisms of the Government. Even if denied by the Speaker, a motion to adjourn may draw public attention to some alleged government failure. See *House of Commons.*

See John B. Stewart, *The Canadian House of Commons: Procedure and Reform* (Montreal: McGill-Queen's University Press, 1977).

"Vertical Mosaic."   The title of John Porter's examination of social class and power in Canada (Toronto: University of Toronto Press, 1965), in which he concludes that power in Canada is concentrated in the leadership of a few institutional structures. Recruitment to elite positions is, according to Porter, selective. It depends on familial, educational, and career linkages; there is a cultural bias towards Protestants of British origin, with junior representation from French Canada notably in the political and so-called ideological elites. In addition, the political and ideological (that is, mass media, education, and church) systems perpetuate the elitism by emphasizing the pluralistic, mosaic quality of Canadian culture (ethnicity and religion) as the most important aspect of Canadians' individual and group rights and aspirations. Porter's preference is for a political system in which "creative politics" (a euphemism for class-based political debate and action) takes precedence over cultural concerns, which are more relevant to a pre-industrial society. He concludes: "Canada is a new society, and should have had great opportunities for institutional innovation, but so far it has been incapable of taking a lead in the changes and experimentation necessary for more democratic industrial societies. A fragmented political structure, a lack of upward mobility into its elite and higher occupational levels, and the absence of a clearly articulated system of values, stemming from a charter myth or based in an indigenous ideology, are some of the reasons for this retardation" (558). See *Bicultural cleavage; Class cleavage.*

Victoria Charter (1971). The agreement reached among the Canadian heads of governments (with the important exception of Premier Robert Bourassa of Quebec) in Victoria concerning constitutional reform; it was subsequently rejected by Quebec. In the Victoria Charter, important parts of the constitution would have been amended by less than unanimous provincial consent. Specifically, such amendments would have taken place by a resolution of the House of Commons and Senate and of at least a majority of the provinces. This would have included: each province with a population at least 25 per cent of the national population; at least two of the Atlantic provinces; and at least two of the western provinces having a combined population at least 50 per cent of all western provinces. Otherwise, Parliament could have unilaterally amended the constitution with respect to the federal institutions; and the provinces could have amended their own constitutions with some exceptions for amendments by combined parliamentary and provincial legislative action. Moreover, the new constitution would have included the entrenchment of human rights in several categories: civil liberties with respect to religion, freedom of speech, and assembly except where limited "in the interests of public safety, order, health or morals, of national security, or the rights and freedoms of others ... "; universal suffrage and free elections; and the declaration of English and French as official languages in Parliament and all provincial legislatures except British Columbia, Alberta, and Saskatchewan. Moreover, both languages would be used more extensively in the provincial courts and government administration. Other provisions included changes in appointments to the Supreme Court, and the abolition of the federal powers of reservation and disallowance of provincial legislation.

Quebec rejected the Charter because of the provision under which Parliament would have been permitted to legislate programmes related to income maintenance and security, but so as not to affect the operation of similar provincial legislation and only after the provinces had been consulted.

Donald V. Smiley has commented sharply: "The failure to secure agreement on the Victoria Charter brought to an end the pretentious and ill-advised exercise on constitutional review, and whatever hopes there may have been either that a major English-French accommodation might emerge from this process or that agreement could be secured on a newer and purportedly better Canadian Constutution." See Smiley's review of the Victoria Charter and Quebec's response in *Canada in Question: Federalism in the Seventies* (2nd ed.; Toronto: McGraw-Hill Ryerson Ltd., 1976), 10-11, 44-52. See also Edward McWhinney, *Quebec and the Constitution 1960-1978* (Toronto: University of Toronto Press, 1979).

Vote of no confidence (want-of-confidence).   The vote on an Opposition motion amending an important Government motion or a vote on the main motion, the Government's loss of which represents defeat in the House. When a Government loses the confidence of the legislature, the prime minister (or provincial premier) either advises the governor general (or provincial lieutenant-governor) to dissolve the legislature and issue writs for an election, or resigns. In the latter case, the governor general (or lieutenant-governor) asks someone else to form a Government which will have the confidence of the House. When the Government party controls more than one-half of the representation in the legislature, votes will predictably favour the Government. In recent years, however, the number of federal minority governments has led to proposals for a stricter definition of what constitutes a want-of-confidence motion. For example, confidence could be specifically limited to the motion on the Speech from the Throne, the budget, estimates, and legislation which the Government designates on introduction as a matter of confidence. In 1968, the minority Liberal Government "accidentally" lost the vote on third reading of a money bill. Instead of resigning, Prime Minister Lester Pearson proposed to introduce a

Government motion seeking the confidence of the House at its next sitting. The Opposition Conservatives accepted the proposal. The Government motion carried, and the Liberals remained in office. In 1979, the minority Conservative Government lost the vote on the New Democratic party's sub-amendment to a Government motion approving the budget. Prime Minister Joe Clark immediately accepted the vote as a loss of confidence and announced his intention to seek the dissolution of Parliament. Thus, the vote of no confidence, enforcing the principle of responsible government, remains a constitutional matter defined by custom and usage. See *House of Commons*.

See John B. Stewart, *The Canadian House of Commons: Procedure and Reform* (Montreal: McGill-Queen's University Press, 1977).

Votes and proceedings. The daily minutes of the proceedings of the House of Commons, including notices to introduce bills in the House.

Waffle, the. A left-nationalist faction within the New Democratic party from 1969 to 1972. The basic thesis of the Waffle was that the only way to achieve national policy-making independence was to regain ownership of major industries from foreign-based, notably United States, multinational corporations. The view of the Waffle was a direct challenge to the strategy of the NDP leadership, which was trying to present a moderate, reformist, social democratic alternative to the Liberals and Conservatives. The Wafflers were so-styled because, in drafting their manifesto in 1969, they "waffled" on the question of nationalization; they ultimately "waffled to the left." Prominent members of the group included Melville Watkins, a university-based economist, who had written a report for the federal Liberal Government on the role of foreign ownership in the economy (*Foreign Ownership and the Structure of Canadian Industry* [Ottawa, 1968]; and James Laxer, an historian, who became a candidate for the federal party leadership representing the group's point of view.

The Waffle's appeal struck a sympathetic chord among the party's membership, especially among those with background in the Co-operative Commonwealth Federation. Its well-honed organization led to a direct challenge to the party's elite. In 1971, Laxer, a political neophyte, was the sole candidate challenging veteran CCF-New Democrat David Lewis for the federal party's leadership on the final (fourth) ballot. The field had originally included several members of Parliament. Two years earlier, Lewis had encouraged a party convention to reject the "ideological straitjacket" of the Waffle. Though Laxer lost the leadership contest, the Waffle continued to pose an organizational as well as personal challenge to the party's hierarchy. In 1972, the Ontario NDP, which was then led by Stephen Lewis, declared the Waffle to be an unacceptable "party within a party"; and it compelled Wafflers to choose between continued party membership and the Waffle's separate identity. While some members remained in the NDP, other Wafflers founded the Movement for an Independent Socialist Canada. See *Continentalism; Economic nationalism.*

For documentation on the Waffle movement up to 1970, see Dave Godfrey and Mel Watkins (eds.), *Gordon to Watkins to You: A Documentary: The Battle for Control of our Economy* (Toronto: New Press, 1970).

War Measures Act (emergency powers). A federal statute which, upon proclamation by the governor-in-council that "war, invasion, or insurrection, real or apprehended" exists, confers emergency powers on the federal cabinet. The Act confers powers upon the cabinet to execute its will during the emergency, and also to declare the emergency's termination, subject to Parliament's approval. The constitutional justification for the emergency powers rests in the "Peace, Order and good Government" clause in the preamble of Section 91 of the British North America Act.

During a period of invocation, the federal government may override the jurisdictional authority of the provinces. Under provisions of the Bill of Rights (1960), the cabinet must bring the proclamation immediately to Parliament if it is in session; otherwise, within fifteen days of the opening of the next session. When introduced, ten members of either the House of Commons or Senate may move revocation and force a debate on the Government's action.

Debate over emergency powers centres on the length of time that the Act should remain in effect following the conclusion of a war and the invocation of the Act in peacetime. The Act was in effect during and following World War One, during World War Two, and until 1954 – though the legislation during the nine peacetime years was of limited scope (Emergency Transitional Powers Act). During the 1945-1954 period, however, a secret order-in-council gave the federal minister of justice the power to arrest, interrogate, and detain anyone likely to behave in a manner prejudicial to public safety "in such place and under such conditions as the minister may from time to time determine" (October 6, 1954). The justification during this time was the Cold War and the spy scare following the defection of a Soviet cipher clerk in 1946. Since the passing of the Regulations Act in 1950, federal orders-in-council and other statutory instruments are published in the *Canada Gazette* unless a category of exemption is published.

In 1970, the federal Government invoked the War Measures Act in peacetime, during the so-called "October Crisis," following the kidnapping and holding for ransom of a British trade official and a Quebec cabinet minister in Montreal by two cells of the *Front de libération du Québec*. Under the declared apprehended insurrection, regulations made the FLQ, successor organizations, and any other organization which advocated force or illegal activity as a means of changing government to be illegal and specified indictable offences for people associated with them. Police and the military were given extraordinary powers of search and arrest, and provincial attorneys-general had the power to enforce three-week detention before a specific charge was required under the regulation. The Public Order Temporary Measures Act replaced the regulations of the War Measures Act in December, 1970. This temporary Act shortened the period of detention and required stronger evidence of adherence to an illegal group. This Act ceased to operate in April 1971, when Parliament could not agree on revised emergency legislation. During the invocation of the War Measures Act and the temporary legislation in 1970-1971, the federal Government asserted that the regulations, though national in scope, had particular reference for Quebec only, and that the provincial government remained chiefly responsible for activities during the emergency under the "normal" powers of the British North America Act (92:14, "The Administration of Justice in the Province ... ").

The Act could be invoked again in peacetime. In 1975, however, leader of the Opposition Robert Stanfield regretted having approved the Government's action. Only the New Democratic party formally opposed the Government, though its caucus was divided. See *October Crisis*.

Wartime Elections Act and Military Voters Act (Canada, 1917). Two federal statutes illustrating the Union Government's flagrant manipulation of the franchise to ensure its victory in the wartime election of 1917. Both acts enfranchised some women for the first time. The Wartime Elections Act gave the vote to wives, widows, and other female relatives of servicemen overseas. The Act disfranchised conscientious objectors, men born in enemy alien countries, and others of European birth speaking an enemy alien language who had been naturalized since 1902. The Military Voters Act enfranchised all Canadian men and women on active service; and it created a floating vote, allowing the military vote to be cast in constituencies which might be suggested to the voters on election day for maximum advantage to the Government.

Wartime Tax Agreement (1941).   An agreement initiated by the federal government under which the provinces agreed to abandon, or "rent," the personal income and corporation tax fields to the federal government until 1946 in return for a rental payment for lost revenue. The federal government also encouraged the provinces not to levy succession duties. The rental payment was based on revenue yields in the abandoned fields in 1941 or on total costs of servicing the provincial debt. Quebec, Ontario, Manitoba, and British Columbia opted for the former; and remaining provinces chose the latter method of calculating the rental payment. The federal government deducted provincial succession duties from the rental payment to those provinces which opted for the servicing of the debt. The federal government had the power, under the War Measures Act, to impose any fiscal arrangement it wished during World War Two. The "agreement" of 1941, however, became the basis for subsequent, periodically negotiated federal-provincial fiscal arrangements. See *Federal-provincial tax-sharing arrangements.*

"Watertight compartments."   A metaphor used by Lord Atkins to describe a narrow interpretation by the Judicial Committee of the Privy Council of federal and provincial legislative competence under the British North America Act. The interpretation gave priority to the enumerated heads of Sections 91 and 92 over the "Peace, Order and good Government" clause in the preamble of Section 91, "Powers of Parliament" (*Attorney-General of Canada* v. *Attorney-General of Ontario,* 1937). Thus, the enumerated head "Property and Civil Rights" under provincial powers (92:13) became an effective source of residual power, except in cases of serious national emergency. See *Emergency powers; Judicial Committee of the Privy Council; Residual power.*

Ways and means.   Legislative consideration of revenue-raising measures which the Government proposes. The budget debate which follows the presentation of the budget to the House of Commons, and which can last up to six days, allows for a general and wide-ranging debate on Government policy. The debate focusses on the minister of finance's motion to approve the Government's budgetary policy. The House then deals with budget resolutions, or ways and means motions, giving notice of amendments to taxation statutes (for example, changes in tax rates, rules, and tariffs). Following the examination of these motions by the House, the tax bills are introduced and similarly debated.

Westminster.   A reference to the British Parliament, which is built on the site of Westminster Palace.

Whig (interpretation of Canadian history).   A reference to a political movement and party in Britain which had some relevance to the reform politics of nineteenth-century Canada (although the term "Clear Grits" was more common in Canada). The Whigs, Grits, or Reformers were generally in favour of granting responsible government to the colonies. The so-called "Whig interpretation of Canadian history" is a pejorative reference to those who see Canadian history as an evolutionary process leading to national independence under the auspices notably of the federal Liberal party and its leaders. As the Liberal party is identified as the chief architect and defender of Canadian nationality according to this "interpretation," the Conservatives are identified as reactionaries opposed to Canada's constitutional development as an independent nation.

Whip (party).   The member of a party's caucus who is responsible for ensuring the presence of party members in the legislature or at committee meetings to maintain adequate representation should a vote be held. The division bells in the House ring for a vote until the whips are satisfied that as many members of their own party as possible are present. Whips arrange the "pairs" among legislators on both sides of the House which allow members to be absent without affecting the relative voting strength of the Government and the Opposition. The party whips are also responsible for arranging the order of speakers in the legislature; this facilitates the Speaker's job of recognizing members in debate.

White paper.   A Government document tabled in the legislature; it outlines Government policy in a particular area and the direction of future action possibly including legislation. Other coloured papers are official documents which discuss policy and alternative proposals and might suggest Government preferences. Should a Government encounter severe opposition to a white paper, it may "withdraw" it. Withdrawing a white paper after a period of "study" is less an embarrassment to the Government than withdrawing legislation. In the early 1970's, for example, the federal Government published white papers on foreign policy, defence, and Indian affairs. The Government withdrew the white paper on Indian affairs in the face of considerable opposition from native groups.

White paper on employment and income (1945).   A federal Government document issued in April, 1945, as World War Two was ending; it outlined Government policy for post-war social and economic reconstruction. In the white paper, the federal Government committed itself to: the maintenance of a high and stable level of income and employment; the acquisition of exclusive powers to levy personal and corporate income tax; the achievement of federal-provincial co-operation to develop a welfare state; and the development of an international economic order based on principles of free trade (*Employment and Income with Special Reference to the Initial Period of Reconstruction* [Ottawa: King's Printer, 1945]). The white paper – along with the report in 1940 of the Rowell-Sirois Royal Commission on Federal-Provincial Relations, the proposals in the green book of 1945, and those of the Dominion-Provincial Conference on Reconstruction in the same year – set the agenda for Canadian national economic development policy and the style of federal-provincial relations which lasted approximately 15 years.

The author of the white paper was W.A. Mackintosh. See his "The White Paper on Employment and Income in Its 1945 Setting," in S.F. Kaliski (ed.), *Canadian Economic Policies since the War* (Ottawa: Canadian Trade Committee, 1966), 9-21.

White paper on sovereignty-association (Quebec, 1979).   A Quebec Government document published in 1979, prior to the referendum to permit the *Parti Québécois* Government to negotiate "sovereignty-association" with the rest of Canada. The white paper discussed earlier accommodations between the anglophone and francophone communities in British North America, and Quebec's experience with federalism, especially federal "invasions" of provincial jurisdiction since World War Two. Of greater interest, however, was the paper's consideration of the definition and implications of national sovereignty for Quebec. The white paper described several instruments in a proposed association with the rest of Canada: a community council of ministers, a commission of experts or council secretariat, a court of justice, and a monetary authority (representation which would be based on the "relative size" of the separate economies). (*Quebec-Canada: A New Deal – The Quebec Government's Proposal for a New Partnership between Equals: Sovereignty-Association.*)

In response, the Liberal party of Quebec denounced the PQ's "use of history for political propaganda . . . half-truths, biased interpretations, historical omissions and value judgments which have no connection with reality" (*The White Paper on Sovereignty-Association: A House of Cards*, 1980). The provincial Liberal party's constitution committee presented its proposed changes to the federal system shortly after the publication of the white paper (*A New Canadian Federation*, 1980). See *Federalism; Parti Québécois; Sovereignty-association.*

Winnipeg Declaration (1956).   The document which redefined the goals of Canada's democratic socialist movement. In the Regina Manifesto of 1933, the Co-operative Commonwealth Federation had declared its goal to be the eradication of "the present capitalistic system" with its "inherent injustice and inhumanity." In 1956, the Winnipeg Declaration defined the goals simply as regulating the economy to improve the quality of life. This "embourgeoiesment" of Canadian socialism was a phenomenon shared with other social democratic parties in the western world; it represented a redefinition of goals which were more consistent with the economic prosperity in the 1950's compared to conditions in the 1930's. In 1961, the organizational metamorphosis took place with the establishment of the New Democratic party. See *Co-operative Commonwealth Federation; New Democratic party.*

Winnipeg general strike (1919).   A strike initially over union recognition in the building trades which gathered general support, including that of city employees. Opponents of the strike were convinced that it presaged the creation of a Communist Soviet in Winnipeg. Prime Minister Robert Borden's Union Government replaced the local police (who were considered too sympathetic to the workers) with the Royal Canadian Mounted Police and the military. A federally authorized arrest of strike leaders led to a workers' march despite a mayoral prohibition. The RCMP dispersed the marchers, but one person was killed and thirty were injured. The strike terminated one week later. At this time, the Union Government amended the Criminal Code to broaden the definition of seditious conspiracy and increase penalties. The Government also amended the Immigration Act to allow for the deportation without hearing or trial of any immigrant, regardless of citizenship or length of residency. The strike and the federal Government's reaction heightened regional and class tensions in the West generally, and in Winnipeg and Manitoba in particular. In 1921, one of the strike leaders, J.S. Woodsworth, was elected to the House of Commons. In 1933, Woodsworth became the first leader of the socialist Co-operative Commonwealth Federation (CCF).

On the general strike, see D.C. Masters, *The Winnipeg General Strike* (Toronto: University of Toronto Press, 1950); D.J. Bercuson, *A Confrontation at Winnipeg* (Montreal: McGill-Queen's Press, 1974); and Kenneth McNaught, *A Prophet in Politics: A Biography of J.S. Woodsworth* (Toronto: University of Toronto Press, 1959).